Contents

Dedication and acknowledgments

This book is dedicated to Celina, without whose patience and support this book would never have seen the light of day; to our children Mark and Melinda and to Luise who have each supported me in all of my endeavours; and to my mother Hannah, in her eighth decade, who has always supported and encouraged each of her children and who is thankfully free of osteoporosis.

Thanks go to those who have offered their assistance in providing information and support. In particular my thanks to my daughter Melinda who has acted as researcher, librarian and co-author during this entire project. Thanks to the Australian Dairy Corporation and in particular Ms Jackie McCann for allowing me to use material originally published by the Dairy Corporation. Thanks to the Health Promotion Unit, Central Sydney Health Service, for permission to reproduce or modify parts of *Staying On Your Feet*.

And finally, my thanks to Susan McCulloch, who encouraged me to write again after I had decided a writer's life was not for me.

Glossary

acupuncture: Ancient Chinese treatment now commonly found in western societies. Involves the placing of fine stainless steel needles into the skin at specific acupuncture locations—known as points. Can also be placed in painful areas or in the skin of the ear. A modern variant is the use of low energy **laser** light stimulation.

adrenal glands: The tiny glands found on top of the kidneys which produce the natural corticosteroid cortisone and adrenaline.

alkaline phosphatase: An enzyme produced in the liver which is increased in your blood in conditions in which there is excessive bone breakdown. Can be raised in the presence of secondary bone cancer.

androgens: The male sex hormones. Occasionally used in the treatment of osteoporosis in men with lower than normal sex hormone levels.

annulus fibrosis: The tough surrounding of the intervertebral disc. When your disc ruptures this structure is often torn, allowing the soft pulp of the disc to protrude onto nerve tissue or the spinal cord contents.

anorexia nervosa: Eating disorder, also known as slimmer's disease. Women and men with this condition virtually starve themselves to death. There are complex reasons for the development of the disease but among them are a distorted body image in which the victim sees him or herself as being grossly obese—despite the obvious emaciation which occurs late in the disease. The menstrual periods cease due to suppression of oestrogen production, increasing the risk of osteoporosis in later life, should the sufferer survive.

anticonvulsants: Drugs used in the treatment of epilepsy. Some may cause loss of calcium from the body. Some, for example Rivotril and Epilim, may be used to treat pain caused by nerve damage. They may cause drowsiness and therefore lead to falls.

antidepressants: Drugs used primarily in the treatment of depression. Also used in the treatment of chronic pain. Antidepressants are non-addictive. Some are sedative and increase the risk of falls. Typical antidepressants include Tryptanol, Tofranil, Sinequan, Anafranil, Prothiaden, Tolvon, Prozac and Aurorix.

arthritis: Inflammation of the joints leading to pain and disability.

biopsy: The removal of tissue from your body for the specific purpose of pathological and other assessments. Bone biopsy may be used to determine bone metabolism under certain circumstances.

bisphosphonates: Drugs developed to reduce the bone removal which occurs during the menopause. **Didrocal osteoporosis therapy** is the name of the preparation of etidronate released in Australia in 1994.

bone: The living tissue formed of complex combinations of calcium and phosphorus, bone cells and blood vessels which is constantly being built up and torn down by the action of the bone cells.

bone 'bank': Consider your bones as a 'bank' for calcium and other minerals. Calcium is simultaneously being deposited or laid down as bone, and being withdrawn in some part of your body. This process is kept in balance by a complex system of chemical messenger substances or hormones.

bone cells: These form the basis of bone. The osteoblasts build bone up and the osteoclasts remove bone and are in a dynamic state of activity with each other. Up to the age of 20–30 there is a tendency for more bone to be formed than lost. After the age of 30 more bone tends to be lost than formed.

bone densitometer: Device which measures the bone density. Various types include: SPA—single photon absorptiometry measures the forearm and heel. Precise but may not give accurate picture of density of spine or hip. Radiation exposure approximately 5 millirems. DPA—dual photon absorptiometry measures spine and hip. Precision is acceptable for diagnosing osteoporosis but not sufficient to detect changes in the individual. Radiation exposure approximately 5 millirems. Superseded by the DEXA—dual energy X-ray absorptiometry—measures spine or hip. Highly precise and can be used to detect changes in the individual. Radiation exposure approximately 2.5 millirems.

bone density: The amount of calcium present in any given area of bone. Determines how strong your bones are. Measured by bone densitometry or absorptiometry.

bone tissue: Compact bone is composed of many rod-like Haversian systems, each containing many concentric cylindrical layers or lamellae surrounding a central blood vessel. The bone cells called osteocytes lie between these layers within irregular spaces called lacunae. Tiny pores or canaliculi connect the osteocytes with one another and with the central blood vessel, allowing oxygen and nutrients to reach the cells. Spongy or cancellous bone has a loose honeycomb-like network of rigid beams or trabeculae. The spaces between these trabeculae contain marrow, which is an important blood-forming tissue.

bone mass: The total amount of bone tissue in a given area of bone or in the entire body.

bone remodelling: The constant process of building up and breaking down of the bone tissue. This process is responsible for the development, maintenance and eventual reduction of your bones.

calcitonin: Hormone claimed to prevent the loss of calcium from the body. Produced by the thyroid gland which sits at the front of the neck. Mainly used in the treatment of Paget's disease of bone.

calcitriol: Synthetic vitamin D developed by Roche Pharmaceuticals as a means of delaying the loss of bone density seen in postmenopausal osteoporosis. Marketed in Australia as Rocaltrol.

calcium: Metallic element which gives bone its strength and durability. Important in the deposition of new bone, in the transmission of nerve impulses and in the clotting of blood. About 99% of your calcium is stored in your bones.

Colles's fracture: Fracture of the bones just above the wrist. Involves the radius and ulna to a greater or lesser extent and usually occurs as a result of a fall on the outstretched hand or arm. Common in osteoporosis because of the increased fragility of the bones.

cortical bone: The dense compact bone which forms the shell or outer part of most of your bones.

crush fractures: Fractures which occur specifically in the spinal bones or vertebras. They occur when the front of the rectangular-shaped spinal bone collapses under the weight of the rest of the spine in patients with osteoporosis. Ultimately responsible for abnormal curvature of the spine—kyphosis.

CT scan: Computerised Tomography. Sophisticated X-ray technique which takes pictures of slices of body tissue. Precision and accuracy quite good. Relatively high radiation exposure— approximately 200–300 millirems.

Dual Photon Absorptiometry (DPA): Measures spine and hip. Precision is acceptable for diagnosing osteoporosis but not sufficient to detect changes in the individual. Radiation exposure approximately 5 millirems. Superseded by the DEXA.

Dual Energy X-ray Absorptiometry (DEXA): Measures spine or hip. Highly precise and can be used to detect changes in the individual. Radiation exposure approximately 2.5 millirems. The most accurate current method of determining bone density.

endometrium: The lining of the uterus or womb. The endometrium is built up and shed as the menstrual loss once a month under the influence of the female hormones.

endometrial cancer: Cancer of the lining of the womb. A definite contraindication to hormone replacement therapy. Claimed by some to be a risk in HRT.

femur: The thighbone. Forms the ball and socket hip joint, with the ball of the head of the femur fitting into the socket of the pelvis. Forms the knee joint between the lower end of the femur and the top of the tibia in the lower leg. The patella sits at the front of the knee joint and is an important component of that joint.

femur, neck of the: Stalk-like portion of the femur which sits at an angle to the main shaft of the thighbone. Carries the round head of the femur. Frequently fractured in osteoporosis—often with minimal injury. Substantial risk of death or loss of independence for sufferers of fractures.

follicles of the ovaries: The follicles are the sites where monthly production of your ova or egg cells occurs and where the female sex hormone oestrogen is produced from the time of onset of your periods—the menarche—to your menopause.

Follicle Stimulating Hormone: Produced by the pituitary gland to stimulate the formation of the ovarian follicles. Increases towards the menopause in response to the reduced number of ovarian follicles.

formication: The sensation of ants crawling over the skin. One of the complaints often made by menopausal women.

fractures: Breaks in the bones caused normally by injury involving violent forces. Frequently occur with minimal or no injury in osteoporosis. Normally extremely painful but can occur in such a manner as to cause little initial pain in osteoporosis and some other pathological conditions.

hip replacement surgery: The usual consequence of a fracture of the neck of the femur. When a fracture occurs the surgeon will remove the head and neck of the femur and substitute an artificial replacement made of strong metal or specialised non-metallic components.

hormones: Chemical messengers produced by one organ or gland to work on distant parts of the body. The female sex hormones or oestrogens play a major role in the formation and maintenance of bone and its bone density.

hormone replacement therapy: also known as HRT or oestrogen replacement therapy. The use of chemical preparations, either synthetic or natural, to replace falling female hormone levels during or after the menopause. Mainly used to reduce the unpleasant consequences of menopause, such as flushing, breast engorgement, dryness of the genital area or a fall in libido. Known to reduce the risk of osteoporosis, cardiovascular disease and strokes.

hydroxyapatite: Bone is created by the production of a soft framework of protein which is hardened by deposits of the special salt called hydroxyapatite which is composed of calcium, phosphorus and other minerals.

hypercalcaemia: Excess calcium in the blood. Occurs in some disease states and is the most common of the uncommon reactions to calcitriol treatment. Results in excessive blood levels of calcium, leading to drowsiness, headache, nausea, vomiting, weakness and constipation. Muscle pain, bone pain and a metallic taste in your mouth may also be indications of excessive blood levels of calcium.

hyperparathyroidism: Excessive production of parathormone or overactivity of the parathyroid glands. Causes excessive breakdown of bone, leading to increased fracture risk.

hysterectomy: The surgical removal of the uterus. Not associated with or a cause of osteoporosis unless the ovaries are removed at the same time as the uterus.

intervertebral disc: The strong yet supple cartilage plate which sits between the spinal vertebras and allows movement and shock protection to the spine.

kyphosis: Abnormal forward curvature of the spine. Initially affects the upper spine and leads to marked loss of height and pressure on the chest and abdominal contents.

laser acupuncture: Uses the principles of acupuncture but uses light instead of the usual needles. Painless and convenient therapy. It may be of assistance in the treatment of pain.

libido: The sexual drive or urge. Can be reduced temporarily at the time of the menopause. Will normalise in most cases but may also be improved by using oestrogen replacement therapy.

light and sound therapy: The latest in microelectronics aimed at producing 'relaxation without ritual'. Uses flashing lights and pulsing sounds to alter brainwave activity.

Magnetic Field Therapy: MFT is claimed by many in Europe to be of assistance in treating the pain of osteoporotic fractures.

menarche: The commencement of the menstrual cycle. The first period.

menopause: Also known as the change of life or the climacteric. The time in a woman's life when she is in transition from the fertile years of her life to those after cessation of egg production. The end of menstruation. Associated with decline and eventual cessation of oestrogen production from the ovaries.

micturition: The passage of urine. One of the features of menopause is increased frequency of passage of urine due to decreased bladder capacity.

oestrogens: The female sex hormones. Necessary to maintain the female secondary sexual characteristics and maintain bone density along with calcium and weight-bearing exercise. The decline in oestrogen levels after menopause is responsible for the rapid increase in loss of bone mass during and after menopause. Also produced by the adrenal glands and the male sex organs, the testicles.

oophorectomy: The surgical removal of the ovaries. If premature, can be associated with declining bone mass and eventually osteoporosis.

ossification: The process of forming bone tissue.

osteomyelitis: Bone infection usually caused by pus-producing bacteria, especially *Staphylococcus* and *Streptococcus*. In past eras, osteomyelitis was caused by tuberculosis and gonorrhoea.

osteopoenia: Reduction in bone density without fracture.

osteomalacia: The name of the adult syndrome of decreased bone density due to insufficient vitamin D, known in children as rickets.

osteoporosis: Condition that is characterised by a reduction in the actual substance of the bones and enlargement of bone spaces. Osteoporosis is defined clinically as loss of bone density associated with fractures following minimal trauma or injury. Osteoporosis is seen as a result of the natural aging process in men and women but is particularly a problem for women after the menopause, during which bone loss occurs at a much accelerated rate compared with that in men of the same age.

ova: The female germ cell or egg. Produced by the ovarian follicles from the early or mid-teens to the premenopausal era or menopause.

ovaries: The female sex glands. Produce fertile eggs and oestrogens through women's reproductive epoch. When the ovaries shut down at the end of this time, no further eggs (ova) are released, and the production of oestrogens declines and eventually ceases.

parathormone (PTH): The hormone manufactured by the parathyroid glands. Controls the concentration of calcium and phosphorus in the blood.

parathyroid glands: four tiny glands found in or near the thyroid gland. Produce parathormone.

Paget's disease of the bone: Also known as osteitis deformans. Common condition in the elderly in whom bones become thickened yet excessively flexible. Controlled in part by the use of the bisphosphonate medication—Didronel.

postural hypotension: Lowered blood pressure which is worsened by posture. Caused mainly by medications which lower the blood pressure such as fluid tablets, some tranquillisers and antidepressants. Blood pressure may suddenly drop on standing up from a seated or squatting position. More likely to affect the elderly and increase the risk of falls.

progestogen: Hormone preparation which is designed to mimic the naturally occurring hormone progesterone. Used in combination with oestrogen in HRT to ensure regular shedding of the intact uterus lining.

progesterone: Hormone released by the corpus luteum which forms after the release of the ova by the follicle. Serves to stimulate thickening of the endometrium in readiness for implantation of the fertilised ova or embryo.

QCT: see CT scan.

rheumatology and orthopaedics: The medical and surgical specialties which are mainly responsible for dealing with the many things which may go wrong with bone.

rickets: Clinical syndrome seen mainly in children due to vitamin D deficiency. The bones become soft and deformed and are subject to frequent fracture. Seen mainly in migrant groups which do not expose their children to light and in people with abnormal or inadequate absorption from the gut.

risk factors: These are the things which make it more likely you will develop a certain abnormal clinical condition. In osteoporosis there are factors you can control which are associated with your lifestyle such as exercise, smoking, calcium intake. There are also those factors which you inherit such as an increased tendency to develop osteoporosis, ethnicity and your genetic make-up.

scoliosis: Abnormal curvature of the spine.

side effects: Unwanted or non-therapeutic effects of drugs.

Single Photon Absorptiometry (SPA): Measures the forearm and heel. Precise but may not give accurate picture of density of spine or hip. Radiation exposure approximately 5 millirems.

steroids: Also known as corticosteroids. Generic name given to chemical substances developed from natural hormones or chemical messengers produced mainly in the adrenal glands. Involved in the control of sugar and its breakdown, the control of stress and the overall control of fluid balance in the body.

steroids, anabolic: Synthetic hormones used to build up tissues and control pain. Used in osteoporosis to reduce pain and further fracture.

tetany: Muscle spasms which occur in the hands and feet in situations where there is a low blood level of calcium.

tibia: The main bone of the lower leg. Together with the femur and the patella, it forms the knee joint above and with the fibula (splint bone) it forms the ankle joint below. Site of the Pott's fracture just above the ankle—this occurs commonly in osteoporosis as a result of twisting on the foot or ankle.

trabecular bone: The spongy bone which forms the inner part of bones and holds the marrow.

transcutaneous electrical nerve stimulation (TENS) units: Small electronic pain-relieving devices which deliver minute electrical currents to the skin and underlying tissues. May be useful for localised pain or pain which is referred from areas of the skeleton affected by osteoporosis.

tranquillisers: Drugs developed to treat anxiety and produce muscle relaxation. May be additional risk factors in producing a tendency to fall. Minor tranquillisers or benzodiazepines are the more frequently used. These include Valium, Serepax, Murelax, Normison, Euhypnos, Mogadon and Rohypnol. May lead to dependence if taken in excess or for prolonged time. Major tranquillisers usually used in the treatment of severe psychiatric disorders include Largactil, Melleril, Serenace and Stelazine.

uterus: The womb. One of the internal sex organs in women.

vertebras: The spinal bones. Roughly rectangular in shape and separated by the intervertebral discs. Subject to compression fractures which lead to forward curvature of the spine in advanced osteoporosis, pain and compression of chest and abdominal contents and nerve tissue.

X-ray: Widely available. Invented in the late nineteenth century to image the bones. Not suitable for early detection of osteoporosis. Translucency of bone indicates potential osteoporosis. Changes on X-ray can be determined only after approximately 30% of bone has been lost. May be required by doctor to rule out other problems of the spine. Radiation exposure for the average X-ray is approximately 50 millirems.

1

Introduction to osteoporosis—the silent thief

As a medical student, more than 30 years ago, I saw my first examples of osteoporotic women in hospital outpatient departments and in hospital beds. Their bent frames, protruding abdomens, shortness of breath, and their tendency to develop fractures with minimal injury seemed to demand measures from the medical profession to prevent this distressing and seemingly unavoidable end to women's lives.

The surgical and orthopaedic wards supplied plentiful examples of fractured neck of femur or fractured hips. Many of these women did extremely poorly after surgery. A significant number died shortly after their surgery as a consequence of blood loss and shock. A large number developed severe chest infection and some of these patients died. In those days hip replacement surgery was inevitably followed by a slow and painful rehabilitation.

Significantly, senile osteoporosis, as it was known in those days, was considered to be an inevitable feature of the aging female.

Later, in general practice, as a young and inexperienced family doctor I was frustrated in trying to manage the problems of frail elderly osteoporotic women and even younger women with osteoporotic fractures of the spine. What was more distressing was the insidious manner in which the fractures occurred. At times, I would be called to the homes of elderly female patients who had been found by relatives lying on the floor of their homes, some for long periods. In most cases they would tell of a fall over a loose object on the floor which had led to an immediate pain in the affected hip and an inability to stand or move from the spot.

Fractures would occur without any appropriate cause. The first thing that brought these women to consult me was not the bending of their spines, which had occurred almost without being noticed. Many women appeared to develop their distressing condition without warning. Many of these women suffered severe back pain and some became bedridden as a consequence.

Others would seek help after breaking their wrists or ankles after apparently minor falls. The only tools available for me to treat these patients were calcium and fluoride tablets, which I hoped might help, and anabolic steroids, which I was taught might control pain if nothing else.

Still later, I became interested in acupuncture and was asked by a number of patients with osteoporosis if I could ease their pain with my needles. This continued when I became consultant acupuncturist at a public hospital where I treated a large number of women with pain resulting from compression fracture.

In the past fifteen years as the director of a pain management facility I have treated a number of patients with osteoporotic pain using the full range of pain treatments available, many of which are described in this book.

In this exciting era we have, for the first time, the means to prevent the next generation of women experiencing the ravages of this largely preventable disease. We understand more about the potentially preventable risk factors which contribute to the loss of bone in postmenopausal women. We have had an explosion of knowledge about the effects, benefits and potential dangers of hormone replacement therapy (HRT). This has been accompanied by utterances of the at times strident critics of HRT. These critics seem to be attacking any new medical discovery or therapy as unnecessary interference in what they believe to be a 'natural' process of aging in women.

We have also seen the introduction of the new antiresorptive agents derived from vitamin D and the group of drugs known as bisphosphonates. These drugs have the potential to stop the 'silent thief'—osteoporosis—robbing multitudes of women of their bone strength. They offer the possibility of a reduction in the numbers of the thousands of women currently requiring hip surgery, who often languish in a dependent state for many years.

We have seen the controversy surrounding calcium and its role in osteoporosis prevention go through various phases. We now have almost universal acceptance of the need for appropriate calcium intake throughout women's lives. As you will see from this book, much of this calcium is available with proper attention to diet but for others it will depend on calcium supplementation.

Finally, as this book is being written, we have the exciting news that researchers in Australia claim to have discovered the genetic structures which determine which women are at risk of osteoporosis. As you will see, the implications of this research include the possibility of predicting at an early age which of you may be at risk. This will allow your treating practitioners to advise you at an earlier age whether HRT or any of the other bone-preserving strategies should be employed to prevent you from being a victim.

Hopefully, with the knowledge currently available, fewer patients will need to seek help for what is now recognised as a largely preventable and unnecessary disease.

Good news for all

This is a 'good news' book for all of those who could have developed the condition. The good news is that action can be taken to prevent this disease. Further good news involves the treatment of those of you who are at risk and those of you who are already experiencing the difficulties of living with osteoporosis.

Osteoporosis

So what is this condition that we are going to explore in this book? Osteoporosis is a condition characterised by a reduction in the substance or mass of your bones and enlargement of the bone spaces. These spaces are an integral part of your bone and are present as part of the bone structure giving your bones their quality of lightness as well as strength.

The loss of bone substance and the thinning of the bony framework around the bone spaces make the bones of your skeleton thinner and therefore more fragile. This can occur as a result of disturbances of your bone nutrition. The process can result from changes in the ways in which the body deals with the absorption and integration of various mineral salts into your living bone tissue.

Osteoporosis is also a condition characterised by a reduction in bone density or strength and flexibility. It leads to a condition where your bones become more fragile. A reduced bone density predisposes to fractures in the presence of minimal trauma or injury. According to the Sydney osteoporosis expert Dr Philip Sambrook, osteoporosis may also be defined as 'a reduction in bone mass leading to an increased risk of fracture'.[1]

It is now possible to measure your bone density precisely. According to some experts, osteoporosis is considered to be present when bone density is below the lowest accepted normal limit in young, healthy subjects.

A related term used for bone loss without fracture is *osteopoenia*. This translates into bone weakness or loss with consequent thinning of the bone. This term is usually used when no fracture has occurred.

Osteoporosis is the most frequent age-related bone disorder in women. It is characterised by decreased bone substance and increased susceptibility to bone fractures. All bones may be affected but it most commonly leads to fractures of the hip, spine and wrist.

As you will read in Chapter 2 the skeleton is made up of numerous bones and joints. The skeleton supports the softer tissues of your body and serves as a sort of 'hanger' or framework to which your muscles and tendons attach. It is the key to all physical activity, enabling you to walk, run, sit down and so on.

One of the most important components of your bone is calcium. Bone is a hard yet flexible living tissue which consists of small crystals of calcium and phosphorus integrated into protein or collagen fibres.

Some 98% of the calcium in our bodies is found in the bone. The calcium crystals provide your bone with resilience and strength, whereas the protein allows for a certain degree of elasticity.

In the young, the process of bone formation (which occurs throughout life) exceeds the process of destruction. As a result, bone mass increases throughout the first 30 years of life. From the age of 30–35 years and over, the process of bone disintegration becomes more rapid and catches up with the process of bone formation. As a result there is a natural loss of bone density. This process is much more pronounced in females and rapidly accelerates with the cessation of menstruation and for the duration of the menopause.

In males, there is a greater bone mass to begin with and a gradual loss of bone mass which is less noticeable and which commences at a more advanced age. Despite this, recent figures indicate that as many as 10% of osteoporosis sufferers are men.

Consequences of a longer life span

Over the past 40 years, the number of elderly people in the United States of America has increased dramatically, and today about 12% of the population is over the age of 65.

According to recent estimates, at the beginning of the 21st century the number of people over the age of 65 will have increased threefold, and 100 000 Americans will be aged 100 or over. It is estimated that in the year 2025 about 20% of the population will be aged 65 or over.

Approximately 10 000 hip fractures were reported in Australia in 1986. The patients involved occupied over 300 000 surgical bed days. It has been estimated by some that by the year 2011 the incidence of hip fracture will increase to 18 000 cases, resulting in an almost doubling of the bed occupancy rate to nearly 600 000. This will see the cost of acute care of these patients increase from $37.8 million in 1986 to $69.5 million annually. These figures do not include the costs for other osteoporotic fractures of the wrists, ankles and spinal vertebras.

As life expectancy increases rapidly, there is a corresponding increase in the incidence of chronic age-dependent or degenerative diseases. The Mayo Clinic has estimated the cost of treatment of these diseases will reach $60 billion in 1990. These expenses will rise proportionately to the growth of the aged population. Public health systems will have to be geared to the demands of an aging population, for example provision of care for fractures, renal problems, low blood pressure, Alzheimer's disease.

Fractures and their cost

According to a recent consensus statement by the Royal Australian College of Physicians:

> Fractures that result from [osteoporosis] lead to considerable distress and disability, and to substantial costs to the health care system. Women beyond menopause are particularly at risk, with present evidence in Australia indicating that 20 to 25% of women who reach the age of 70 will have been hospitalised with a fracture of the upper limb, spine or lower limb.[2]

The report goes on to state that occupation of hospital beds by patients with hip fractures is exceeded only by that of patients with mental disease, cardiovascular disease and cancer. The Australian figures suggest 16% of patients suffering hip fractures will die within six months, and 50% will require long-term nursing care. The direct cost of age-related fractures in Australia has been estimated to be $175 million per annum. The incidence of hip fracture exceeds that of cancer.

In the United States of America in 1984 it was estimated that the national cost of fractures due to osteoporosis was US$6 billion. The population most at risk is the age group over 65 years. One-third of the female population and one-sixth of the male population with a life expectancy of 90 years will incur osteoporosis-related fractures.

After an incident of fracture, 15–25% of the population who were self-reliant will require institutional nursing care for a year or more. Some 25–35% of this population will depend on other people or mechanical means for their movements.

The cost of treatment of fractures is expected to rise significantly over the coming years.

In the United States of America 20–25 million people are estimated to be suffering from osteoporosis. Annually this leads to 1.3 million fractures of the hip, spine and wrist. It has a large social cost as well as the suffering, immobility, chronic pain and death associated with fractures due to the osteoporosis.

In the United Kingdom in 1985 there were 44 000 admissions to hospital for the treatment of hip fractures. The average hospital stay was 34 days, at a total cost of £164 million.

By the age of 60 one in every four women in the western world will have been affected by osteoporosis to the point of having a significant bone loss. Most will show no signs or symptoms in the early stages—they will be asymptomatic.

Osteoporosis is a 'silent epidemic'!

Osteoporosis is recognised as a 'silent epidemic', which like other epidemics is capable of control; once the condition and its many causes are recognised they can be controlled. In many postmenopausal women bone is being steadily lost; some women have no warning of this before the first osteoporotic fracture occurs. The implications of this epidemic are frightening.

Approximately one in every four western women over the age of 65 will sustain a spinal fracture. By 75 years of age one in every four women will have had a fractured hip due to osteoporosis. One in three of these will die within six months—due to the fracture and its consequences.

In Australia a 100-bed hospital could be filled every day with fracture cases resulting directly from osteoporosis.

Fractures of the hip and neck of femur

Women are twice as susceptible to fractures of the stalk-like neck of the femur when age is adjusted. The incidence of hip fracture increases with age—it doubles every five years. Fractures of the hip in osteoporotic patients usually occur in the presence of only moderate degrees of injury.

Some more statistics

At 60 years of age, women have a life expectancy of nineteen years with a 15% chance of a hip fracture. At 80 years of age there is a life expectancy of 9–10 years with an additional 15% chance of a fractured neck of femur. At 90 years of age there is a 33% chance of women having had such a fracture.

Hip fractures not the end of the story

Mortality after surgery for fractured neck of femur is up to 40% compared with a 5.8% mortality in an equivalent population of the same age. It is most marked in the first four months after the surgery.

The aim is for optimum bone density

It is known that peak bone mass is reached in the mid-thirties. We must therefore aim at optimum levels of bone density, well before the onset of rapid bone mineral density loss at the time of the menopause in all women.

Early recognition and prevention

It is now recognised that there are effective treatments to prevent or reduce the severity of osteoporosis. However, a precondition for success is an accurate and reliable diagnosis of the disease and its severity. The consequences of our failure to take effective measures will be further generations of unnecessarily bent and deformed women.

This book will deal with the multiple factors involved in the prediction of those of you at risk of developing this largely preventable disease and its consequences. The controversy surrounding the use of treatments such as calcium supplementation (Chapter 9) and HRT (Chapter 10) will be covered in detail.

Is hormone therapy a reliable and safe method of controlling osteoporosis in the women who accept this form of therapy, or is it just another example of the medicalisation of normal aging phenomena, as claimed by some prominent writers on what they term the 'menopause industry'?[3]

One of the aims of this book is to provide up-to-date information on these areas so that you the reader can make informed judgements as to whether you should accept the advice of your medical advisers.

In Chapter 8 we will deal with the new medications involved in preventing the bone-robbing effects of your menopause. The increasing numbers of these which are becoming available to your medical practitioners will help fight this largely unnecessary condition. Your choices are therefore increased as you make decisions based on the most up-to-date information available.

The introduction of sophisticated scanning devices (Chapter 5) which measure accurately the amount of calcium in your bones, has created almost as much controversy. On the one hand we now have an apparently safe and simple approach to the diagnosis of calcium loss; on the other hand, critics claim it is as yet unproved technology and that women are being once again used as guinea pigs in the cause of largely male science. Recent government decisions will make this technological development more accessible to those in need.

This book will present both sides of the case for and against the use of these approaches and the possibility of mass scanning as a preventive measure.

Chapter 7 concentrates on the need to prevent falls in the mostly elderly population of women at risk of osteoporotic fractures. Details on how to 'fall-proof' your home and a list of drugs which may increase the risk of falls are given.

The most recent treatments for the prevention of osteoporosis and the risk factors for osteoporosis are detailed in separate chapters. Although pain is not an early feature of osteoporosis, it is a common cause for the sufferer of osteoporosis to seek assistance from their medical adviser. In Chapter 13 details of some of the new and alternative treatments available from the medical profession are detailed. Their availability and costs are described.

Throughout the book, patient vignettes are used to emphasise points raised about the presentation, complications and treatment of real people with established osteoporosis. Some of these have been drawn from among the author's patients and family. In all cases the identity of those described will be obscured to preserve confidentiality.

The resources and reading list provided at the end of the book will enable you to seek out appropriate assistance to determine if you have osteoporosis, and to look for appropriate care if the diagnosis is established.

Finally, the book provides you with a glossary of the sometimes technical terms used by those who advise you about osteoporosis. Although jargon has been avoided as much as possible in this book, some is present where it is necessary. Explanations in simple English should make it possible for the reader to understand these terms and how they are used. The reading list will enable those of you who are interested to increase your knowledge of osteoporosis and the menopause.

2

Bone—a tour around your skeleton

Bone is the special form of tissue that makes up the skeleton on which all your other body tissues hang. Your bones are living organs made largely of this tissue and surrounded by a tough membrane called the periosteum. Bones consist of a dense outer shell (cortex) inside which is the honeycomb-like structure of the trabecular bone. The cortex is thin and the holes of the honeycomb are enlarged in the bones of people with osteoporosis.

Bone is a living, growing, dynamic structure in which new material is constantly being built and old material is constantly being eliminated and replaced. The strength of your bone depends on three key requirements throughout your life. The first of these is regular weight-bearing exercise. The second is an adequate intake of calcium, a major component in bone, throughout your life. The third is the presence of adequate levels of sex hormones. In women this is the female hormone oestrogen; in men the male hormone, testosterone. These make up the pillars of bone strength.

All three of these factors must be present. Calcium alone will not guarantee strong bones throughout your life.

Bone tissue is a unique tissue because it contains living cells embedded in a hard crystalline medium. Bone is created by the production of a soft framework of protein which is hardened by deposits of a special salt called hydroxyapatite which is composed of calcium, phosphorus and other minerals. This is held together by the special protein known as collagen, and other organic substances.

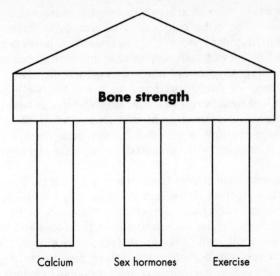

Calcium is a major ingredient in building new bone and assists in creating bone strength. Almost all of your body's calcium, approximately 99.9%, is contained in the bones and teeth. Yet, the total amount of calcium in your bones is only about 1 kg or a little over two pounds.

Your skeleton doesn't function simply as a type of clothes hanger on which all of the outer components of the body are laid. Nor does your skeleton simply remain unchanged until it deteriorates in old age. The skeleton, and its component bones, is a dynamic structure which is constantly changing. It is being built up and broken down continuously by the bone cells that it contains.

By the time you finish reading this book your skeleton will have changed in a number of subtle ways. You will not have exactly the same skeleton that you had when you started this book. Yet it will still have the same strength to enable it to resist compression, twisting and bending.

The ideal qualities for structural framework will have been fulfilled. Your bone will possess inherent lightness, strength and flexibility resulting from its unique internal structure.

Bone tissue—compact and spongy

Two major types of bone tissue exist. *Compact bone tissue* is composed of many rod-like Haversian systems, each containing many concentric cylindrical layers or lamellae surrounding a central blood vessel. The bone cells called osteocytes lie between these layers within irregular spaces called lacunae. Tiny pores or canaliculi connect the osteocytes with one another and with the central blood vessel, allowing oxygen and nutrients to reach the cells.

The *spongy* or *cancellous bone tissue* has a loose honeycomb-like network of rigid beams or trabeculae. The spaces between these trabeculae contain marrow, which is an important blood-forming tissue. Young marrow is red due to the many new blood cells forming. Older marrow becomes yellow with the deposition of fat cells.

Your bone tissue is constantly renewing itself throughout your life, constantly tearing down and rebuilding its mineralised framework. Chemical substances secreted by the cells of the immune system help regulate the balance between bone loss and formation.

Bone-absorbing cells known as osteoclasts dissolve or break down old tissue, and bone-forming cells or osteoblasts deposit new tissue. Once bone tissue hardens, the osteoblasts undergo change into mature osteocytes.

Bones—support and protection

The single most important function of your bones is the support of the softer tissues of your body. The action of your voluntary muscles on your bones and joints is what produces your ability to move and to walk.

A second important function of your bone is the protection of softer structures, especially those of your nervous system.

A third is the production of blood cells in the marrow. Cells there which are called stem cells are the ultimate source of all types of blood cells. These were finally isolated in the bone marrow in the late 1980s.

Bones also store calcium salts, and the tiny bones in the middle ear of higher animals conduct soundwaves and make hearing possible.

In summary, bone serves a number of important functions:

- It supports the soft tissues.
- It protects the inner organs and tissues.
- It produces many of your blood cells.
- It acts as a store for your calcium.

Bones—varieties and shapes

There are a number of types of bone. The bones can be long, as in the main bones of the limbs. These *long bones* include the humerus of the upper arm and the femur, tibia and fibula of the lower limbs. The *short bones* occur in the wrist or ankle. Typical examples of these include the carpal bones of the palm and the tarsal bones of the arch of the foot.

Your spinal bones or vertebras are examples of *irregular bones*, and the bones of the skull are typical *flat bones*. The kneecaps or patellas are typical of bones laid down in tendons—the *sesamoid bones*.

Most limb bones are long and roughly cylindrical. The shaft consists of a shell of compact bone—the cortex—surrounding an interior of spongy bone and marrow. The ends of the limb bones are mostly spongy bone tissue, capped by cartilage at the joints. During our youth, rapid growth occurs in the specialised epiphysial cartilage, which lies between the flared section of the bone and the epiphysis—the growing end of the long bones.

The process of forming bone tissue is known as *ossification*. A further type of bones are the *dermal bones*, which ossify within the connective tissue of the skin. The clavicle or collarbone is typical of these dermal bones.

The above may be summarised as follows:

- Your bones can be long—as in the limb bones.
- Your bones can be short—as in the bones of wrist and ankle/foot.
- Your bones can be flat—as in the skull.
- Your bones can be irregular—as in the spinal bones (vertebras).
- Some of your bones grow in connective tissue—they are dermal bones.

Peak bone mass and your 'bone bank'

The maximum deposition of calcium into your bone occurs at about twenty years of age in women and men. By your mid to late twenties your bones will contain as much calcium as you will ever have. Your bones are then at their greatest strength and density or 'peak bone mass'. The term 'bone mass' means the amount of bone material in a given area of bone.

Consider your bones as a 'bank' for calcium and other minerals.

Calcium is simultaneously being deposited or laid down as bone and being withdrawn in some part of your body. This process is kept in balance by a complex system of chemical messenger substances known as *hormones*.

The strength of your bone at peak bone mass is partially determined by factors you inherit and which you can't change. These include the level of your sex hormones, your ethnicity, and your family history.

Bone strength also depends on lifestyle factors which you can have an influence on, such as exercise, diet, smoking, alcohol consumption and probably others which are not currently recognised.

Up to the time of your peak bone mass, new bone is being added to your skeleton faster than old bone is removed.

Once your peak bone mass is achieved there is a period of stabilisation where your calcium gain and loss are in a state of balance—gain and loss are basically equal. Then, from about the middle of your third decade, gradual bone loss starts to occur. Calcium is now being removed from your bones at a faster rate than it is replaced. This gradual loss of bone as we get older is a natural process.

The greater your peak bone mass, the greater the protection you will have against osteoporosis in your later years. As the major build-up of bone in girls occurs in the earlier teenage years, it is particularly important for girls in their early teens to exercise regularly and get plenty of calcium in their diet.

Menopause and bone loss

Women start to lose bone at a much faster rate after menopause, which usually occurs between age 45 and 55. For some women this may start as early as the middle of the third decade and for others it may be delayed into the late fifth decade. In others, early menopause occurs as a result of surgical removal of the ovaries, hormonal suppression or as a result of eating disorders such as anorexia nervosa.

During the first five years following menopause, bone loss for women is far greater than for men in the same age range. This is because the ovaries virtually cease producing oestrogen, which plays such an important part in the generation of new bone.

14

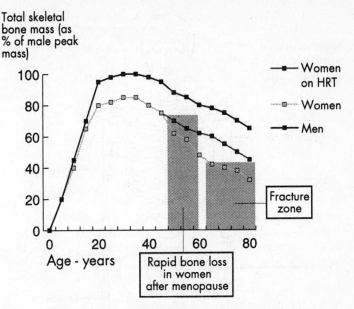

Changes in bone mass with age

Fracture threshold

For many women and some men, a 'danger' level of calcium in the bones is reached in the later years. This leads to the increased probability of your bones breaking more easily. This is sometimes called the 'fracture threshold'. Once you have crossed this threshold the risk of you having a fracture, due to the weakened and more brittle osteoporotic bone, increases.

Whether you reach the fracture threshold depends on how much bone is deposited in your 'bone bank' at peak bone mass, your rate of bone loss after peak bone mass and what age you have reached.

Your skeleton

To explore your skeleton further you need some background knowledge to have some understanding of the amazing structure which is your skeletal system. The next section will take you on a brief tour of the skeleton, emphasising those areas most commonly affected by those fractures which unfortunately characterise osteoporosis.

The human skeletal system is comprised of individual bones and cartilage that receive a supply of blood and are held together by

15

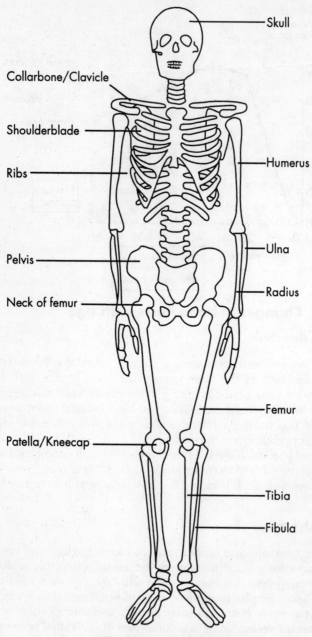

Skull

Collarbone/Clavicle

Shoulderblade

Ribs

Humerus

Pelvis

Ulna

Neck of femur

Radius

Femur

Patella/Kneecap

Tibia

Fibula

Skeleton (front view)

fibrous connective tissue, ligaments, and tendons. The three main functions of the skeletal system are protection, motion, and support.

Your skeleton protects the body by enclosing the vital organs. It permits you to move by responding at certain joints to the contractions of your muscles, and it supports your body by serving as a framework formed by the bones and their various projections.

The bones and their various spines and prominences enhance the natural system of support and leverage to which tendons and the covering membranes of the muscles—the fascia—are attached. The so-called skeletal muscles, internal organs or viscera, and skin are enabled to obtain a secure attachment.

As already noted, your skeleton also serves as a depot for calcium, which is vital to proper functioning of cell membranes, and for phosphorus, which is needed to ensure the health of cells throughout the body. In addition, the skeletal system is important because the bone marrow produces blood cells.

At birth your body has about 275 bones, but as the body develops many of these bones fuse together. In the adult human the skeleton consists of 206 name-bearing bones and a variable number of largely unnamed sesamoid bones which develop in the capsules of certain joints or in tendons.

The tendons hold muscle to bone, and the specially developed sesamoid bones provide special support or reduce friction where the tendons cross over your joints. Fractures of these bones may be the only thing to draw our attention to their presence. The best-known sesamoids are the patella (kneecap) and pisiform (one of the wrist bones).

Not all bones are affected by osteoporosis. As osteoporosis does not usually affect the bones of your skull these will not be dealt with in this brief review of the human skeleton. The disease which mainly affects the skull of the elderly is Paget's disease, which causes the bones to become dense yet too flexible.

The areas most effected in osteoporosis, leading to their increased incidence of fractures, are the spine or spinal column, the bones of your wrist, ankle and foot, and the major bone of the thigh, the femur.

Of particular importance is the stalk-like neck of the femur, which connects the ball of the femoral head to the upper shaft of the thighbone. Fracture is a major source of illness and even death.

The spinal column

The spinal column of most adults consists of 26 bony segments or vertebras. Occasionally people are born with one or more absent or extra vertebras, or some vertebras will be fused together, as a result of developmental problems or injury or degeneration.

There are seven vertebras in your cervical or neck area, twelve in the thoracic or chest area, and five in the lumbar or lower back area. The three bones of the sacrum are fused to form a single triangular mass and the last small vertebras of the tailbone or coccyx may be separate or be fused into one or more pieces.

Each vertebra, except the first and last, has a body which is roughly rectangular in its cross-section. These bodies are held in place by strong muscles, tendons and ligaments in a more or less gentle S-shaped curve. The vertebral bodies function to bear weight, as in standing or sitting, and to allow all of the movements necessary to allow you to bend, straighten, twist or lift.

The vertebras are separated from each other by an intervertebral disc. This remarkable structure has a tough yet strong outer lining— the annulus fibrosis—and a soft gelatinous pulp. The discs, made of a fibrous elastic cartilage, cushion the vertebras, lubricate the joints between vertebras, and act as shock absorbers, unless disease or injury occur.

Two stalks, called pedicles, arise from the two sides of each vertebral body. The pedicles of one vertebra lie next to those of the adjoining vertebra. Between the pedicles is the space or canal through which the spinal nerves emerge.

In addition to a vertebral body and pedicles, all vertebras except the coccyx possess a vertebral opening or foramen through which the spinal cord passes, and various bony protuberances that, together with their attached ligament and muscle, limit the kinds of movements the spine can make.

The most common fractures seen in the osteoporotic person are compression fractures. These may occur without warning or pain and lead to gradual forward curvature of the spine which is typical of the person with advanced osteoporosis. The more acute and painful fractures of this type can occur with minimal trauma or injury.

In this type of fracture the front edge of the vertebra is compressed in such a way that it loses height compared with the more normal height of the back portion of the vertebra. This leads to the characteristic wedge-shaped vertebra of the osteoporotic person.

The changes which occur in the vertebras with compression create other problems due to the involvement by pressure on the tissues of the nervous system.

Severe compression of the spinal nerves or even the contents of the central spinal canal—the spinal cord and the nerve roots—

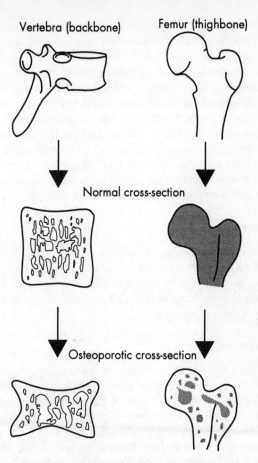

Vertebra (backbone) Femur (thighbone)

Normal cross-section

Osteoporotic cross-section

Process of bone loss

often leads to the typical pain experienced in sciatica—pain down the leg and foot. In more serious cases, compression of the lower nerve roots may lead to difficulties in bowel and bladder activities, with incontinence being a possible consequence.

The rib cage

Your rib cage is made up of twelve pairs of ribs, the twelve thoracic spinal bones, and the sternum (breastbone). The first seven pairs of ribs are called 'true ribs' because they join directly to the sternum.

The eighth to tenth ribs are called 'false ribs' because they do not attach directly to your sternum. Instead, they are joined with each other and with the seventh rib. The eleventh and twelfth ribs are called 'floating ribs' because they do not join anything else at their front ends.

In people with advanced osteoporosis the rib cage and its contents—the lungs and heart—are put under great pressure by the forward bending of the upper or dorsal spine. This may occur to the extent that it becomes difficult for the person to breathe owing to the effective squeezing of the lungs into the markedly reduced space between the spine, the ribs and the diaphragm.

Some experts in the treatment of advanced osteoporosis have resorted to the surgical removal of the lower ribs in an attempt to reduce the pressure on the chest contents.

The shoulder girdle

The shoulder girdle consists of two shoulder blades or scapulae and the two collarbones or clavicles. The entire apparatus, together with its muscles, permits you to raise your hands skyward. It also assists humans to perform functions that most animals, except primates, are incapable of performing.

The upper limbs

Each of your upper limbs consists of an upper arm, forearm, and hand. The upper arm contains a single bone, called the humerus. The head of the humerus forms a ball-and-socket joint with the shoulder blade by way of a large depression in the shoulder blade known as the glenoid cavity, or fossa.

The forearm contains two bones, a radius and an ulna. The hand, wrist and fingers contain 27 bones consisting of eight carpal bones (the wrist), five metacarpal bones (the palm), and fourteen phalanges (the finger bones). The metacarpals, whose distal ends are known as knuckles, form the palm.

The most common fractures in the upper limbs occur at the wrist, particularly at the ends of the radius and ulna, closest to the wrist. This type of fracture, known to doctors as a Colles's fracture, commonly occurs when the person tries to break a fall with the outstretched hand. The hand is commonly forced forward or backward, leading to a fracture in one or both of the forearm bones just above the wrist. The osteoporotic person is also more likely to fracture the long humerus bone in the upper arm.

Healing of these bones usually occurs with rest and immobilisation, either in a splint or with a sling.

The pelvic girdle

The pelvic girdle or pelvis supports your trunk or body on the thighs while standing, permits sitting, and provides protection to your urinary bladder, ovaries, fallopian tubes, uterus, and rectum.

The pelvis is formed from two hipbones, a sacrum which lies between the hipbones, and a coccyx or tailbone. Each hipbone consists of an ilium, ischium and pubis, which are joined together in adults to form one bony mass.

The pubis forms the front region of the hipbone, where the two hipbones unite by way of a cartilage bridge known as a pubic symphysis. Where the three components of each hipbone unite, a socket is formed. Known as an acetabulum, this socket receives the head of the femur.

Fractures of the pelvis occur much less frequently than those of the neck of the femur owing to the greater bone density of the pelvis compared to that of the femur. Fractures of the pelvis are seen more commonly after motor car crashes.

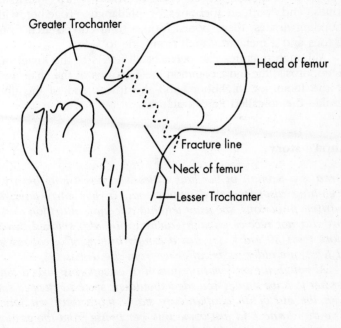

Front view of fracture of the right femoral neck.

The lower limbs

Each lower limb is composed of a thigh, lower leg and foot. The femur is the bone of the thigh and is a large, heavy, long bone that connects the hipbone to the shinbone of the lower leg at the knee. The thighbone consists of a long shaft with the end that fits in the socket of the hip joint, forming a ball that sits on the angled neck of the femur. The bottom end of the thighbone ends in a wider area which together with the tibia and patella forms the knee joint.

The knee joint between the femur and tibia is provided with some protection by the kneecap or patella, which is a sesamoid bone embedded in the tendon of the large quadriceps muscles at the front of the thigh.

In addition to a shin bone or tibia, the lower leg contains a splint bone or fibula. Whereas the shinbone allows the leg to bear weight, the fibula enables you to make certain movements at the ankle, which is the joint between the shinbone, the fibula, and one of the bones of the ankle, the talus.

The foot contains seven tarsal or ankle bones, five metatarsal bones, and fourteen toebones or phalanges. Together with surrounding tissues, these bones form a long curved arch from heel to toes and a metatarsal arch from side to side.

Although fractures can occur at all levels of the lower limbs in osteoporosis, the most common are fractures of the shaft and neck of the femur or thighbone, and the lower end of the tibia and fibula—the so-called Pott's fracture.

Anna's story

Anna is a woman in her late sixties who has a long history of the breathing disorder called emphysema. In her early days, due to wartime privations, she went without adequate nutrition and therefore did not receive enough calcium. She also smoked heavily for more than 30 years. She has a family history of osteoporosis, with at least one older sister suffering from the disease.

Although the only manifestation of osteoporosis was a tendency for her to have slightly rounded shoulders, she had stopped smoking with the aid of an acupuncture staple more than ten years ago. One day Anna had just come into her house from the garden and was about to change her shoes. She had stepped out of one pair of shoes and had put on one of the next pair. She then twisted around to put the second shoe on and was surprised to find herself on the ground in agony. She had fractured her leg just above the ankle, and one of the bone fragments protruded through her skin.

The fracture was set in plaster but, instead of six to eight weeks, it took more than three months for the fracture to heal and it was a further three months before she was able to bear weight fully and return to her normal activities.

Fractures of the neck of the femur are the most likely to cause severe problems for the victim. These include loss of independence and more importantly, for a large proportion of sufferers, death.

3

More problems with bone

Bone diseases most directly influence our ability to walk or to move any part of the body. They are also often associated with disorders or disease of the joints. Diseases of the joints—or arthritis—should not be confused with osteoporosis, although both may exist in the same person at the same time.

The medical specialties focusing on bone disorders are rheumatology and orthopaedics. They are mainly responsible for dealing with the many things which may go wrong with bone. These problems include the usual categories considered in medicine, that is, congenital, infectious, metabolic, nutritional, toxic, and neoplastic diseases.

Problems occurring at or around birth

There is a wide spectrum of birth defects or congenital bone diseases. These range from mildly bowed legs to severe lesions such as spina bifida, in which the lower end of the spine fails to develop properly and the baby is born with paralysis and misshapen vertebras.

Congenital diseases may have a hormonal basis such as in fibrous dysplasia. In this relatively uncommon condition, fibrous tissue replaces that of some bones and often results in bone deformity. In addition, some girls with this disease physically mature so early that they are capable of pregnancy and childbirth at the age of seven.

Congenital defects may also have genetic bases, as in families who have extra fingers or toes (polydactyly), or in the disease osteogenesis imperfecta, in which children have such brittle bones that many are fractured. The life expectancy of these children can be affected by the disease.

Disorders of growth and development include several kinds of dwarfism and gigantism. These are usually caused by abnormalities of the pituitary gland in which an excess or abnormal amount of the growth hormone necessary for normal growth is produced.

Abnormal curvature of the spine (scoliosis) may occur for unknown reasons. Abnormal growth of the ankle and foot may lead to club foot. Bones or limbs may develop deformity as the result of known causes, such as the infection poliomyelitis.

Infections

Bone infection is called osteomyelitis and is usually caused by pus-producing bacteria, especially *Staphylococcus* and *Streptococcus*. Before the development of antibiotics children frequently contracted this disease. Today bone infections are introduced primarily through fractures and during surgical operations. In the past, people infected with syphilis, tuberculosis, leprosy or yaws were also susceptible to bone damage.

The typical extreme forward curvature and shortening of the spine seen in tuberculosis of the spine leads to the typical portrayal of the hunchback—Pott's disease.

In the past, syphilis was often associated with destruction of the larger joints such as the knee. This occurred because the disease selectively destroys those nerve fibres which carry pain signals from the effected area to the brain—denying the sufferer the necessary acute pain which acts as a warning that damage in the joint is occurring.

Arthritis

Inflammation of the joints leading to pain and disability is known as arthritis. Most forms of arthritis will lead to joint deformity and possibly enlargement. This may occur as the result of actual inflammation when the joints become hot and swollen and the lining tissues of the joints are destroyed, as in rheumatoid arthritis or the arthritis associated with gout (a metabolic condition associated with abnormal breakdown of certain amino acids).

The spinal arthritis condition of ankylosing spondylitis occurs more commonly in younger males and leads to the development of a stiffened and bent spine at an early age. X-rays of this latter condition show a spine looking like a bamboo pole, with the individual spinal bones being fused into a single unit.

The chronic skin problem of psoriasis is associated in a small but significant number of people with a generalised arthritis linked in most cases with the destruction of the smaller joints.

Bob's story

Bob, aged 43 years, attended a pain clinic because he was experiencing severe neck and shoulder pain following a motor car accident two years previously. Despite a wide variety of treatments, including conventional physiotherapy, chiropractic, osteopathy and naturopathic remedies, Bob complained of increasing pain and stiffness in the neck, upper back and both shoulders.

Bob has a long history of a chronic skin condition in which his skin shows many areas of itchy, dry, flaking skin. This has been diagnosed as psoriasis—a chronic condition which is of unknown origin and which runs in families.

Medical examination revealed marked stiffness of the entire spine. His neck was almost rigid, and his left shoulder joint was extremely restricted in its range of movement. He was extremely tender to the touch over the neck, upper spine, and the top and back of the shoulders.

As part of his assessment and prior to his referral to the pain clinic he had been referred for X-rays of the whole spine. These X-rays showed that Bob's spine appeared to be less dense than normal. There were other features shown on the X-ray films which suggested the possibility of osteoporosis. These took the form of a number of compression fractures in the upper or dorsal spine. There was wedging of the affected vertebras resulting from the fact that the anterior or front of the bones were shorter in height than the posterior or back of the affected bones.

The medical condition of ankylosing spondylitis—a severe form of mainly spinal arthritis, seen more commonly in men—was also suspected because of the apparent fusing together of a number of the vertebras. This led to the development of the typical 'bamboo' spine seen in X-rays of this condition.

Bob was sent for a bone density scan as a result of these X-ray findings. It now appeared likely that these changes had resulted from the large does of steroids given to Bob as treatment for his painful shoulder condition. The scan revealed a marked reduction in bone density in his hip and spine. Bob is now at great risk of a fracture due to osteoporosis.

Metabolic disorders

Metabolic abnormalities often involve defects in the storage of minerals—particularly calcium and phosphorus—in the skeleton. Diseases of the kidney can cause a metabolic imbalance of phosphate and calcium so that weakening of the bone occurs. Other metabolic bone diseases are osteoporosis, gout, and Paget's disease of bone.

Parathyroidism

Parathormone (PTH),[1] the hormone manufactured by the parathyroid glands, controls the concentration of calcium and phosphorus in the blood. It increases blood levels of calcium by increasing the bone-robbing removal of the mineral (calcium) from the skeleton, increasing absorption of calcium from the bowel and reducing the reabsorption of calcium in the kidneys. It also increases the manufacture of vitamin D and lowers the blood phosphorus levels by increasing its rate of excretion.

Under normal conditions in your body, PTH levels rise as the blood calcium falls. Abnormally raised PTH levels may result from a parathyroid tumour known as an adenoma (primary hyperparathyroidism) and conditions which cause a tendency toward low blood calcium levels, for example chronic kidney failure (secondary hyperparathyroidism). If secondary hyperparathyroidism becomes longstanding, the glands may secrete excess PTH (tertiary hyperparathyroidism).

Patients with mild hyperparathyroidism may have no obvious symptoms or complaints. Clinical features in the more severe cases are related to excessive blood calcium, and patients will complain of feeling generally unwell, loss of appetite, nausea and vomiting, drowsiness or confusion. Peptic ulcers and acute inflammation of the pancreas may be the initial complaints in some people.

Kidney involvement may present with extremely painful renal colic from the presence of stones, blood in the urine or frequent day and night passage of urine from kidney damage. Bone pain suggests involvement of the bones—backache is common. Gout-like symptoms may occur.

The blood levels of calcium may be high and those of phosphorus low. The blood level of the enzyme alkaline phosphatase is raised, reflecting the increased activity of the bone-growing osteoblasts in response to bone loss. Changes in the X-rays in the early stages include increased translucency of the bones and erosions under the periosteal covering of the bone in the fingerbones and toebones. It is important to exclude other causes of excessive blood levels of calcium such as malignancy (particularly multiple myeloma), sarcoid and drugs, not forgetting excess vitamin D.

The diagnosis of hyperparathyroidism can be made when PTH is detected by the use of radioisotopes in the presence of excessive calcium in the blood. The second stage in making the diagnosis is the finding of the tumour or tumours. The best approach to treatment is a surgical operation on the neck. In experienced hands, this type of surgery has a 90% success rate in locating and removing the tumour, thus completely treating the condition.

Paget's disease of the bone

This condition, which is also known as osteitis deformans, is common in the elderly (up to 10%). The cause is unknown, but there is a weak tendency for Paget's disease of bone to occur in families. Geographical clustering of this condition, for example in North Lancashire in England, emphasises the possible importance of environmental factors.

There is an increase in bone-robbing osteoclastic activity, compensated for by an increase in bone-building osteoblastic activity, which results in disorganisation of the normal bone architecture and an increase in the bone blood supply. Any bone can be affected, but the legs, spinal bones and the skull are most commonly involved.

Patients are often without symptoms and Paget's disease of the bone is commonly discovered during consultations for unrelated conditions, or when arthritis or pain are investigated. Those who complain of problems due to their Paget's disease complain of constant and localised bone pain, unrelieved by posture or rest. There may be bone deformities such as enlargement of the bone of the forehead, distorted facial features and bowing (bending) of the shinbones or tibia. The affected bone may feel warm to touch, and when the doctor listens with a stethoscope he or she may be able to hear the blood flowing through the enlarged blood vessels of the bones.

Complications of Paget's disease of the bone include blindness caused by pressure on the nerves to the eyes; deafness due to abnormal bones in the middle ear or to pressure on the nerves of hearing caused by the enlarging bone; secondary osteoarthritis, and pathological fractures.

Investigations show raised activity of the enzyme alkaline phosphatase, reflecting the increase in bone-building activity in the presence of normal calcium and phosphate levels.

Drug treatment is indicated only when patients become symptomatic or develop complications. In such cases, calcitonin and disphosphonates such as Didronel may be used. Conservative measures, such as the use of simple pain-killers, physiotherapy and correction of any inequality of leg length, are also required.

Nutritional disorders

Vitamin D deficiency

Vitamin D has until recently been regarded as one of the vitamins known to be soluble in fats. It is now considered to be a hormone or chemical messenger rather than a true vitamin. It is largely responsible for the formation, growth and maintenance of bones and teeth, in combination with calcium and phosphorus, and it is known to be involved in the regulation of these minerals in your blood. In this case the hormone, vitamin D, is manufactured in your skin as the result of the interaction between your skin and some of its cells and the ultraviolet light in sunlight.

Despite its importance vitamin D is present in appreciable amounts in almost no foods. Egg yolk, butter, herring, mackerel, sardines, shrimp and tuna contain very small amounts of vitamin D. Fish liver oil is the best source of extra vitamin D if this is medically required.

Fortunately for most of us, almost all of the vitamin D in our bodies is produced in our skins as result of exposure of the skin to sunlight. This makes it all the more important to expose some of our skin to the sun each day.

Deficiency of vitamin D in adults is known as osteomalacia and in children as rickets. This vitamin deficiency is now fairly uncommon in the western world although it may occur in some immigrants and the elderly, as a result of a combination of dietary insufficiency and lack of exposure to sunlight.

It may also be caused by poor absorption or malabsorption from the stomach and intestines. Therefore, those with a history of previous gastric surgery, coeliac disease and deficient bile salt production are at higher risk. Other less common causes include chronic use of long-term anti-epileptic drugs known as anticonvulsants, liver and kidney failure, and inherited or familial conditions such as vitamin D-resistant rickets and X-linked hypophosphataemia.

The main function of vitamin D is to ensure an adequate concentration of calcium for the formation of calcium salts in your bone. Deficiency of vitamin D results in a deficiency of the deposit of minerals in the bone, and a reduction in the strength and flexibility of bone.

Childhood rickets usually presents with bone deformity or failure of adequate growth. Signs include an enlargement of the front and sides of the upper skull bones, delayed closure of the anterior fontanelle (the soft spot at the front of an infant's head which serves to allow the growth of the skullbones), rickety rosary (enlargement of the growing end of the rib cartilages), pigeon deformity of the chest and bowing or other deformities of the legs.

In the adult, the osteomalacia may produce skeletal pain and tenderness and spontaneous bone fractures. Muscle weakness is often present and there may be a marked weakness of the muscles closest to the trunk.

In both conditions, tetany shows itself by the presence of spasm of the muscles of the hands and feet, and by facial twitching. Investigations show low or low to normal amounts of calcium in the blood plasma, low phosphorus levels, and increased levels of one of the enzymes found in association with bone loss or breakdown—alkaline phosphatase.

X-rays show thinning or less density of bone due to defective laying down in the bone of minerals and almost transparent bands of bone which may look initially like fractures, particularly in the pelvis, ribs and long bones.

In children, there may be additional changes in the epiphysis or growing ends of the long bones. These areas become broadened. Bone biopsy may sometimes be required for diagnosis in adult cases.

How should vitamin D deficiency be managed? Prevention is better than cure. Education and living standards should be improved in the susceptible populations. Free access to and adequate dietary intake of vitamin D should be ensured. Supplements should be given to epileptic patients on certain long-term anti-epileptic drugs. High replacement doses of vitamin D are required in patients with kidney disease and those with inborn resistance to vitamin D.

Scurvy

This long-time scourge of the seafarer, caused by a lack of vitamin C, also affects bone tissues. The condition was recognised by authorities in the eighteenth century and resulted in all seagoing vessels carrying fresh fruit or vegetables containing vitamin C. It is rarely seen in the western world except in groups with special problems, such as the isolated elderly, the demented, alcoholics and food faddists. Vitamin C deficiency results in the failure of the body to manufacture the collagen fibres which are an essential component of most body tissues, including bone.

The most obvious findings in scurvy relate to the deficiency of collagen in the blood vessel walls, leading to severe bruising of the body and bleeding from the gums.

Other minerals may also be important

A study in the late 1980s indicated that the mineral boron is nutritionally important. Apparently, it reduces loss of the bone minerals calcium, phosphate and magnesium and helps to maintain adequate blood levels of oestrogen and testosterone, which play a role in bone health.

Copper is another mineral involved in bone development. In some mammals and birds manganese deficiency is associated with bone abnormalities. Selenium poisoning is recognised in animals grazing on high salt pastures and *itai itai byo* or 'ouch-ouch' disease is a medical condition that has been found in some Japanese women who have drunk water contaminated with cadmium from industrial effluent.

Toxic diseases

The importance of toxic conditions of bones to public health became evident because of such tragedies as thalidomide-induced birth defects and radium poisoning. The drug thalidomide was given to pregnant women throughout the world as a sleeping-pill and to treat nausea. It caused an epidemic in which thousands of babies were born with deformed or missing limbs.

Women employed during the 1920s as painters of luminescent clock dials were unwittingly exposed to radium from the paint as they licked their brushes. Many died, either from anaemia or from bone cancer, alerting doctors to the dangers of radioactivity and subsequent radiation injury. Other types of toxic bone disease include fluoride and lead poisoning and overexposure to X-rays.

Kidney diseases

The condition of renal osteodystrophy occurs in some patients with different forms of kidney failure. The result of the kidney failure is the development of osteomalacia, forms of parathyroid overactivity and even alternating areas of increased and decreased production of bone in the spine. The kidneys lose their ability to manufacture some forms of vitamin D and their ability to control the blood levels of calcium.

Liver diseases

Chronic conditions associated with liver damage almost inevitably are associated with bone or calcium loss. 'Cirrhosis' is the term used when the liver is chronically damaged as a result of chronic alcohol abuse, chronic hepatitis or another condition where the body is unable to deal with iron—haemachromatosis. In these conditions, the end result of damage to the liver tissue or the ducts which transmit bile leads to a decrease in the amount of calcium absorbed from the blood.

The damaged liver is also unable to convert the vitamin D produced in your skin to its final active substance. The loss of calcium produced by liver disease may be counteracted in some patients by the use of the synthetic vitamin D drug, Calcitriol.

Tumours

Bone tumours, although not common, are not rare; benign tumours are more common than malignant ones (sarcomas). Metastatic tumours or secondary cancers are those which arise primarily in another tissue.

They spread by the blood or lymphatic fluid to the skeleton, where they usually grow in many places at once. They are very common in bones, although tumours originating *in* bones are not. The skeleton is second only to the lung as a site for metastases of cancer. More fatalities and greater pain are associated with metastases of bone than with any other type of cancer.

Fractures

Fractures or broken bones are the most common bone disorders. They can occur as the result of an accident or can be secondary to metabolic diseases. Fractures may be life-threatening to older people with osteoporosis. Many women with osteoporosis may break a hip during a fall and often lose their independence or even die from complications.

Treatments

Treatments for bone diseases vary as widely as the causes. Physical disorders often require mechanical therapy—for instance, plaster casts for fractures, and braces and splints for support. Drugs are used for metabolic problems, and antibiotics for infections. Corrective surgery benefits many people having such diseases as scoliosis. Therapy can also involve rehabilitation medicine, in which victims of injury, deformity or amputation can learn how to function as normally as possible.

How can medications contribute to bone loss?

The following list includes the types of medication which have a negative effect on your bone mass and may therefore contribute extra risks to your development of osteoporosis:

- Thyroid hormone preparations; thyroid replacement therapy; thyroid weight loss therapy; thyroid treatment of PMS syndromes
- Glucocorticoids
- Anticonvulsants
- 'Loop' diuretics
- Phosphate-binding 'antacids'
- GnRH-agonist therapy for endometriosis, hirsutism
- Testosterone-blocking agents; cyproterone acetate
- Oral tetracyclines
- Isoniazid

Thyroid medications

Drugs used in the treatment of thyroid gland disorders may hasten the loss of bone. These drugs increase the metabolism of the body and they have been prescribed at some times in the past for weight reduction. There is no current indication for this use in Australian medical practice. Their use should be restricted to the treatment of thyroid gland underactivity.

The steroids

The glucocorticoids are also known as steroids or 'cortisone drugs'. As we have seen, these are mainly produced in the tiny adrenal glands which sit on top of the kidneys. The main function of these hormones is the regulation of carbohydrate, protein and fat metabolism in the body. They also have influences on the immune system and on the body's capacity to fight inflammation.

They are mainly used in the treatment of chronic illnesses such as chronic severe asthma and rheumatoid arthritis. They cause an increase in the loss of bone calcium, particularly if they are taken over a period of time.

Anti-epileptic drugs

Some of the drugs used to treat epilepsy may also result in loss of bone density. These include the commonly prescribed medicine, Dilantin. You should inquire of your treating doctor what your risks are and take measures to prevent bone loss. These may include the use of calcium supplements, increasing weightbearing exercise, or the use of alternative anti-epileptic drugs if this is possible.

You should not, under any circumstances, stop your anti-epileptic medication without discussing the matter fully with your treating doctor.

Diuretics—fluid tablets

If you need to take tablets to reduce fluid in your legs and body—the diuretic drugs—you should be aware that some of these are associated with an increased loss of calcium from the kidneys. The particular group of diuretics associated with additional risk of calcium loss are the so-called 'loop diuretics'. Included in this group of drugs are Lasix and the host of generic drugs it has spawned. These include Urex and Uremide tablets.

On the other hand, the widely used thiazide diuretics conserve the body's calcium and may actually protect against osteoporotic fracture in the elderly. The thiazide diuretics include Chlotride, Dichlotride, Hygroton, Navidrex, Moduretic and Diazide.

Antacids

A large number of antacid preparations also interfere with the absorption of calcium from your gastrointestinal system. Those that contain aluminium cause an increase in the excretion of calcium and thus contribute to bone loss. These include Almacarb, Aludrox, Amphogel, Digene, Gastrogel, Gelusil, Mucaine and Mylanta.

Anti-oestrogens

If you have either endometriosis or hirsutism, you may be prescribed drugs which act against the effects of hormones. Medications such as the GnRH drugs may be given to you to assist in these conditions. Unfortunately these medicines increase the rate of bone loss. You may therefore require a non-hormonal treatment which slows the rate of bone loss. The major treatments available are Calcitriol, Didrocal and Calcitonin.

Some males may be at extra risk of developing osteoporosis when they are prescribed drugs to counter the effects of the male hormone, testosterone. Some of these men may benefit from the non-hormonal anti-bone-robbing drugs such as Calcitriol and Didrocal.

Long-term antibiotics

The tetracycline group of antibiotics may contribute to the loss of calcium if taken for prolonged periods. Tetracycline interferes with the laying down of new bone. Those at most risk are those taking long-term treatment for conditions such as acne and chronic bronchitis. Drugs in this group include Achromycin, Doryx, Ledermycin, Minomycin, Mysteclin, Rondomycin, Tetrex and Vibramycin.

The use of the drug isoniazid in the long-term treatment of tuberculosis is also associated with osteoporotic bone loss.

Many of these drugs appear to have their negative effects on bone calcium because of their effects on the kidneys' ability to excrete or retain calcium.

These actions are shown in the table as follows:

Drug	Decreased absorption of calcium	Increased excretion of calcium
'Loop' diuretics		x
Tetracycline antibiotics	x	x
Anticonvulsants	x	x
Glucocorticoids	x	x
Antacid preparations	x	x
Thyroid hormone medications	x	x
Isoniazid		x

Summary

In this chapter we have seen that osteoporosis is just one of the many problems which beset our bones. There are many bone diseases which may contribute to the loss of your bone calcium. These conditions increase the loss of calcium or decrease its absorption. Some contribute to bone fragility, thus increasing the risk of fracture. Treatments are available in many of these conditions to reduce bone loss and hence fracture risk.

4

Osteoporosis—what are the features and risks?

As populations age, diseases of the aged assume a greater importance in society. This is becoming evident in most western countries and is reflected in increased media and public interest in osteoporosis, dementia and other diseases of aging. The increasing public health importance of and community concern about these diseases mean that those at greatest risk and their treating medical practitioners need to be aware of new concepts regarding their causes and treatment.

In advanced osteoporosis with fractures, current therapy is relatively ineffective. Therefore prevention must be the major thrust in the management of postmenopausal osteoporosis. Doctors, and particularly family physicians, must be able to identify individuals at increased risk of osteoporosis at a relatively early age so that appropriate preventive measures may be taken. Risk factor assessment, particularly family history and lifestyle evaluation, is an important first step in this process.

Prevention is to be preferred over treatment in any circumstances, but is especially important when no generally satisfactory treatment for a disease exists. Such, for example, has been the case with poliomyelitis and this is the case with osteoporosis today.

Types of osteoporosis

Two main types of osteoporosis are often described. These are classified as Type I or postmenopausal osteoporosis, and Type II or senile osteoporosis.

Type I occurs in a ratio of one male to six females aged 50–75 years of age, mainly in the delicate trabecular bone inside the more dense outer layer or cortex of the bone. It is characterised by rapid bone loss with frequent fractures in the spinal vertebras. There is low absorption of calcium from the gastrointestinal tract, and the major causative factor is the menopause.

Type II occurs, according to this classification, in patients over the age of 65 years in a ratio of two females for every male affected. Both the inner trabecular and the outer cortical bone are affected, and the rate of bone reduction or loss is slower than in Type I. In Type II osteoporosis, frequent fractures occur in the vertebral bones and in the neck of the femur. Calcium absorption is slow, and the major cause is old age.

Increased bone loss in women

Bone mass peaks in both men and women at about age 30 to 35, and five to ten years later begins to decline, roughly in parallel with a decline in total muscle mass. The fractional rate of total skeletal loss in men is about 0.3% per year and remains essentially constant throughout the remainder of life.

In women the rate is initially the same as in men, but at menopause it increases sharply to as high as 2.2–3.0% per year for the whole skeleton. The results of this continuous loss of bone become apparent after some fifteen years, usually at the end of the sixth or the beginning of the seventh decade of life.

Between the ages of 50 and 70 a woman may lose up to 50% of her bone mass—a fall at this age is associated with a great risk of bone fracture, particularly of the femur.

For the one in three women and one in six men who are liable to sustain this type of fracture, the consequences are severe. They include surgery with the introduction of artificial hip joints, prolonged hospitalisation and a higher incidence of post-operative mortality. About half of these patients remain chronic invalids requiring nursing care. Mortality has been said to be as high as 40% in the first six months after the occurrence of a fractured hip. At this stage, there is little that can be done to remedy the situation.

This chapter will discuss the major features of osteoporosis and describe in detail what we know of the risk factors for osteoporosis. We will cover those factors which you can do little or nothing about, and also those which you as an individual can prevent or alter.

We need first to describe the major problems which arise as

osteoporosis develops and progresses. Hopefully, many of you reading these words will be able to change some of the lifestyle risk factors which will enable you to avoid the consequences of this largely preventable disease.

Age-related bone loss—a condition

Certain skeletal regions, such as the centre of the lumbar vertebral bodies, have been reported to show immediate postmenopausal losses as high as 6–7% per year. This postmenopausal acceleration of loss in women produces a reduction of total skeletal mass amounting to 20–30% over a twenty-year period.

The immediate postmenopausal loss gradually becomes less severe, so that by age 70 the rate of loss in women is roughly the same as in men once again.

These figures apply to all races, all occupational classes, all nutritional classes, and to all bone regions and bone types studied to date, at least when large numbers of individuals are taken as a group. Some individuals do appear to move contrary to the general trend for at least short periods of time, but, taken as a group, all people lose bone (and muscle) as they age.

Modern methods of measuring bone mass make it possible for the first time to look at various skeletal regions and even different bone types, that is, cancellous and compact bone. As a result, it is now recognised that certain individuals may lose compact bone more rapidly than cancellous, and others may lose cancellous bone more rapidly than compact; further, apart from bone type, some may lose more rapidly from certain regions (e.g. spine) than others.

Thus, within the general trend of bone loss from the entire skeleton, we now recognise distinct patterns in which certain regions or types of bone are lost more rapidly than others. These patterns of loss appear to be related to the type of fracture that may develop.

Osteoporosis—a diagnosis

As has been pointed out previously in this book, the term osteoporosis is generally used to refer to the occurrence of fracture following minor injury or trauma. These fractures occur in people (or body regions) with reduced skeletal mass. Osteoporosis does not usually refer to the reduction in skeletal mass itself.

This way of describing osteoporosis is largely due to the fact that patients first come to medical attention because of fracture. Until recently, it was difficult to detect decreased bone mass in a reliable way in someone without fracture. Thus, for most physicians, fracture itself was and is the principal diagnostic evidence of osteoporosis.

Do you have osteoporosis? What are the major features of osteoporosis?

Fractures

The major feature of osteoporosis, whether it is postmenopausal or due to advanced age or other factors, is the occurrence of fractures of the weakened and more fragile bone. Unfortunately, until bone breaks osteoporotic bone doesn't hurt. When a bone is broken or crushed, whatever the cause, it will cause some degree of pain. In osteoporosis, bone fractures occur most commonly at the wrist, hip and spine.

Less commonly, fractures occur in the upper arm or pelvis. Some of these fractures occur in the absence of any particular injury. This is the situation which occurs commonly in fractures of the spinal vertebras and leads to one of the other major features of osteoporosis—spinal deformity. Other fractures occur more commonly as a result of falling onto the wrist or hand or onto the hip.

Crush or compression fractures A specific type of fracture occurs in the spinal bones or vertebras. When the bone weakens as calcium is lost and the fine structure of the internal part of the bone loses its substance, the bone literally collapses under the body weight. This process affects the front of the spinal vertebras, causing the spine to collapse forward.

The most common consequence of this process is backache. This can occur at any level of the spine, but is particularly common in the upper back or dorsal spine and in the lower back or lumbosacral spine.

The pain is due to what are known as 'crush fractures' of the vertebras. The front part of a vertebra crushes because of loss of bone strength and the forward bending of the body.

Kyphosis or 'dowager's hump'

One of the more distressing features of advanced osteoporosis is the presence of severe bending forward of the upper spine leading to the deformity known as the 'dowager's hump' or the medical term—kyphosis. This results from spinal crush fractures occurring in the upper back or dorsal spine. This leads to a loss of height and deformity of the rib cage with pressure on the contents of the chest and abdomen.

Severe spinal deformity associated with osteoporosis eventually involves the entire spine. When this occurs, chronic back and neck pain will be experienced as a result of the fractures and also as a result of pressure on or stretching of the nerves as they emerge from the spine. Severe pain can be experienced in the arm or leg—sciatica—as a result of nerve damage. In fortunately less common situations, nerve root pressure or pressure on the spinal cord may result in paralysis or lack of bladder or bowel control.

Shortness of breath and regurgitation

As the upper spine collapses and bends forward, the chest contents are forced downwards and forwards onto the diaphragm, leading to increased breathlessness. The results of the pressure on the contents of the abdomen include hiatus hernia, in which the stomach is pushed up into the chest through the diaphragm. This leads to severe indigestion and acid regurgitation, which may be particularly severe at night when lying down in bed.

Pot belly

The stomach seems to bulge forward, forming the typical 'pot belly', and the lower ribs may touch the top of the hipbone. As a result of the compression of the entire abdominal contents, incontinence occurs or is worsened.

The severe forward bending of the neck can be so severe that the chin is permanently rubbing against the upper chest—at times causing ulceration of the skin.

All of this has major implications for increasing the risk of falls. A woman or man with severe osteoporosis will have a centre of gravity in front of, rather than directly along, the spine. This increases the tendency to fall forward and hence increases the risk of fractures of the wrist, spine and hip.

Loss of height

The loss of height due to excessive forward spinal curvature can be as much as 15–20 cm (8 inches). The earliest signs of this occurring may be the discovery that dresses or skirts which were previously at a certain length now seem to be longer. Later problems may emerge when the osteoporosis sufferer tries to reach above the head into tall cupboards or to hang washing.

In more advanced or severe cases it becomes difficult for the osteoporosis sufferer to lift their eyes due to the severity of the forward-bending deformity of the neck and upper back.

Factors in osteoporotic fracture

There are probably factors, both in the bone itself and external to the bone, that contribute to fracture in patients diagnosed as having osteoporosis. The bone factors include decreased skeletal mass, altered architecture of the bone elements such as the girder-like trabeculae, and reduced strength of the skeletal material itself. Among the outside factors a principal one is the increased risk of falls. The relative contribution of each factor is unknown; in general, though, decreased mass is probably the single most important factor in most patients.

Decreased skeletal mass

Osteoporosis suggests there is a causal relationship between decreased bone mass and increased fragility. All studies of patients with osteoporotic fractures have shown that, on average, such patients exhibit values for bone mass well below the peak adult normal range, and generally lower than those of groups of people of the same age without osteoporotic fractures. Thus, bone mass is a moderately good discriminator between those likely to fracture and those not.

The fact that some people with seemingly low bone mass do not suffer from fractures has led to the need to look at other factors in the development of osteoporosis. These are known as *risk factors* and they may be genetically determined or they may be what are known as lifestyle factors.

These considerations are important in the prevention of osteo-porosis because most measures currently thought of as preventive relate principally to the control of age-related bone loss. To the extent that factors other than bone mass are important in osteo-porotic fracture, such preventive measures must inevitably prove not to be completely effective.

Altered internal architecture of your bone

Bone has a number of features which give it strength and flexibilty, yet still provide a lightweight living organ. The internal struts of bone are known as trabeculae, and their distribution and alignment are important to bone strength. Alterations in the bone architecture typically result in fracture in disorders such as Paget's disease.

Until recently, architectural abnormalities were not thought to play a role in osteoporotic fracture. However, several examples with probable applicability to osteoporosis can now be described. During aging, the diameter of the long bones expands. This inevitably makes the long bone shafts stiffer and less resilient. As a result, normal bending stresses tend to be transferred to the ends of the bones, where rapid growth occurs during adolescence. This appears to contribute to the increased risk of hip fracture in the elderly.

Two patterns of trabecular bone loss have now been identified. In one form, commonly found in patients with vertebral crush fracture, the total number of trabecular elements is reduced. Specifically, the trabeculae which act as cross braces disappear. This is the pattern seen in postmenopausal osteoporosis.

In the other form, the total structure remains, but all elements are thinner. The second pattern is typical of the age-related bone loss that occurs in men. Even though the bone mass in affected men and women is identical, this second pattern is architecturally stronger. This may explain the lower incidence of osteoporotic fracture in men.

Reduced material strength

The bone material may be weakened altogether apart from the effects of reduced bone mass. According to experts, inadequate skeletal repair of fatigue damage to bone appears to result in exactly this kind of defect. There is a failure to repair microfractures and to remodel areas of dead bone.

As a result, structural defects that are brought on by sporadic bursts of unusual mechanical stresses continue to occur until a major break develops in response to minor trauma. In this manner bone is similar to most solid materials which develop stress cracks—like metal fatigue.

Normally bone repairs such microscopic defects by local bone resorption and subsequent deposition of fresh bone, but if resorption of the damaged area is delayed, loading stresses are concentrated at the defect and the crack grows until the entire bone is put at risk of fracturing.

Increased tendency to fall

This is a more important factor than has been commonly recognised. It will be covered in some detail in Chapter 7. Factors involved in increasing your risk of falling range from environmental influences, such as slippery floors and obstacles in the living space, to inadequate shoes, postural hypotension, and various medications interfering with balance and alertness.

Long-term outlook

Without proper care and treatment of osteoporosis there is the increased risk for many people of fracture, disability, pain and loss of mobility. The prolonged immobility which follows hip fracture in many sufferers is often associated with other chronic medical conditions. A major consequence of this prolonged immobility is, of course, an increased risk of worsening bone density loss.

Social and psychological problems can arise due to the loss of independence and need to rely more on others, and social isolation can result because of a fear of falls away from home. For some, the point is reached where admission into a nursing home is necessary.

Further facts about osteoporosis

Females are affected far more often than males. In females it is estimated that approximately one in three over the age of 60 will go on to develop an osteoporotic fracture. For males, the incidence of osteoporosis is approximately one in six over the age of 75.

In females osteoporosis rarely occurs before 40 years of age. It is particularly common after menopause. In men osteoporosis rarely occurs in isolation before 60 years of age. If osteoporosis occurs before 60, other causes, such as excessive alcohol usage and male hormone deficiency, need to be examined.

Whatever the gender, more than half of the population can expect some symptoms of osteoporosis if they live long enough.

So who is at risk?

One of the important developments in the study of osteoporosis is the realisation that some of us are more likely to develop osteoporosis than others. Knowledge of these risk factors is important if we are to prevent or treat the condition.

Risk factors are the things which increase your chances of developing osteoporosis. Researchers have identified a number of these factors which help to predict if you are at risk. Having one or more of these does not necessarily mean you will develop osteoporosis or have a fracture, but the chances of this happening are increased.

It appears sensible for those at risk to be aware of the possibility of decreasing bone density and for those at minimal risk to be vigilant. Osteoporosis may still develop in those who initially are thought to have little risk.

Estimates of cumulative life risk of osteoporotic fracture vary, largely because good epidemiological data are not available; but it seems safe, from available evidence, to estimate that a white female in Australia who reaches 60 years of age has a risk of 25–50% of sustaining one or more osteoporotic fractures before she dies.

Factors that appear to increase risk of fracture or, alternatively, that mark the women at increased risk include:

- Slight or slender build
- Fair skin
- Family history of osteoporosis or osteoporotic fracture
- Small muscle mass
- Sedentary lifestyle
- Small peak adult bone mass (late 20s to early 30s)
- Low calcium intake
- Early menopause or oophorectomy (surgical removal of the ovaries)
- Cigarette smoking
- Excessive consumption of protein, alcohol, fibre or caffeine
- One or more prior osteoporotic fractures

Factors that aggravate age-related bone loss or that superimpose another bone-losing mechanism on age-related loss include:

- Thyrotoxicosis or excessive thyroid therapy in the treatment of hypothyroidism
- Glucocorticoid or 'steroid' therapy
- Malabsorption syndromes

- Excessive use of aluminium-containing antacids
- Miscellaneous disease states, from kidney failure to disseminated collagen diseases

Although in Australia as in other western countries the principal ethnic group affected is Caucasian, it must be said that worldwide, brown- and yellow-skinned people are also notably at risk. Afro-Americans, on the other hand, are relatively immune, and among Caucasians, those of Northern European extraction seem to be more at risk than those from around the Mediterranean basin. So far as is now known, these ethnic differences in susceptibility are explained principally by differences in peak adult bone mass.

As has been pointed out elsewhere in this book, osteoporosis is the end point of many different possible processes; it is therefore difficult to make sweeping statements about the likelihood of *your* developing osteoporosis. Certainly, we observe osteoporosis in women who do *not* fit the foregoing profile. All any set of risk factors can do is place people into two groups: those who possess several of the risk factors and are more likely to develop osteoporosis than the general population; and those who possess none of the risk factors and are therefore less likely to develop osteoporosis than the general population.

Female gender

Women are far more likely to develop osteoporosis than men. There are several reasons for this. Girls and women generally have thinner, lighter bones than men. We have already seen that women have an accelerated rate of loss of bone mass during menopause due to a fall in the production of the female sex hormone oestrogen. Even though this rapid loss slows down and becomes closer to the male rate by age 70, women generally have a longer life span than men. This implies that women starting from a lower base level of bone mass have a greater risk of fracture due to bone loss.

However, Adelaide researcher Dr Alan Need was recently reported as stating that despite the emphasis on osteoporosis in women after menopause, there were indications from a four-year study at Adelaide's Institute of Medical and Veterinary Science that osteoporosis was on the increase in men aged over 50. The report in the Melbourne *Herald Sun* newspaper stated that the risk of men in this age group developing osteoporosis is as high as 10–12%.

Genetic factors in osteoporosis

Many studies have shown that dark-skinned races are generally at minimal risk of developing osteoporosis. It is also recognised that people of fair-skinned (Caucasian) race and Asians are at greater risk. It is recognised by some experts that these differences may be related to geographical and cultural factors as well as race or ethnicity. Many cultures do not eat a great deal of dairy food, others keep themselves covered to the extent that very little vitamin D is made in the body because of the exclusion of sunlight.

Recent studies[1] on identical and non-identical twins have shown that the genetic control of your tendency to develop osteoporosis may originate from as few as one set of genes or even a single gene. These studies measured the bone mass in the upper arms, the neck of the femur and the lower spine. They showed a significant correlation of these measurements in identical versus non-identical twins.

The discovery of the 'osteoporosis gene' may assist in the detection of those at risk. As this book is being written, the research mentioned above has made its way into the Australian mass media. Researchers at Sydney's Garvan Institute for Medical Research, led by Professor John Eisman, have now claimed the discovery of the gene which determines whether or not you are at risk of developing osteoporosis. The gene—called the calcitriol (vitamin D) receptor gene—is said to control bone density by regulating the rate of bone cell turnover. The gene acts directly on the bone-removing osteoclasts and on the bone-building osteoblasts.

As a consequence of this discovery, it is now thought by many that the genetic factors you are born with may predominate over your levels of exercise, calcium intake and lifestyle. Genetic study may assist the future early detection of those at risk. A number of studies have confirmed the importance of a family history of osteoporosis in identifying a high-risk patient group.

In the future, DNA analysis of a single blood sample may be used to identify individuals at risk of osteoporosis as a result of inherited genetic factors. Since an individual's gene pattern is constant throughout life, identification of high-risk individuals would be possible in young adulthood (or even in childhood). This would allow early lifestyle (e.g. exercise, diet) and therapeutic interventions to minimise the development of clinical disease.

Genetic differences account not only for overall body size, but for the relative massiveness of the bone elements. Some people are large-boned, others small-boned. For example, dark-skinned people generally have heavier skeletal structures than do Caucasians or people of Asian ethnicity. Mechanical, nutritional, and hormonal factors can alter this genetic endowment, but they cannot eliminate its fundamental importance. Heavy-boned people (particularly Afro-Americans) are relatively immune to osteoporotic fracture to any significant extent, irrespective of wide variations in nutritional adequacy.

Thus, each individual has his or her own genetically determined 'normal' amount of bone for body size and for mechanical loading, and it is this 'normal' value about which he or she varies. If that amount is large, then age-related bone loss works from a high peak mass, and by age 70 to 80, the individual still has relatively more bone than a person of the same age who started with a smaller skeleton.

Your age

In general, the longer you live the more risk you have of developing osteoporosis. This is particularly so for women, although we have seen that men also appear to be at greater risk. Your bones are at the peak of their strength at about 30–35 and the bone mass declines from that time on. Although it is recognised that calcium intake, hormone levels and exercise levels are important in maintaining optimum bone density, your bones will continue to lose more calcium than they retain with advancing age. Men will generally not develop osteoporosis before 60 years of age and women will seldom develop it until after 40 years of age.

Family history

The discovery of the so-called 'osteoporosis gene' confirms what has been observed for years. Women whose mothers have a history of osteoporosis are at greater risk of developing the condition themselves. It therefore makes sense to reduce the lifestyle factors which are recognised as increasing your risks. This includes smoking, excessive alcohol intake and eating disorders.

Inadequate body mass and eating disorders

A certain amount of body fat is necessary for the adequate production by the woman of oestrone, a weak oestrogen produced in fat. When the ovaries have ceased production of the female sex hormones, the oestrone produced in the fatty tissues of the body continues to help protect against osteoporosis.

Obviously this does not imply that all women should carry excess weight any more than men should. The health problems associated with excessive weight are known to include high blood pressure, diabetes and the development of osteoarthritis.

However, women who are excessively thin may have some degree of eating disorder such as anorexia nervosa. Estimates of incidence of eating disorders in as much as 40% of the female population of the USA have been noted in some recent literature. In many of these women the effects of the disorder include cessation of the menstrual periods—amenorrhoea. This is a reflection of the lack of oestrogen and represents premature menopause. Anorexic patients leave dairy foods and many foods with dietary calcium out of their diets. This will often result in significant loss of bone. (Resumption of menstruation will usually occur if body weight can be regained.) A typical example of this can be seen in many professional ballet dancers.

Ballet dancers exercise to excess in their quest for perfection—excessive exercise is itself a risk factor for osteoporosis. The ideal low body mass which is required of them is also a risk factor. In addition, it is recognised that many develop amenorrhoea as a result of their low body weight. They are also at much greater risk of stress fractures in the feet than many athletes.

This problem has also been recognised in many female professional athletes. Active campaigns have been launched in Australia in the past few years to make our athletes aware of the increased risks of osteoporosis which are associated with their pursuit of athletic excellence.

Joan's story

Joan is a 23-year-old competition athlete who fell from a horse while on vacation. As a result she sustained a twisting injury to her right knee. Initial investigations and assessment suggested Joan had sustained ligament injuries to the knee, and she underwent arthroscopic surgery. Her surgeon introduced a fine instrument into the knee which enabled him to look into the knee and detect or repair any problem. Unfortunately for Joan the injuries seemed more related to stretching and straining of the knee rather than any rupture or tear of the knee structures.

She was advised to embark upon an intensive exercise program in which she attempted to build up the strength of her thigh muscles to build up strength and stability of the leg muscles. However, a disturbing set of problems began to arise. Her pain continued and actually became worse, both at rest and during activity.

Her knee continued to swell alarmingly and she began to notice the knee would be hot or cold to touch alternately. The pain then developed a burning quality and the skin took on a shiny look. The skin over the knee could tolerate pressure, yet it could not tolerate being brushed with a feather or tissue.

A diagnosis of reflex sympathetic dystrophy (RSD) was eventually made after tests confirmed she had now developed problems related to the function of the sympathetic nerves which control the flow of blood in the blood vessels (among many other functions). By this stage Joan was unable to put any pressure on her affected knee.

Despite a large number of treatments for her RSD, including transcutaneous electrical nerve stimulation (TENS), acupuncture and treatments aimed at reversing the problems in the sympathetic nervous system, Joan has complained for over two years of continuing pain and disability. Her major complaints have been associated with pain in the knee and the right hip. During a trip overseas she was even provided with a supply of intra-nasal salmon calcitonin by a medical specialist. This was prescribed to control pain and possibly reverse her RSD.

However, recent investigations, including bone density scanning, have shown the development of localised osteoporosis in the affected right knee and right hip. This is thought to be related to the prolonged immobility and lack of weight-bearing following Joan's RSD. Fortunately the bone density of her spine remains within the normal range of values expected for her age. The only treatments suggested at present are increased and prolonged calcium intake and maintenance of her oral contraceptive regimen.

Over the past months Joan, with the encouragement of her medical adviser, has started to increase her weight-bearing exercise. She is now walking for twenty minutes per day and aims to increase this eventually to 40 minutes per day. She is also taking two 600 mg Caltrate tablets each night to supplement her dietary intake of calcium.

Rheumatoid arthritis and other auto-immune diseases

Inflammation in rheumatoid arthritis, lupus erythematosus (known as LE) and other auto-immune conditions contribute to bone loss. In these conditions the body tissues seem to be at war with themselves, leading to the development of bone and soft-tissue inflammation and scarring. The tendency to exercise less, inadequate nutrition, and the use of cortisone-type drugs also contribute to accelerated bone loss in these people.

Premature menopause

Any situation which leads to a premature cessation of the normal menstrual cycle or menopause increases a woman's chance of developing osteoporosis. When this occurs there will be more years during which the bones are not protected by oestrogen, the hormone which plays an important part in the manufacture of new bone.

Conditions which may lead to early menopause include the surgical removal of the ovaries which produce oestrogen. Early hysterectomy is claimed by some to contribute to an earlier menopause. However, if the ovaries—or at least one ovary—are left by the surgeon, natural hormone production should continue. Supplementation by hormone replacement therapy (HRT) may still be required.

The use of drugs which suppress the menstrual cycle may also contribute to an early menopause. Endometriosis is one condition in which these drugs, known as GnRH drugs, may be used to halt the spread of the disease and to reduce the pain caused by the condition. These drugs include the preparations known as Superfact, Synarel, Lupron and Zoladex.

Exercise and bone mass

While heredity plays a major role in determining bone mass, environmental factors clearly modify the inherited bone mass potential.

We have already seen there is an important relationship between mechanical force exerted on the skeleton and bone mass. With humans, however, there are obvious limitations on experimentation and a lot of our knowledge has come from observations of changes in bone and its calcium or mineral status as a result of the extremes of physical activity.

Immobilisation is well recognised to be a leading cause of an increase in urinary calcium loss, due to an increase in the bone-robbing osteoclast cells as well as a decrease in the bone-producing osteoblast cells.[2] This can result in a loss of your bone mass which may be as high as 1% per week, which appears mainly to affect your weight-bearing bones. Similarly, it is recognised that the weightlessness experienced by astronauts in space causes increased urinary loss of calcium and an associated decrease in bone mineral density.[3]

Other examples of this relationship are seen in the hypertrophy of both bone and muscle in the dominant arm of tennis players and in the legs of ballet dancers, and the atrophy of both bone and muscle that occurs on prolonged bed rest, in space flight, and with paralytic syndromes such as poliomyelitis and quadriplegia.

Which factors determine bone loss?

The mass of your total skeleton or of certain skeletal regions is determined by a number of factors: your genetic program; variation in mass around that genetic level, determined by the amount of mechanical loading you place on your spine—the level of physical stress you place on your skeleton; and the intake of adequate nutrition, including calcium.

The factors that appear to be responsible for age-related bone loss and that predispose to osteoporotic fracture are basically the same as those that determine bone mass, i.e. genetic, mechanical, and nutritional/hormonal factors.

Mechanical factors

Mechanical factors are probably the most important determinant of age-related bone loss, although, as we have seen, there are important interactions between mechanical and nutritional/hormonal forces. In general, physical activity declines with age; even those individuals who continue athletic or other physical activities tend to become more sedentary overall. Thus, integrated 24-hour mechanical loading of the skeleton certainly declines with age, both in the population at large and in virtually all individual members thereof. Since bone mass is a function of mechanical loading, it follows that bone mass must inexorably decline with age. Preventive measures in osteoporosis have to be visualised against that reality.

Nutritional factors

There is a large, if mixed, body of evidence that indicates that nutritional factors play important roles in age-related bone loss. Calcium is the most important of these factors. Contrary to older notions, calcium remains an important nutrient throughout adult life. Perimenopausal women who have chronically low calcium intakes or who absorb it inefficiently have been shown to be in negative calcium balance.

Those who take more calcium in food or as supplements or absorb it more efficiently are in more positive balance. In fact, there appears to be a clear relationship in women at time of menopause between level of calcium intake and calcium balance.

Chronically low calcium intake   Calcium is a major building block of bones and adequate calcium intake is therefore essential for strong bones in childhood, teenage years and early adulthood. Calcium is necessary to help prevent bone loss from your late twenties and early thirties on.

Surveys carried out in Australia have shown that many girls and women consume far less than the recommended daily intake of calcium. This is of particular concern in lactating women in whom calcium requirements increase dramatically.

A recent article in the *Medical Observer*[4] dealt with the issue of calcium and exercise. It examined the preliminary data from a three-year study by Professor Ego Seeman and Ms Shona Bass of Melbourne's Austin Hospital. They are studying the diet and exercise routines of 25 young female gymnasts.

Professor Seeman had already carried out a study of young female ballet dancers. The recent study is reported to show that too much exercise during puberty may be too much of a good thing. Most of the dancers were reported to be suffering from abnormal menstrual function—either loss of their periods or insufficient periods—intense physical activity and low body weight. Despite having normal bone density in the spine and legs, their bone density was less than normal in the ribs, skull and arms. Professor Seeman is quoted in the article as stating this shows weight-bearing sites in the skeleton are protected to some extent from the bone-robbing effects of low oestrogen.

The study shows that the longer the absence of periods in the dancers the more rapid is the bone loss. This occurs despite the increased exercise these young women undertake. Seeman believes the increase of bone density seen before puberty is markedly reduced by the ballet dancers' subsequent delayed puberty. Professor Seeman is further quoted in the article as follows:

> We believe the important health message is this—if girls want to participate in sport, they should be encouraged to do so before puberty, but then should slow down for a few years. At about 15 they can pick it up again. During puberty let's leave nature alone. Let the kids grow to their full potential; let their menstrual cycles become established.

Inefficient calcium absorption Anything which interferes with the normal absorption of calcium from the intestine can contribute to increased risk of osteoporosis. The intake of cortisone-type drugs, deficiency of vitamin D, and diseases of the thyroid gland and liver are all associated with abnormal calcium uptake by the body.

Excess protein can increase your risk of developing osteoporosis. Protein intake is also a factor of importance. Excess dietary protein is, of course, metabolised and either used immediately for energy or stored as fat. In the process of conversion the sulphur-containing amino acids yield sulphate, which is excreted in the urine. Either the sulphate alone or the associated acid load, or both, are responsible for an increase in urinary clearance of calcium.

The effect of increases in pure protein intake on urine calcium is quite dramatic: a doubling of protein intake results in an approximate 50% increase in urine calcium. This full effect is rarely apparent, however, for protein never occurs in isolated form in the normal diet, but in varying combination with phosphorus. Thus, increases in protein intake are normally associated with increases in phosphorus as well, and the effect of the increased phosphorus in this situation is the same as when phosphate is used pharmacologically: it reduces urinary excretion of calcium.

Oestrogen loss also results in a deterioration of calcium balance, which is due both to decreased absorption efficiency from the diet and to decreased renal retention of calcium. Oestrogen appears to act as a stimulant to the action of the parathormone (PTH) produced by the parathyroid glands. It increases the blood levels of bone-robbing PTH and at the same time increases the levels of the naturally occurring vitamin D. Vitamin D increases the absorption of calcium from the gut and the PTH increases the retention of calcium by the kidneys.

When menopause occurs the balance is tipped towards a loss of calcium from the bones and the body itself. Without oestrogen the levels of PTH and vitamin D fall and the bones lose more calcium. The excess calcium is lost in the urine as the kidneys allow more calcium to leave the body.

It is widely recognised that even after the menopause the negative effects of lowered oestrogen can be at least partially counteracted by increases in calcium intake. Some studies suggest that total skeletal bone loss following menopause can be retarded by high calcium intakes. However, it takes almost a doubling of your calcium intake in the absence of oestrogen to produce the same level of calcium balance as could be obtained with a small oestrogen supplement.

Other lifestyle and dietary factors

Other lifestyle or diet-related factors probably also play a role in aggravating the tendency to age-related bone loss.

Smoking

Women who smoke are often thinner and may have an earlier menopause. They also have lower levels of oestrogen. Unfortunately we have seen recently that even passive smokers—those who inhale other people's smoke—are at risk of health problems.

A recent study on the effects of smoking on women was reported in the *New England Journal of Medicine* and summarised in the *Australian Doctor Weekly*.[5] The study was carried out by Professor Ego Seeman and Judith Hopper, an epidemiologist. The study made use of the Australian Twin Registry and found that women who smoked a packet of 20 cigarettes a day experienced a loss of bone density of 2% per decade. According to the study, if you are a heavy smoker, by the time you reach 50 years of age your bones will be ten years 'older' than they would be if you did not smoke.

The mechanism by which cigarette smoking decreases your calcium levels and thus your bone mass is not precisely known. However, the study authors suggest smoking leads to a reduction of oestrogen production and an increase in oestrogen breakdown. Theoretically this could lead to menopause occurring two years earlier.

Recent well-publicised cases in Australia and overseas have established a legal link between the development of lung cancer and lung diseases such as emphysema in people who have never smoked yet have been exposed to other people's smoke. The link of smoking to osteoporosis as well as its link to cancer, heart disease, stroke, emphysema and blood circulation problems is yet one more reason to stop smoking or never start.

Overuse of alcohol

Alcoholism is now recognised to be a common problem, but too often goes unrecognised in middle-aged women. It contributes to the osteoporosis problem in a number of ways, including generally reduced calcium intake and excess urinary loss of calcium. Alcohol is probably also as toxic for the bone remodelling apparatus as it is for the liver and brain cells. In any case, bone loss is severe in alcohol abusers, with both men and women alcoholics exhibiting bone mass values similar to those found in individuals of the same sex, but 40 years older.

High caffeine intake

A large intake of food containing caffeine, such as coffee, tea or cola drinks, is thought to increase loss of calcium from the body.

Thyrotoxicosis and liver disorders

Thyrotoxicosis, or overactivity of the thyroid gland, and cirrhosis or chronic liver damage due to excessive consumption of alcohol and other factors, may be potent contributors to the later development of osteoporosis.

Inadequate absorption from the gut

Medical conditions which interfere with absorption of nutrients from the gut such as the malabsorption syndromes and some gastrointestinal surgery can lead to increased risk.

Treatment with steroids (cortisone-type drugs)

High doses of these drugs taken long term, i.e., over six months or more, may interfere with calcium absorption and formation of bone. Such drugs are used to treat a variety of conditions including arthritis, asthma, eczema and certain cancers. Cortisone-type drugs are a synthetic type of hormone belonging to the class of hormones known as corticosteroids—commonly called steroids. The natural hormones are produced in the small adrenal glands which sit on top of the kidneys. The body uses them to regulate the circulation, control inflammation and to cope with stress.

Since many sufferers of arthritis and severe asthma are restricted in their capacity for weight-bearing exercise they face a double jeopardy in terms of their risk of developing osteoporosis.

People on cortisone drugs should not discontinue their medication suddenly, nor should the dose be reduced without consulting a doctor.

If you have any concerns about this type of medication, discuss them with your doctor. If you have to be on these drugs you may be able to use other medication to reduce the possibility of osteoporosis.

Hormones

If you have not been pregnant or used oral contraception your risk may be higher. One of the natural features of pregnancy is the increased level of oestrogen circulating in the blood. We know that, along with exercise and adequate calcium intake, oestrogen plays a vital part in building bone strength.

The use of oral hormone contraception may have a protective function against osteoporosis because of the increased level of oestrogens available to the woman using it.

Dietary and hormonal factors play a role in two ways: firstly, they help determine peak adult mass, and hence the level from which age-related loss occurs; and secondly, they influence remodelling rate. Both oestrogen and calcium supplements suppress remodelling of bone. In contrast, excess protein or caffeine intakes, by increasing calcium loss, lead to an internally stimulated increase in remodelling, and thus the loss of bone mass.

Importance of prevention

Once the disease is present, effects of gravity and exercise on your skeleton are even further decreased because of the discomfort and disability caused by accumulated fracture damage. The chances of producing an effective increase in skeletal strength by the use of drugs or calcium are also further reduced.

I am a young woman. How can I prevent osteoporosis in my later years? Preventive care in the young adult woman should be directed at two ends: achieving your bones' full genetic potential and developing dietary and lifestyle habits that will serve you in good stead years later. The prescription is simple enough: maintain a high calcium intake, exercise regularly and vigorously, and avoid excesses of protein, alcohol, smoking and caffeine.

The need for calcium in the years from cessation of growth to age 35 has, for some inexplicable reason, been inadequately recognised by most authorities, even though the data supporting this need have been available for many years.

Rapid growth during adolescence produces what is at first a relatively fragile skeleton, simply because the periosteal envelope of the skeleton has expanded at a faster rate than bone mass could be provided to fill in the skeletal structure.

Much reorganisation of skeletal structure then occurs for at least another ten years after cessation of growth, and if the adult skeleton is to achieve its full genetic potential, the individual must ingest adequate calcium and must continue to load the skeleton mechanically during these years. Failing these inputs, the woman is left with a small peak mass at age 35 and begins the age-related downward decline from a level of skeletal mass that may be quite inadequate, but a level that in any case is less than could have been achieved.

I think I am going through menopause. How can I prevent osteoporosis? If you are nearing or experiencing the effects of menopause and have a relatively small bone mass you are clearly at a disadvantage. There is little or no evidence to suggest than any known program will give you substantially more bone mass at this stage of your life than you possess when treatment is started.

Hence, efforts are necessarily directed at preventing loss to the greatest extent possible. In the premenopausal years this is best accomplished by ensuring a high calcium intake, in the order of 1000 mg/day or more. In the postmenopausal years, your calcium intake should be increased to at least 1.5 g/day if no oestrogens are used.

Alternatively, protection can be more easily accomplished by oestrogen, in a daily dose of about 0.625 mg conjugated equine oestrogen or its equivalent. Current evidence suggests that the risk of developing cancer of the lining of the uterus—endometrial carcinoma—is greatly diminished, if not abolished altogether, if oestrogen is accompanied by a suitable progestogen. HRT will be discussed further in Chapter 10.

Mechanical loading of the skeleton needs to be maintained at as high a level as possible. As pointed out earlier, you have only as much bone as you need for resisting applied mechanical loads. Oestrogen and calcium can help ensure that you achieve this level of bone mass and slow, to some extent, its loss from that level. In the last analysis neither agent can cause a skeleton to be heavier or sturdier than required by the uses to which its owner puts it.

Finally, both in the premenopausal and postmenopausal years, it is worthwhile also to control intake of drugs and nutrients that interfere with effective utilisation of calcium. The alternative is to plan to compensate for such agencies by significant daily supplements of calcium.

Things which increase your loss of bone mass include, as we have seen above, high protein intakes, smoking, high caffeine intakes, excessive alcohol consumption, and aluminium-containing antacids.

Strict vegetarian diets and low sodium diets create a similar problem for the postmenopausal woman, because they are almost always low in total calcium intake. These diets effectively demand some sort of calcium supplementation to ensure an intake of calcium in the 1.0 to 1.5 g/day range or higher.

I am now over 65 years of age. Is it too late to prevent osteoporosis? The typical elderly woman will already have lost a great deal of the bone she once had—often you will have lost as much as one-third or more of your peak bone mass. While it will probably never be possible to give you the skeleton of a 35-year-old, it is quite wrong to take a fatalistic view about prevention of fracture.

All of the strategies described for younger women remain important for the elderly as well. Regular vigorous physical activity and programmed exercises are particularly important. Exercise not only slows further bone loss, but it provides the background stimulation needed to remodel fatigue damage. It helps maintain the structural integrity of the reduced skeletal mass you are left with.

Many experts now think that HRT should be considered an option in all women at risk of osteoporosis. As you will see in Chapter 10, there are advocates of the notion that women should be placed on HRT within ten years of the menopause and should remain on HRT for the rest of their lives. The rationale for this recommendation is the protection HRT provides against cardiovascular disease and osteoporosis in those who choose to accept this method of improving their quality of life in their latter years.

It is in older age that attention to adequate vitamin D status becomes more important. Vitamin D deficiency becomes more and more common in older people, particularly among the institutionalised elderly. Walking for the 40 minutes three or four times weekly necessary to give you adequate weight-bearing exercise should also stimulate the skin to produce adequate vitamin D.

If you feel you need vitamin D supplements a sufficient dose would be 400 to 600 IU/day. Doses above 1000 IU/day should be avoided. Vitamin D deficiency in the elderly is an easily preventable problem, and now that we recognise its importance there can no longer be any excuse for its existence.

Finally, your attention needs to be directed at falls and at those environmental and body mechanical factors that lead to fracture. These include attention to:

- drug therapy that may be contributing to postural hypotension or to confusion and poor concentration;
- unsafe environments such as inadequate night lighting, inadequate handrails in bathrooms and on stairways, and objects on the floor (such as throw rugs) could that lead to tripping or slipping;
- unsafe shoes;
- unsafe practices for lifting and carrying.

While unglamorous, such efforts will likely produce a better preventive outcome in terms of fracture risk than many seemingly more dramatic interventions. Falls prevention is dealt with in detail in Chapter 7.

Osteoporosis and men

Although many of the medical problems associated with osteoporosis occur in women, one-fifth of all hip fractures occur in men. Osteoporosis in men is therefore an important and relevant health problem about which there is relatively little information.

Health authorities and researchers[6] have noted a marked increase in fracture incidence rates in men over the past decades, and data have shown an increase in fracture frequency at multiple sites with advancing age. It is said that by age 90, one in six men will be hospitalised due to hip fracture. Some 12–20% of these unfortunate men would be expected to die as a direct or indirect result of their hip fracture.

As in women, a hip fracture can lead to long-term nursing home care for up to half of those men who survive it, and the direct and indirect costs of osteoporosis in men have been estimated at approximately $1 billion annually in the United States. Studies in normal men have identified that bone loss in the spinal bones occurs twice as rapidly as that at the ends of the arms and legs.

Male sex hormones are crucial for the preservation of skeletal strength and function in men, and testosterone deficiency has been associated with the development of clinical fractures. Androgens— the male sex hormones—have been found to have a positive effect on bone density and calcium absorption in women as well as in men. However, the use of anabolic steroids in women is unfortunately associated in some with the side effects of masculinisation—facial hair growth, acne and lowering or hoarseness of the voice.

Some 7–30% of men presenting with compression fractures of the spinal bones, in the absence of injury, are due to the lowering of sex hormone production. The Melbourne endocrinologist Dr Ego Seeman studied 105 men who presented with vertebral fractures due to spinal osteoporosis and compared them with age-matched controls. Of these patients 7% demonstrated proven underactive hormone production, and an additional 12% had either testicular atrophy or other signs consistent with failure of the testes.

Low male sex hormone production is therefore a major causative factor in the development of clinical fractures in adult men. Blood levels of testosterone are significantly lower than normal in elderly men with osteoporosis. It has been increasingly recognised that diseases of the pituitary gland and the adjacent hypothalamus region of the brain are a cause of such lowering of the male hormone levels in these patients.

As in women, there is also an increasing occurrence of medically induced low male hormone production due to the use of radiation, chemotherapy, and more recently through the increased use of GnRH analogues.

How does bone loss occur in men?

Puberty has a major impact on male bone mass. The outer cortex of the long bones increases in thickness under the influence of the male sex hormone, testosterone, which is being produced in increasing amounts at this time. In laboratory tests it has been found that the male hormones directly stimulate bone-building osteoblasts, and this increased growth is accompanied by higher levels of the enzyme alkaline phosphatase. Conversely, other substances known to be important in the breakdown of bone, such as hydroxy proline and osteocalcin, are found in increased amounts in the urine of castrated males.

Can treatment help?

There are a few studies on the reversibility of bone mass in men with underactive hormone production. The findings show that reversal of male hormone production to more normal levels is associated with an improvement in the bone mass in the cortex of the bones.

Bone mass has been reported to increase in men treated for primary testicular failure.

Men with the congenital Klinefelter's syndrome have been found to have a decrease in cortical bone density associated with lower serum levels of the hormone calcitonin. Male hormone therapy in men with underactive sex hormone due to congenital or developmental causes may cause an increase in serum calcitriol and bone formation.

A study on the effects of calcium and vitamin D supplementation in men with normal bone loss showed that the administration of these supplements did not affect the rate of bone loss.[7] The authors concluded that much has still to be learned of age-related osteoporosis in men.

Ray's story

Ray is a 60-year-old retired man with a long history of back problems. He was forced to retire from work nearly ten years ago after injuring his back while lifting. A surgical operation to relieve pressure on one of his spinal nerves failed to ease his pain. Years of acupuncture for pain control followed. Although tests of liver function showed longstanding abnormal liver function, a liver biopsy did not show any cirrhosis.

One day when attending for his regular acupuncture treatment he complained of severe pain in the middle of his back, just above his waist. This pain had begun several weeks earlier, without any preceding injury. The pain also spread around the side of his trunk to the left side of his body. When Ray was examined there was an extremely tender area over the ninth thoracic or dorsal vertebral bone.

His treating doctor was concerned about the possibility of a spontaneous fracture of the spinal vertebra due to a secondary cancer and referred Ray to a major hospital for specialist opinion.

X-ray confirmed the presence of a fracture of the ninth vertebra and that it was a typical compression fracture associated with osteoporosis. All spinal bones appeared on X-ray to be lacking sufficient calcium.

Further investigations, including blood levels of calcium, liver function tests and tests for bone tumours failed to determine the reason for Ray's osteoporosis. Ray's subsequent treatment has consisted of regular injections every six weeks of the anabolic steroid Decadurabolin and calcium supplements. In the two years since the fracture Ray has had no further fractures.

Summary

We now know a great deal about the risk factors involved in the development of postmenopausal osteoporosis. This should enable you to determine whether changes in your lifestyle may prevent you from developing this largely preventable condition and reducing your risk of fractures in your later years.

We have also seen that male osteoporosis is related at least in part to the presence of lower than normal male sex hormones and that preservation of adequate hormone levels is necessary to prevent premature fracture related to decreased bone density.

Our knowledge of these risk factors will also enable our struggling healthcare system to reduce the burden on it caused by the increasing numbers of elderly persons occupying hospital beds for the treatment of fractures and their sequelae.

We may also be able to ensure that women's later years can be lived to their full potential and their skeletons continue to serve their role unimpeded into old age.

5

How is osteoporosis diagnosed?

As you read this book you may have asked yourself—do I already have osteoporosis? This chapter offers you the latest information on some of the new concepts and new techniques which have revolutionised the diagnosis of osteoporosis.

Strange as it may seem, osteoporosis did not gain prominence as a 'silent epidemic' until the mid-1980s. We might ask—why is it that a condition, which was previously ignored as undiagnosable and untreatable, began to arouse so much interest?

One reason for the increase in interest was the advent of technology that enabled bone density to be measured both reliably and in a reproducible manner. In this way, osteoporosis is no different from any other area of science. Major advances have often been preceded by our ability to measure important aspects of the condition being studied.

Unfortunately, facilities to measure bone density are not available in all major teaching hospitals as yet; therefore, this chapter will discuss not only the use of these measurements but will also refer to approaches which are not dependent on bone densitometry. Later in the book you will find a list of osteoporosis centres and the location of bone density scanning units.

According to Dr Richard Prince,[1] Senior Lecturer in Medicine at the University of Western Australia, and Consultant Endocrinologist in the Department of Endocrinology and Diabetes at Sir Charles Gairdner Hospital, bone density measurement should be seen as occupying 'a similar position in relationship to osteoporosis as the measurement of haemoglobin to the management of anaemia, or plasma creatinine to the management of renal failure'.

He goes on to state, 'As in anaemia or renal failure, the clinical diagnosis of osteoporosis is considered, and then either confirmed or refuted by appropriate investigations'. In his view and in the view of many prominent osteoporosis experts bone density measurement is the most appropriate approach to diagnosing osteoporosis.

Definitions

Recent rapid advances in our understanding of osteoporosis have left considerable areas of controversy. Therefore it is important that we again attempt to define what is meant by osteoporosis.

Our current clinical definition of osteoporosis is the fracture of any bone after minimal trauma or injury. This is associated with low bone density, and may lead to pain and/or deformity. Your skeleton is considered normal if it is strong enough to withstand the normal stresses of our everyday life.

Abnormality or osteoporosis occurs when these normal stresses cannot be withstood without structural failure or fracture. Prince considers the diagnosis of osteoporosis as occupying the equivalent position in endocrinology (the study of the body's chemical messengers and their relevant glands) as heart failure does in cardiology (the study of the heart and blood vessels). He goes on to state 'Indeed, at a clinical level osteoporosis could be defined as bone failure'.

The diagnosis of osteoporosis requires a sophisticated level of diagnosis compared with some medical conditions. This extra level of sophistication indicates a greater degree of understanding of the process, e.g., osteoporotic fracture due to oestrogen deficiency. Prince emphasises the fact that, even when this so-called symptomatic clinical definition is used, many patients with the condition are being ignored.

A second approach to the definition of osteoporosis already covered elsewhere in this book is to define osteoporosis as being present when the bone mass is lower than a predetermined amount. This is the case whether clinical symptoms are present or not.

The amount of bone below which osteoporosis is considered to be present can be decided when we assess the amount of bone required by most people for normal everyday life—the so-called 'theoretical fracture threshold'. Current work in various osteoporosis centres is being directed towards determining this density for the various sites and the various techniques of bone density measurement. There are clear advantages in intervening at the earliest stage with effective preventive treatment.

It is possible that abnormalities in the microscopic structure of the bone may also play a role in its structural failure. It is also important to realise there are factors other than bone density involved in fracture, for example injury or trauma. Nevertheless, bone densitometry appears to be the most effective method of investigation to confirm the diagnosis and determine the risk of fracture.

Two common categories of bone loss have been defined. These two groups are not mutually exclusive in deciding what the abnormal process is, but they do help with clinical decision-making.

The first is postmenopausal osteoporosis, which is the main subject of this book and which is related to bone loss resulting from oestrogen deficiency. This bone loss may continue for as long as twenty years after the last menstrual period but is most rapid in the early postmenopausal years. Postmenopausal osteoporosis is typically associated with bone loss in the fine trabecular bone, which is inside the more compact shell of the cortex. This bone loss can be prevented by oestrogen replacement.

The second category is age-related bone loss. The pathological cause of this is uncertain, but it is the major cause of continuing bone loss after the age of 75. Typically it is associated with bone loss in the outer compact cortex or outer shell of the bone. This type of bone loss is seen in both men and women alike.

Diagnosis

The clinical diagnosis of osteoporosis according to many osteoporosis experts depends on the recognition of bone fracture after minimal injury. The discovery of a fracture is usually not difficult. However, fracture of the spinal vertebras may occasionally cause spinal deformity with little or no pain at the time of fracture. For this reason, X-rays of the whole thoracic or dorsal spine and the lower or lumbar spine are required.

The decision as to whether the injury which has led to a fracture is minimal or not is often difficult. Generally, minimal injury is considered to be a force roughly equal to or less than that involved in your falling from a standing height. A typical osteoporotic fracture may occur in a person with lowered bone strength simply through the act of standing up from bed or twisting on an ankle.

The latest in bone density analysis

In 1988 the US Food and Drugs Administration (FDA) gave the American electronic manufacturer Lunar permission to market their new instrument called the DPX. The Lunar DPX is a dual photon X-ray bone densitometer based on the use of X-ray rather than radioactive agents, as used in earlier bone-scanning instruments.

The DPX uses two wavelengths of radiation—one is absorbed by bone and the other passes through fat and other tissues. The computer which is linked to the scanner is able to determine the exact amount of bone mass and its density. The accuracy is within 0.5%, which means a very high accuracy consistent over a number of measurements. This bone density measuring instrument was designed and built to fulfil the most stringent and accurate requirements. The DPX and the other instruments which have followed are now able to provide an accurate and reliable assessment of bone density in osteoporosis.

The Lunar DPX is able to measure bone density in any part of the body. It is without risk to you as the subject, or to the radiographer who is carrying out the necessary measurements by operating the equipment. There is minimal radiation in the bone density measurement—less than or equivalent to a dental X-ray—and most importantly it has extreme accuracy compared with other techniques.

Other units currently in use employ the principle of single photon absorptiometry (SPA), dual photon absorptiometry (DPA) or computerised tomography (QCT), and are much less accurate, time-consuming and may expose the patient and radiographer to unnecessary radiation.

Dual energy X-ray absorptiometry (DEXA) enables the prediction of future fractures at sites separate from those sites which are scanned. It is particularly useful because it may be used at spinal sites and also those of the limb bones, e.g., spine, femoral neck and forearm. Its great sensitivity means it is particularly useful for following the treatment of spinal osteoporosis.

The unique accuracy of DEXA means that it is possible to ascertain the extent and rate of bone loss if serial tests are carried out. Changes occurring as a result of treatment programs can be seen with this technique within months rather than the year or two it takes with older approaches to measurement of bone density. It is therefore possible to assess the benefits of medication and prescribed exercise programs.

With the assistance of DEXA we are able to scan the vertebral column, the neck of the femur and indeed any part of the body if the appropriate software is used.

The examination is named bone densitometry and the DPX is a bone densitometer. It is able to determine very precisely and accurately the degree of your bone density. The information on bone density gathered is fed into a computer and compared with a database consisting of information on various age groups, a group of people matched with your age and a reference group of young females. The computer is then able to demonstrate very precisely the risk category to which you belong (see photo section).

In a lumbar scan the computer screen shows an image of your spine from the first lumbar vertebra up to and including the fourth lumbar vertebra—the results are calculated at these levels, which are the most significant in spinal osteoporosis. In the femoral neck scan, an image of the femur is shown, and the comparison shown between your bone mass and that of the reference groups stored in the computer's database.

The results can be handed to you and a more detailed analysis sent on to your referring doctor. Where treatment is indicated, its efficacy can easily be monitored by repeat scans, due to the accuracy of the instrument. These can be carried out six months after the previous examination.

Single photon absorptiometry Single photon absorptiometry (SPA) is usually carried out on the forearm bones and occasionally the heel (calcaneum). SPA enables the prediction of future fractures at sites separate from those sites which are scanned. However, SPA cannot be used at those bone sites in what is known as the axis of the body such as the spinal vertebras. Its greatest value is in following the effects of treatment of osteoporosis of the limbs.

Typically, the forearm is scanned in at least two sites by a single energy level beam of charged particles—photons from a radioactive source—which is collected and analysed. The greater the bone density, the less energy passes through the bone and thus the weaker the photon beam which is collected. Placing the affected wrist in a water bath helps to allow for the soft-tissue effects around the bones. Two sites are chosen representing bone which has a larger proportion of the thicker cortex and the thinner or less dense trabecular bone.

Computer-assisted quantitative tomography Computer-assisted quantitative tomography (QCT) requires what is known as a phantom standard. The equipment is more expensive and allows spinal sites to be scanned. The process produces X-ray slices, known as 'tomographic cuts', through the vertebral bones. Unfortunately, QCT produces much higher radiation than DEXA.

Plain X-rays   Plain X-rays are also useful in the diagnosis of osteoporosis. Fracture of any of the vertebral or spinal bones may occasionally occur without pain or disability. The radiologist or your specialist may suspect osteoporosis if the X-ray appears to show a more transparent or less dense appearance than normal. Fractures which have occurred in the absence of severe trauma would also raise suspicion of osteoporosis.

When pain does occur it is often poorly localised. In other words, pain caused by a vertebra collapsing as a result of a fracture may produce a vague ache or pain in the area of the spine. This is very different to the pain caused by a fracture of, say, the wrist or the ankle, in which the area that is damaged is obvious.

It is important your doctor X-rays the whole of your thoracic spine and your lumbar spine. This means that your entire spine from your upper back to your lower back must be X-rayed to exclude fractures. There is a considerably greater radiation dose than with the above methods. Despite this, plain X-rays can detect only severe spinal bone loss. To detect severe bone loss from the spine requires radiation doses of up to twice that required in the more sophisticated technique of QCT.

New work[2] by Melton on fracture definition suggests that for a wedge-shaped fractured vertebra to be diagnosed it must have a front height of at least 20% less than its rear height. This rule is changed for the fourth lumbar vertebra (L4) where it must be 30% and for the fifth lumbar vertebra (L5) where 5% is sufficient. A central or concave fracture can be diagnosed using similar criteria. A crush fracture is said to be present where the rear height of the vertebra is 20% less than that of the vertebra below.

A sound way to measure bone density   Another recent advance in the measurement of bone density is the use of ultrasound. In this approach, soundwaves are passed through the relevant bone—commonly the calcaneum or other bone site—and the bone density is measured according to the way in which the soundwaves are bounced back to the detector. The technique is said by its supporters to have an accuracy similar to that of the DEXA scanners without exposing you to X-rays. It also has the advantage of portability compared with the large machines needed for DEXA. At present these ultrasound scanners are being introduced in a few centres only.

So which bone density measurement should become the standard?

The relative strengths and weaknesses of the various approaches have become clearer over time. All of the currently used measurement techniques appear to produce a valid measurement of bone mass and are probably all predictive of future fracture and therefore of clinical use. However, DEXA has the flexibility to measure any area or all of the skeleton that none of the other approaches has. This technology also has great speed and accuracy, and the added advantages of relatively low cost and low radiation exposure. It has certainly replaced DPA, which uses the radioactive substance gadolinium.

Who should have bone density analysis?

Sambrook[3] in a recent issue of *General Practitioner* suggests that bone densitometry should be carried out in certain defined situations. These indications have generally been accepted by the Government Panel set up to advise on the introduction of new medical technology. These specific indications include:

- Oestrogen-deficient women in whom the bone density result will influence decisions regarding future treatment, such as the use of HRT.
- Patients with fractures occurring in the absence of injury or low bone mass as determined by plain X-rays. The bone density scan in these cases will be used to diagnose spinal osteoporosis and assist in the medical management of these patients.
- Patients receiving long-term steroid therapy in whom the scan can be done to guide the future therapy.
- Patients in whom there is an excessive production of parathormone and in whom there are no symptoms. This will assist in the diagnosis of hyperparathyroidism and help to determine those patients in whom surgery is necessary.
- Bone densitometry can be used to assess the progress of therapy in those persons diagnosed with osteoporosis.

Now the technology exists, many would argue there is a good case that every woman should have a bone density scan on reaching the menopause, to assess the degree of bone density and the rate of bone loss. There are authorities who also feel that women who have not had a bone density test on cessation of the menopause should have one at any age after that. There have been suggestions that men over the age of 65 should also be tested.

Some osteoporosis experts have recently advocated that every woman between the ages of 30 and 50 should be tested for bone density. Some women in this age group lose more bone mass than others before reaching the menopause.

To date, governments around the world (including the Australian Government) have failed to adopt the procedure of universal screening of bone density in menopausal or postmenopausal women. Many believe that such screening should be a part of preventive health measures for women in a similar way to Pap smear testing and breast screening programs.

To counter the arguments for more widespread bone density screening, Coney has raised several valid points. She asks which women will be offered screening, particularly in New Zealand where there were so few scanners at the time of writing her book in 1991. She also asks what treatments would be offered to those found deficient in bone calcium. Her final point was to question the number of serious fractures which screening would prevent.

Coney goes on to query whether HRT is to be offered to all women with low bone density after their scans. Her doubts regarding this are expressed as follows:

> Several recent major reviews of the question of screening for osteoporosis have concluded that mass screening cannot be recommended until a protocol for such a programme is formulated and its effectiveness justified.
>
> Screening all postmenopausal women also raises the question of what you would do for women whose bone density was shown to be low. There is really no point in measuring for bone loss unless you can do something about it.
>
> Hormone replacement therapy is being promoted as a way of preventing further bone loss and women who already show significant bone loss could be offered HRT. But such an approach would result in large numbers of women taking a drug that is still the subject of considerable controversy over long-term safety, and we do not know how acceptable the long-term therapy needed would be to women. Even if a woman used HRT, this would not give her a guarantee that she would not have a fracture, as HRT can only reduce her risk, not eliminate it.[4]

For a final word on the controversy surrounding universal bone density screening, Associate Professor Sambrook recently stated:

Screening remains a controversial area . . . bone densitometry is generally considered not to be sufficiently sensitive and specific for use in an unselected population. Therefore, universal screening is not appropriate at this time.

Further studies are needed to determine the optimum densitometric method, appropriate intervention and cost benefit before universal screening can be justified.[5]

In March 1994, the Australian Government introduced a fee rebate of $75 for bone density scanning. This occurred after recent Budget decisions proposed that bone density scanning should become available as a means of assisting in the prevention and management of osteoporosis in postmenopausal women. The Medicare Benefits Advisory Committee recommended the rebate be available under set circumstances. The rebate will be available for those previously diagnosed with osteoporosis and in whom the diagnosis requires confirmation. It will also become available for the monitoring of previously diagnosed osteoporosis.

Laboratory techniques

Sensitive blood tests can be used to measure the amount of calcium in the fluid part of the blood known as the plasma. Total plasma calcium or albumin-corrected calcium can be measured but are only a crude screening method for osteoporosis.

Plasma calcium The measurement of total plasma or albumin-corrected calcium is said by some experts to be adequate as a crude screening method for lowered or increased levels of calcium in your blood. However, 40% of the calcium in your blood or serum is combined with the albumin protein in the blood and is therefore biologically inactive. Specialised tests[6] for calcium are therefore necessary if abnormal calcium levels are not to be missed.

Bone turnover Blood tests measuring the amount of bone turnover have been developed. These involve the measurement of levels of natural hormones and enzymes in your blood. The two most common of these currently are the measurement of osteocalcin and alkaline phosphatase. Of these serum osteocalcin may replace alkaline phosphatase as a measure of bone formation. Levels of the substance hydroxyproline in your urine may also be useful as a measurement of bone resorption or breakdown.

Variation in these measurements can be useful to the treating specialist in making a diagnosis. Prince has given the following examples. He states raised bone formation and resorption are typical of early postmenopausal osteoporosis, whereas low bone formation with raised or normal bone resorption are typical of alcohol-induced osteoporosis. Very high bone turnover is typical of osteoporosis associated with overactivity of the thyroid gland.

Hormone measurements Hormone measurements also have their role in the diagnosis of osteoporosis under certain situations, for example the levels of the various thyroid hormones can be measured in patients suspected of thyrotoxicosis, testosterone in hypogonadism, oestradiol and follicle-stimulating hormone in menopause, parathyroid hormone in primary hyperparathyroidism and 25-hydroxy vitamin D (calcitriol) in sunlight-deficient 'nutritional' osteomalacia.

Sophisticated tests for proteins specific to certain bone tumours may be necessary in the diagnosis of abnormal bone fracture. For instance, the bone tumour of multiple myeloma can be diagnosed by the presence of Bence-Jones's protein by using the technique of electrophoresis of blood and urine.

Laboratory measurements of female hormone levels in your blood or urine are often useful in diagnosing the cause of osteoporosis.

Bone biopsy Recently biopsy of bone taken from the hip has become an even more accurate way of determining the presence of lowered bone density. Before the bone specimen is taken from your iliac or hipbone under a local anaesthetic, you would be given two oral doses of the antibiotic tetracycline. The first is given three weeks before the biopsy and the second several days before the bone being taken. The attraction for this antibiotic to growing bone means it is possible for the specialist to measure the rate of bone growth accurately from a small specimen of your bone. This technique has been shown to be of value in the assessment of alcohol-related loss of bone density.

Summary

This chapter has dealt with the exciting developments in the diagnosis of osteoporosis. We have discussed the introduction of the new approaches for imaging the bones and determining the level of calcium. It is now possible for your specialist to measure your bone density with a greater degree of accuracy and safety than in previous times. Earlier diagnosis should also mean that corrective steps can be taken early enough to prevent, in many cases, the development of the classical deforming features of osteoporosis.

Recent decisions by Australian health authorities have opened the way for more women diagnosed with osteoporosis to have access to bone density scanning for the purposes of diagnosis and management. We still await the advent of universal screening of menopausal women.

6

Preventing osteoporosis

Fortunately, for all of you at risk, there are many things you can do to protect yourself against osteoporosis. At the same time you will be creating a better overall health base for yourself. In this chapter we will cover many of the key things that are necessary for you to minimise your possibility of developing osteoporosis.

The National Osteoporosis Society of the United Kingdom emphasises in its manual for GPs that to help maintain their bones in a healthy state in the years after menopause, there are four key areas to which a patient should be encouraged to pay attention. These are:

- Regular exercise
- A balanced diet, rich in calcium
- Stopping smoking
- Decreasing alcohol intake

Although none of these measures appears to replace the need for HRT when osteoporosis is due to oestrogen deficiency, lifestyle advice may be useful and important in the following circumstances.

As you will see HRT is not always appropriate and may in fact be contrary to your general health. It is vitally important you consider all available information and discuss the pros and cons with your doctor. To be effective in preventing bone loss, it is now believed therapy should begin within ten years of the onset of menopause.

Bone mineral density measurement may be appropriate, depending on your risk of developing osteoporosis and your age, and may indicate who should commence HRT. Generally, if it is considered appropriate to use it, measurement of bone density is taken around the time of your menopause to establish your baseline levels. You should discuss bone density scanning with your doctor.

The importance of lifestyle changes

Lifestyle changes may assist other prescribed means of preventing osteoporosis. The same lifestyle changes can make a contribution to building peak bone mass in younger people and assist in maintaining skeletal health in adults. These changes can also go a long way to empowering you to do something to assist your own future health.

It is very important to understand that there is not one activity you can choose to do alone and disregard all the others. For example, you need both regular weight-bearing exercise and adequate calcium. Choosing one or the other may prove quite inadequate in protecting you against osteoporosis. Adequate oestrogen levels are now widely accepted as being as important as the other two factors in preserving bone health.

Protecting yourself against osteoporosis

Studies have shown that regular weight-bearing exercise can increase bone formation.[1] Conversely, immobilisation or lack of weight-bearing exercise, such as occurs in astronauts in weightless conditions, is known to cause bone loss.

Physical activity

Bone tissue responds to the stress being placed upon it. This comes from weight going through the bones and the impact of muscles pulling on them. Weight-bearing exercises are particularly beneficial for bone strength.

The term 'weight-bearing' means the activity is carried out while your body weight is on both of your feet. In this way the force of gravity acts through the entire skeleton.

High impact activities increase this force, because at some stage both feet are off the ground, for example running and jumping. Although these are necessary during your earlier and more healthy years, they may not be suitable for the frail elderly. In this latter group, walking on a regular basis (at least three to five times weekly for 30–40 minutes) may constitute sufficient exercise.

Physical activity and bone loss   As we have already indicated, it is important to realise bone is a dynamic tissue which is regulated by hormones, nutrition and physical activity through all the phases of your life. The relationship between bone density and physical activity was first described in 1892.

Over this century, athletes of all ages have been shown to have greater bone density than sedentary individuals of the same general age grouping. Bone thinning occurs in the elderly who do not exercise, and in the young who exercise inadequately.

The amount of bone density in athletes correlates closely with the level of stress exerted, so that among athletes, weight-lifters will have the most dense bones and swimmers the least. Despite the fact that swimming is not the best exercise for bone health, elderly swimmers show increased bone density in their arms and vertebras compared with elderly people of the same age who do not exercise.

Bone loss and inactivity   In contrast to the increased bone density in athletes, inactivity and immobilisation lead to bone loss. A complete lack of physical activity, such as occurs during confinement to bed because of illness or the immobilisation of a limb after injury, leads directly to a reduction in bone density. It makes sense that you preserve as much bone strength as possible by resuming physical activity as soon as you can. During the early recovery phase of illness or prolonged injury you will need to take extra care to avoid falling. So don't attempt too much too soon. You should seek guidance from your doctor or physiotherapist about a safe and sensible program.

Lost in space—the calcium story   The past three decades have seen an explosion of activity in the space race. This has also brought a great deal of knowledge about the effects of weightlessness on bone density and the calcium balance. Very early in the exploration of space, scientists discovered only a few days in the weightlessness of space could cause massive bone loss.

Yet, since the Russians placed the Mir space station in orbit around the earth, Russian cosmonauts have spent in excess of 300 days aboard Mir without the skeletal deterioration expected following earlier space flights. The Russians have achieved this reduction in expected bone loss by a combination of medication and exercise.

The exercise is done for an hour a day on a bicycle ergonometer—basically an exercise bike in space! Other exercise is done in a complicated strap harness which forces the cosmonauts to move against resistance in any direction.

Bone gain and activity The benefits of exercise on increased bone density are seen at specific sites of bone. They are more prominent in those body areas subjected to higher stress levels. This is particularly seen in the development of the dominant limb. Thus, a right-handed individual is more likely to have increased bone density in the forearm bones on the right side of the body than in the left non-dominant arm.

Elderly male cross-country runners have shown a 20% greater bone density in their lumbar vertebras and in their legs than a control group of elderly males who do not run. Other studies have shown a significant increase in total body calcium in postmenopausal women who exercised regularly for a year. This contrasted with a control group who did not exercise and in whom total body calcium fell in the same period.

Although the reasons for the effect which exercise has on bone are not fully understood they may be related to what is known as the piezoelectric phenomenon.

This theory explains why exercise increases bone mass in a very specific manner. It explains that the bone growth associated with exercise is due to bone responding locally to stress. It does this by developing minute electrical currents at the point where the bone is being bent or compressed. This results in a realignment of the individual bone units in the direction of the force the bone is being subjected to. There is also local production of a hormonal skeletal growth factor.

It has long been recognised that the application of magnetic fields to bone stimulates the development of new bone growth. This has been proved in numerous studies where pulsating electromagnetic fields (PEMF) have been used to heal some fractures and pseudoarthroses. This knowledge has led to the development of therapeutic PEMF devices which have been used to treat bone pain in some osteoporotic patients.

Postmenopausal women and exercise Studies of women who have osteoporosis have shown bone growth after their involvement in exercise programs. Exercises in postmenopausal women should be aimed at increasing extension of the spine rather than at flexion.

Thus, exercises will aim at backstretching rather than bending forward, which may increase the risk of compression fracture.

In all exercise programs for the postmenopausal woman you will be advised to start gently and slowly. You will be asked to increase your exercise intensity gradually in ways which encourage rather than discourage the continuation of the exercise program. In fact, swimming may be a good beginning exercise for both men and women, particularly those who have not exercised in a while.

Swimming may not improve bone density, but for most it can be a fun exercise and it can assist in the development of the endurance and strength necessary to maintain an exercise routine. Hydrotherapy and/or water exercises may be available at a local or community level. For those who wish to know where hydrotherapy is available in their local area we suggest you contact your local Arthritis Foundation as given in the list of resources later in this book.

Exercise has been shown to increase confidence in the elderly group most likely to suffer from the effects of osteoporosis. It does this because it assists balance, coordination and flexibility. These may help to reduce the chance of falls and thus the possibility of fractures due to the osteoporosis.

The bonus of increased exercise lies not only in improving the health of your bones, it also increases the health of your heart and blood vessels and your respiratory system.

It must be stressed that you will require at least three sessions a week of brisk exercise, such as walking, to ensure health for your heart and bones. A certain amount of time and effort is required for you to gain the greatest benefit from your exercise program.

Research has clearly shown that women who exercised at least three times a week had higher bone density than inactive women. This increase in bone density occurs in women aged from twenty to 80 years. Other research indicates that people who exercised at least three to four hours per week had a 50% less risk of hip fracture.

The intensity of exercise has been shown to be important. As a general rule, the more intense your exercise activity is, the more your skeleton will benefit from the stress on it. Brisk walking is thus much better than a leisurely stroll.

Individual benefits of increased physical activity The degree to which physical activity affects your bones depends on a number of known factors. Firstly, your age is important. As we have seen, the most important period for building up your maximum bone density

79

is in your late teens to early twenties. It is then you will achieve your 'peak bone mass'. This is the time of the peak deposits to your 'bone bank'. Your bones are at their maximum strength at this time of your life. Regular exercise will assist you in maintaining this over the years before the period of accelerated bone loss during the years of the menopause.

This loss of bone density and strength starts to occur in both men and women during your mid-thirties, but undergoes a major acceleration in women during their late forties and fifties. You will therefore need the maximum levels of bone density possible to protect you against future bone fracture.

Fortunately, exercise helps you reduce the amount of bone you may lose around the time of menopause, and in the years afterwards. You should continue to be as physically active as possible, allowing for other health factors such as the health of your heart, arteries and blood pressure and the presence or absence of arthritis or chronic illness.

Exercise and calcium are not enough in isolation As well as regular exercise, adequate levels of sex hormones and calcium are necessary to maintain bone strength. Recently, a study carried out in Western Australia found that for a group of postmenopausal women several factors emerged. The study found that combining exercise and HRT increased the bone density of the participants. Exercise with the subject taking at least 1000 mg of calcium per day also slowed bone loss. However, exercise alone did not slow bone loss.

Extreme exercise regimens, such as are common among 'fitness fanatics' or those who indulge in excessive dieting, may lead to irregular menstrual cycles and even an absence of the normal menstrual cycle in premenopausal women. If you exercise or diet excessively and your periods cease, this is an indication of inadequate levels of sex hormones, which will result in loss of bone if not corrected.

In our community this is a possible danger for some female athletes, ballet dancers and gymnasts who take part in very high levels of repetitive exercise. One of the chronic problems associated with the low body weight and intensive exercise programs of would-be ballerinas is the absence of menstrual periods— amenorrhoea—which has been associated with stress fractures in the feet and spines of dancers in their late teens and early twenties.

With prompt medical treatment the hormonal balance can be corrected.

How physically active are you at present?

Now is the time to review your current level of physical activity. If your lifestyle is very sedentary, any reasonable increase in your physical activity is likely to benefit your bone health.

Any form of physical activity might count as exercise. Exercise can range from a leisurely walk in the park through to an intense work-out in a gymnasium. To achieve the many benefits associated with exercise you will need to devote a reasonable amount of effort and time to it.

If you already exercise actively and regularly, then try to maintain or even increase your level of activity.

Osteoporosis and exercise If you already have osteoporosis, your degree of physical activity is likely to be restricted. You should work within the bounds of safety and aim for as active an exercise program as you can. If you are uncertain, you will be able to discuss this with your medical adviser, physiotherapist, or the coordinator of your osteoporosis prevention/management program. An exercise program derived from clinical experience, as described later in this book, will:

- make a useful contribution to the overall health of your bones;
- improve your balance and coordination to safeguard you against falls;
- help maintain your general health and wellbeing.

Other chronic conditions The health of your bones may be impaired by the lack of physical activities imposed on you by the presence of chronic medical conditions. These include arthritis, diabetes, asthma, heart disease and other physical disabilities.

In many of these conditions, regular exercise is an important component of the overall management. A regular exercise program is important to counter any negative effects such chronic conditions may have on bone strength and general health.

Reducing the risk of falls Keeping mobile and active contributes to better balance, coordination and mental alertness. Research into falls and fractures in the elderly suggests these factors help reduce the incidence of falls and hence the likelihood of fractures. The improved general health associated with regular exercise may also reduce the need for certain medications, some of which affect balance and mental alertness. This will be covered in Chapter 7.

Smoking

Smoking is known to increase your risk of developing osteoporosis after menopause. It is therefore important you stop smoking as soon as possible. As previously described, smoking has a direct detrimental inhibiting effect on the cells which rebuild bone. Women who smoke may also have an increased chance of their menopause occurring up to five years early. Fortunately, we now have a number of methods to assist you to quit smoking once you have chosen to do so.

It is important for you to realise the responsibility for quitting smoking is always your own. Your author has assisted many hundreds of patients to quit smoking over the past twenty years, using autohypnotic and acupuncture-based treatments. Hypnosis is widely practised in Australia by members of the Australian Society of Hypnosis (ASH).

Hypnosis—self-help for smokers The Australian Society of Hypnosis has members in every Australian State. They are all doctors, psychologists or dentists who have undergone an extensive training program in hypnosis and its application in their specialist areas of practice. In most States of Australia (the exception is NSW), hypnosis is limited by Government Acts to the members of these three professions.

Hypnosis is normally used to enhance positive feelings regarding your ability to cease smoking and never to smoke again. Your use of hypnosis will also help to increase your feelings of self-confidence and self-esteem. It will not help you if you do not really want to stop smoking.

Normally you will need a small number of sessions which may be taped for you to use as a future support. The aim is always to teach you a technique that becomes a part of your own support structures, and an alternative means of relaxation.

Your State branches of the Australian Society of Hypnosis are listed in the *Yellow Pages* in all States.

Patches and chewing gum—gradual withdrawal More recently, nicotine chewing gum and patches have been introduced to assist those who feel they require a gradual reduction of nicotine rather than immediate cessation. Your general practitioner or local anti-cancer organisation or Quitline will be able to advise you further. When used with a comprehensive support program, such as that provided by the manufacturers of Nicabate, these patches have a role in assisting some smokers to quit permanently.

There are also group approaches to quitting, such as 'Smoke-enders', which appear to have a high success rate and may appeal to some of you.

Acupuncture for smoking cessation? According to acupuncture specialists, your body has numerous specific acupunture points over its surface. Your ears also have numerous points which can be stimulated by needles and, more recently, by low-powered lasers.

Stimulation of the so-called 'lung points' in the centre of your outer ears has been used by medical acupuncturists for over twenty years. These points are relevant to smoking cessation because they are supplied by the only branches of the vagus nerves to emerge onto the surface of the skin. Stimulation of this point on the ear is claimed to reduce drug withdrawal by stimulating the parasympathetic nervous system. This counteracts the effects of stress and thus reduces the unpleasant withdrawal symptoms.

Stimulation of the lung points has been shown to produce high levels of the body's natural endorphins—chemical messengers which have a pain-relieving and sedative effect on your body. Usually the medical acupuncturist will combine needles in the outside of your ears with needles in other body points to assist in reducing withdrawal symptoms and to help relax you. Stimulation of these points by laser acupuncture is also claimed to be effective, according to its proponents.

Another treatment variant is the placement in your ears of semi-permanent needles which can be left in place for several days to assist you in getting over the acute withdrawal.

If you are interested in any of these approaches, you should contact your State branch of the Australian Medical Acupunture Society (AMAS). The numbers are listed in your *Yellow Pages*. All members of the AMAS are medical practitioners and you will be referred to your nearest qualified medical acupuncturist.

Decrease excessive use of alcohol

There is no doubt that excessive use of alcohol contributes to a greater risk of postmenopausal osteoporosis. This occurs because alcohol impedes the absorption of calcium. Excessive alcohol intake is one of the leading causes of liver damage and it also damages the cells which build up your bone. Increased alcohol intake is also a major factor in falls and road traffic crashes.

Again, hypnosis and/or acupuncture in conjunction with counselling may be of assistance. Organisations such as Alcoholics Anonymous can be of great support to those who have a major alcohol addiction and who are therefore at greatest risk of liver damage.

The role of the physiotherapist

Physiotherapists have a role in educational and preventive programs of physical activity for the middle-aged and elderly. They may do this on an individual basis or take a key role in the development of community-based programs for osteoporosis prevention, such as that run by the Arthritis Foundation of Victoria.

The physiotherapist also has a role in the rehabilitation of those of you who already have osteoporosis. This role involves developing programs of exercise as well as the treatment of the complications of established osteoporosis.

Preventive programs   The physiotherapist is in an ideal position to help you, the public, understand that bones need a moderate amount of stress throughout life if they are to remain strong and healthy.

All the evidence now available clearly shows that elderly bones and joints must have the continuing stresses of exercise if they are to remain strong and active. This contrasts with the earlier view that exercise is risky to elderly people. The earlier view also held that light exercise was enough and that age in itself was a barrier to exercise.

The more modern message must now be carried to the elderly, and activities must be promoted to enable skeletal health to be maintained in old age.

Programs such as this have been in place for the past ten years in Western Australia and have been described by Professor Lance Twomey.[2] These are run by physiotherapists and include a component on health education, stressing the need for continuing relatively high levels of exercise activity throughout life for all elements of the heart and blood vessels and musculoskeletal systems. According to Twomey, physiotherapists have an excellent knowledge of pathology and human movement and are ideally suited to be involved in these programs.

As previously noted, exercise programs for frail elderly patients with possible microfractures or compression fractures of vertebral bones should be introduced only after a proper evaluation on an individual basis. Exercise may then proceed with due caution.

Initial periods of exercise should be brief and in a safe and secure environment. Hydrotherapy is an ideal starting exercise. However, it is no substitute for even 5–10 minutes of weight-bearing activity. Exercise should aim at strengthening the trunk and limbs after first emphasising joint mobility.

Controlled backward stretching movements should be encouraged rather than forward bending or flexion movements. This is because flexion is in the direction of the often present forward curvature of the spine (kyphosis). Any additional forward movement of the spine might therefore increase the possibility of vertebral microfracture and damage.

Exercise also helps to maintain the integrity of all of your joint structures throughout life. There is thus a valuable role for gradually progressed exercise in the management of those joints involved in inflammation (such as rheumatoid arthritis) and degenerative disease (such as osteoarthritis) as well as the 'normal' joints.

Specific physiotherapy approaches Physiotherapy techniques include heat treatment (both dry and moist) and ultrasound therapy. As detailed elsewhere, the physiotherapist will also assess posture and function of your musculoskeletal system and prescribe and supervise exercise programs.

Often, treatments found to be ineffective when used in isolation are extremely effective when combined with other approaches, for example, TENS therapy used together with heat treatments such as microwave therapy and hot clay packs. Physiotherapists may also supervise or refer you on to hydrotherapy—water-based exercise or monitored swimming programs.

A number of the approaches available from physiotherapists and medical practitioners are described in detail in Chapter 13, on the treatment of pain. These include approaches such as TENS, laser stimulation and magnetic field therapy.

Healing hands—therapeutic massage

Gentle therapeutic massage may assist in the reduction of tight muscles and also be useful simply as a means of relaxation. Various styles of massage, from the typical European style of massage to the Oriental-style shiatsu therapy, may be useful in the overall management of pain. The main difference from conventional massage is that shiatsu uses the points and principles of acupuncture.

The occupational therapist and osteoporosis

Occupational therapy may be useful to provide patients with assistance in the necessary activities of daily living, for example in the form of aids such as tap-turners, special chairs or rails which can be used by some patients in the home to increase mobility. Occupational therapists may also run useful self-help groups.

7

Preventing falls

Statistics show that one in every three people over 65 can expect to fall in the next twelve months. Of course, older people are not the only ones who fall—children do it all the time—but the consequences are much more severe for older people. Not only is serious injury a more likely consequence, but the chances of recovery are not as good and healing will take longer. As the number and proportion of older people in Australia are increasing very rapidly at present, the distressing statistics can only get worse unless we try to change things.

The purpose of this chapter is to alert you to the dangers of falls later in your life and the possible causes and remedies of those dangers. By giving you information on the known causes of falls, and suggestions on what you might do to prevent them, it is hoped you will be able to choose what you can do to keep yourself safer from falling. I also hope to show that it is possible to make these choices. Older people should not accept the belief that falling is a natural part of growing older.

This chapter closely follows the booklet *Staying On Your Feet* published by the Health Promotion Unit of the Central Sydney Health Service. They have kindly allowed reproduction or adaptation of much of their booklet here.

There are seven major causes of falling. By concentrating on these seven causes and their remedies it is hoped you will not join those unfortunates who fill the orthopaedic wards of our hospitals.

The seven main causes of falling by older people are:

- Unsafe footwear

- Changes in eyesight or eye disorders
- Poor balance and gait
- Inappropriate medication use
- Chronic health conditions
- Hazards inside the home
- Hazards in public places

Any one of these items presents a danger, but imagine how much worse it is when several are combined—an older person wearing ill-fitting shoes, feeling dizzy from a mixture of medicines and trying to negotiate a particularly bumpy footpath!

Myrtle's story

Another example from clinical practice is Myrtle. She is a previously fit 78-year-old who had noticed she was having more and more difficulty in reaching high cupboards and hanging out the sheets. One day, as she stood on a low step to reach one of the top cupboards, she apparently lost conciousness and fell to the floor. Luckily, all drawers were closed and she had sensibly remodelled her kitchen so that most corners were rounded.

She came to some time later, lying stretched out on the floor, experiencing considerable pain throughout her neck and back. When she felt able, she got up and slowly walked to her bedroom where she waited until her husband returned from his shopping. Although she was badly bruised from her neck to her lower back, she was too embarrassed to seek medical attention.

Several weeks later, when she attended her family doctor complaining of continuous pain, she was found to have a compression fracture of one of the spinal vertebras in her upper back.

Just as there are seven dangers leading to falls, there are seven remedies which will help to save you from many of these dangers:

- Wearing safer shoes
- Making the most of your eyesight
- Exercising appropriately to maintain balance and walking ability
- Managing your medicines wisely
- Managing chronic health conditions as well as possible
- Modifying your home to make it safer
- Making changes in the world outside your home

Take good care of yourself

In general terms, at all ages, the better your overall health, the safer you will be from falling. When we consider health we mean of course not simply your physical health, but also your mental and social wellbeing.

To maintain your best level of physical health you need the following:

- A nutritious diet
- Appropriate physical activity
- Regular medical checks (including dental, podiatry, eyesight and hearing)
- A good balance of rest and activity

It is particularly important to have your vision and hearing tested regularly and properly corrected. A simple thing such as having earwax removed can improve your balance and therefore help keep you safer from falling.

Mental wellbeing is probably a more individual thing. We're all familiar with the expression 'a healthy mind in a healthy body', but what the words 'healthy mind' mean will vary from person to person. For one it may mean doing a crossword puzzle each day, for another playing draughts with a friend, for another attending classes at a School for Seniors or University of the Third Age. But whatever form it takes, there is no doubt that a mind which is active and stimulated is a key feature in positive, successful aging.

Falls often have a very injurious effect on mental wellbeing. This can result from an actual fall or even the fear or the expectation of falling. Some older people have been known to withdraw from activities and social contacts because they knew someone who had fallen or because they feared they might fall themselves. They have decided they will be safer if they stay quietly at home. Unfortunately, this is not the case.

At times those who isolate themselves are just increasing the feelings of loneliness. By becoming less active, they will cause their muscles and joints to weaken, thus increasing their susceptibility to falling. This is the kind of situation where the support and encouragement of friends and family can be very helpful.

Unfortunately, it is also the kind of situation where well-meaning friends and family will often discourage an older person from being active, and this can be very unhelpful. Friends and family may need to set their own fears and anxieties aside and concentrate rather on the wellbeing of the older person instead.

Mental and social wellbeing are closely linked—since humans are basically social creatures it is clearly more difficult for a person who is isolated and lonely to maintain a positive healthy mental outlook than for one who has a lot of contact with other people. Staying in touch with life seems to be the key—taking part in activities and clubs, pursuing a hobby, joining a gentle exercise group, taking care of pets, continuing education, reading, listening to music, writing letters are just some of the possibilities.

Nevertheless, it must happen that there will be times of distress and depression as friends and loved ones become ill or die, or your financial situation worsens or other life events which cannot be predicted or controlled take place. At these times of stress, you are less likely to be taking good care of yourself and so will be more vulnerable to some kind of accident. Try talking about your feelings with a friend. Often we think our problems will be a burden to our friends but this is the case only if we expect other people to fix the problem. Many friends or family members will be only too happy to talk through problems with you. They may well be insulted if you do not allow them this privilege.

If you cannot talk to a friend, then you might try one of the caring, confidential, anonymous telephone services that are available. It is worth remembering that bottled-up feelings act like a pressure-cooker, so letting them out in a safe way will be beneficial.

Recent publicity on radio and TV in Australia highlighted the benefits of pets for older people. Dramatic improvements in function have been seen when nursing home residents were brought in contact with dogs and cats. Unfortunately, smaller pets also increase the risk of falls, and larger dogs may be too boisterous for the frail elderly.

Falls have been known to occur because the victim was simply not concentrating at the time of the fall. The person fell because they were too impatient or did not take adequate care. So, teach yourself to recognise risky situations and assess your capacities realistically. It may be possible to climb a ladder and fix the gutter but it may not be wise—weigh the risk against the inconvenience of waiting. On reflection, Myrtle told her doctor she should have waited until her husband was home to support her before attempting to reach her upper cupboards.

Wear safer shoes

The better your shoes fit, the less likely you are to fall. Well-fitting shoes are one of your greatest aids in the fight to prevent falls.

Making a wise choice in shoes is probably the easiest of all the steps you can take towards being safer from falling and one which can make a big difference.

Many older people will admit that, although they know lace-up shoes are the best choice for fit, they find shoelaces difficult for people who have arthritis in the hands. Velcro fastenings are an excellent second choice in this case. Some of our patients have recently proudly shown casual shoes which have neither laces nor Velcro. These shoes use an ingenious system in which the shoe is tightened with a large, easily turned knob which is connected with a sturdy nylon cord.

Sole design for safer shoes

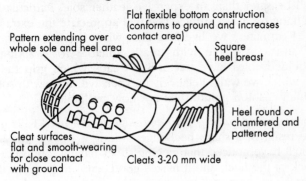

Flat flexible bottom construction (conforms to ground and increases contact area)

Pattern extending over whole sole and heel area

Square heel breast

Heel round or chamfered and patterned

Cleat surfaces flat and smooth-wearing for close contact with ground

Cleats 3-20 mm wide

Unsafe sole design

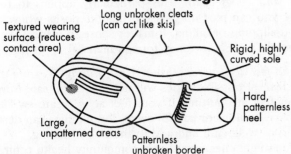

Long unbroken cleats (can act like skis)

Textured wearing surface (reduces contact area)

Rigid, highly curved sole

Hard, patternless heel

Large, unpatterned areas

Patternless unbroken border

As well as being a good fit, here are some other points to look for in shoes:

- *Ideally your shoes need a large area of contact between the sole and the ground.* The more contact there is, the safer the shoe will be. Flat shoes are the wisest choice, so this does not raise a difficulty for men but many women may feel reluctant to give up heels. Clearly, high heels are not safe, but that doesn't mean that women need give up heels altogether—there are lots of shoes about with wedge heels and you might like to consider them.

- *Soles should be flexible and relatively soft.* This kind of sole will travel better over uneven surfaces than a hard, smooth sole.

- *Tractor-like treads give some extra grip.* The grip may be provided by the material used or by a pattern, or both. This means that a cheaper synthetic sole with a stud pattern, for instance, will be safer than an expensive leather sole. Particularly when walking on a wet surface you will appreciate the extra security.
  Fortunately we live in a time when there is a large variety of shoes available with treads suitable for walking. These moulded soles have tractor-like treads which grip the surface on which we walk. Relatively inexpensive shoes with soft inserts which cushion painful feet are now available.

- *Shoes should have a rounded edge to the heel.* Falls are often the result of a sharp heel-edge striking a wet or shiny surface. You'll have noticed that jogging shoes have a round edge at the back of the heel, and it makes good sense to look for the same feature in your walking shoes. The modern casual or walking shoe makes use of this feature to make it less likely you will catch your heel on uneven surfaces or pavements.

- *Keep your shoes clean.* This particularly applies to the soles, where you can pick up grease or fatty deposits which can lead to you slipping or falling. It makes sense to inspect your shoes frequently and remove any foreign material.

- *Painful feet also increase your risk of falling.* Wearing the safest and cleanest possible shoes will not make you safe from falling if your feet are hurting. If your feet ache or are swollen, or if you have bunions or painful corns, these things can destroy any feeling of wellbeing and add to the risk of falling.
  You might check your local community health centre to find

out if it provides a podiatry service. If you have trouble with your feet, for instance if it is difficult for you to cut the nails or deal with corns, a visit to a podiatrist may be the kindest thing you could do for yourself.

Make the most of your eyesight

There can be no doubt that the better your vision is, the safer you will be from falling. This implies that we all should make the best of our eyesight and this is particularly important as we grow older. Wearing spectacles, particularly if they are new or have multi-focal lenses, can lead to falls through the misjudging of steps and obstacles.

The known causes of eye problems, at any age, are:

- Poor nutrition
- Poor lighting
- Mental strain
- Not carrying out enough eye exercises

Here are some tips on each:

- *Nutrition:* We know that green and yellow vegetables are vital for healthy eyes. Vitamins E and A are important, so a wholefood, unrefined diet is indicated, and one including plenty of fruit and green leafy vegetables.
- *Poor lighting:* All eyes need adequate light so they can work without strain, and this is especially so for older eyes. Skimping on lighting is false economy. If you are having problems, consider simply replacing a 60-watt globe with either a 75- or 100-watt globe. More light will then reach the retina at the back of your eyes, and this may make a significant difference to your problem.
- *Mental strain:* There may be debate as to the extent of the damage mental stress does to the eyes, but there is little doubt that it does have some effect. Techniques which relax mind and body also help relieve eye strain. You may have noticed that when you are under stress, you blink less frequently than normally and your eyes become fixed and strained. It can help if you consciously make yourself blink every ten seconds or so, particularly if you are concentrating hard or doing close work or reading.

  Simple relaxation techniques can help to reduce your overall level of stress. Since many of these are carried out with your eyes closed, this can be of assistance. Some of these approaches are outlined in Chapter 11.

- *Wearing spectacles:* It is important you have your eyes checked regularly by a properly qualified eye specialist. The presence of cataracts and retinal detachment should be excluded or corrected. It is also possible you may not need to wear spectacles if your eyesight has stabilised. So, don't throw away your spectacles, but you may sometimes find you are wearing them when you don't need them for the task in hand. Proper advice should always be sought before abandoning their use.
- *Eye exercises:* Many people believe that we allow our eyes to become lazy—and it is certainly true that eyes often respond well to simple exercises. It may be helpful to ask your eye specialist or optician whether you can be given some simple exercises to enhance your eye fitness.

Natural changes

It is normal and natural that eyesight slowly becomes less acute as people grow older. The change is gradual, so it does not have a particularly marked effect on most of the daily activities of older people. However, it does increase the risk of falling, as any worsening of vision must do.

If you do not see clearly when you are dealing with potential hazards such as steps, carpet edges, kerbs, door thresholds and wet floors, the inherent danger in these things is magnified. When normal aging changes interact with environmental factors such as these, the result can be a greater risk of falling.

Another normal change in older eyes is that the pupils become smaller and respond more slowly to change. This means that their adjustment to different levels of light and dark takes longer. You may have noticed that nowadays your eyes need a little more time to adjust when you come inside on a sunny day, or when you go out into the sun.

Glare is also more of a problem for older eyes. They have become more sensitive to glare, so very bright or unshielded lights will be troublesome. You will probably find you need to take a little more care than previously in getting the balance right so that you have enough light in your house to enable you to see everything but not so much that you find it glary.

Another age-related change in eyesight is that it becomes more difficult to gauge height and depth. This can mean you have a problem negotiating steps or placing objects on shelves or benches, and it explains why you may be helped by a marker strip on the edges of stairs, for instance. The problem with height and depth is compounded when there is no contrast or shading—as, for example, in a flight of stairs carpeted uniformly from top to bottom, or low tables of similar colour and material as the floor they stand on.

With these changes in mind, the following suggestions should assist you in preventing falls resulting from these natural changes:

- Provide plenty of lighting throughout your home, making sure if possible that the lights are shielded rather than bare.
- Try to have switches ready to hand as you enter each room, just inside or outside the doorways. A light switch next to the bed is a sensible option. An alternative is to have a lamp on the bedside table with the switch within easy reach of your bed.
- Light switches should always be located at the top and bottom of stairways.
- Think about using night-lights in the bedroom and bathroom and on the route between them—not only to help you see at night but to ease the transition from dark to light.
- Be aware that when you go from light to dark or vice versa your eyes will need time to adjust. It may be on entering a dark room or going from the house out into bright sunlight—perhaps on these occasions you could give yourself a moment or two of stillness to allow your eyes to catch up with your feet.
- If it is possible, could you have the edges of steps and stairs marked with paint or brightly-coloured adhesive?

If you notice any changes in your eyesight, it would be wise to talk to your doctor or an optometrist. It is in any case a good idea to have your eyes checked each year, and it is worth noting that an eye-test from an optometrist does not cost anything for people with a Medicare Card.

Eye disorders

There are also eye disorders many people may experience as they grow older. These, too, add to the risk of falling. Some eye disorders may be temporary, the result of changes in blood pressure, of heart palpitations, an increase in pressure within the eyeball or insufficient arterial blood flow. Any of these conditions can reduce vision for 5–10 minutes, after which it gradually returns to normal.

There are other disorders which are more progressive and long-lasting. Conditions such as glaucoma and cataracts, as well as nutritional disorders from vitamin B_{12} and thiamine deficiency, can lead to symptoms such as a halo appearance around lights or smoky, hazy or cloudy vision. These problems progress slowly, so they are often not noticed at first. This makes it even more important to have regular eye examinations.

Various treatments are available, ranging from eyedrops and vitamin supplements to surgical corrections and laser treatment. Apart from cataracts, it is fair to say that the earlier the condition is recognised, the less your eyesight will be affected.

Exercise appropriately to maintain your balance

Your body is constantly balancing and rebalancing itself as you change position, stand up, walk, sit down or bend. Human bodies are designed to maintain effective balance and movement, and to do this they need help from pelvic and leg muscles that are as supple and strong as possible.

Exercise is the key to keeping muscles supple and strong so that you are in control of your bodily movements and can keep your balance. Most people have a sense of uneasiness when they suspect that something is not quite right with their bodies, and this applies to balance as well as all our other functions.

A doctor or physiotherapist can check your balance for you, but there is a simple way of testing yourself at home which will give you a rough guide. It is suggested you do the test with another person present or a chair or table handy to keep yourself safe.

Try standing on one leg, count to 30, then stand on the other leg and count to 30 again. If you can stand for 25–30 seconds, your balance is quite adequate, so exercise for you would be a matter of maintaining that good level. If you can stand for 15–25 seconds, your balance is fair but would improve with appropriate exercise.

Simple, safe, sensible exercise includes walking, bowling, Tai Chi, Feldenkrais (awareness through movement), aquarhythmics (gentle water exercise), yoga, gardening, square dancing and ballroom dancing. Some older people say that an enjoyable activity for them is dancing or moving and stretching rhythmically to music in the privacy of their homes. These activities will not offer the same benefits as regular moderate exercise but not everyone can or wants to take up regular exercise.

As you begin to exercise, either to maintain or to improve your balance, it is as well to remember that bodies which have not been exercised for some time need to be treated gently while they adjust to the new demands being made of them. Working slowly and safely will allow gradual improvement, even though you may feel some discomfort at first. Listen to what your body tells you—if you have discomfort, you are trying to do too much.

Be creative in thinking about exercising. What can you do while you're still in bed for instance? (Stretching of arms and legs, fingers and toes, circling of ankles and wrists, pressing head into pillow are some exercises that come to mind.) What can you do while you're waiting for the bus? (Shoulder raising and dropping, neck stretching, pelvic floor exercises . . .) While you're sitting watching TV? (Stretching, circling, squeezing eyes shut and opening, screwing face up and relaxing it . . .).

Manage your medicines

The best way to manage medicines is to learn about them, what they are, what they can do, what they can't do and what side effects they might have. They often have long and involved scientific names, so medicines can seem a bit mysterious and complicated, but they also have common names and you may prefer to think of them that way. Learning about medicines is not really so different from learning about the foods you eat.

Talk to your doctor or chemist about the medications you are taking. Some medications affect balance and coordination. You should always be told by your doctor if side effects are likely to affect you in any way. Problems are more likely if you are taking a number of different medications. Unfortunately, this is more likely as we get older. It is not uncommon for older people to be taking medication for a variety of medical conditions such as heart and blood pressure problems, arthritis and gastrointestinal conditions.

Most medicines have side effects, and some medicines can increase the likelihood of falling. But every person is an individual and responds slightly differently to medications, so we cannot say what the effect of a particular medicine will be for a particular person. Also, since many people take a combination of medicines and since one medicine can interact with another, it is impossible to make predictions about the effect of combinations.

Therefore responsibility rests with you to learn all you can about your own medicines, study your reactions to them and in particular watch out for any side effects.

You may like to know that medicines which can increase the possibility of falling include some drugs used to lower blood pressure or treat heart conditions, some used to relieve stress and anxiety (tranquillisers) and some used to treat sleeping problems (sedatives).

As well as the expected side effects from a medicine itself, you need to be aware that there are also circumstances that may cause side effects. Some of these circumstances might be:

- A change in the type or brand of medicine you are taking
- A change in the number of tablets you are taking
- The addition of a new medicine to those you are already taking
- Minor illnesses such as colds, flu or diarrhoea
- Times when you are feeling unusually tired or worried or depressed

If you notice that you are feeling dizzy or out of kilter, then ask your doctor to see if the medicine might be causing the dizziness or adding to it. When you visit your GP do you make sure you take with you all the information that is needed or useful? It is a good idea to have on hand a list of all the medicines, both prescribed and over-the-counter, that you are currently taking and in what quantity and strength. You should also make yourself a list of all your symptoms.

The questions you ask your doctor could also be asked of your pharmacist. If you have a regular pharmacy, is it one which keeps a computerised record of your medications? This is a very useful new development and one worth looking out for. Those pharmacists who provide a typed sheet of information and advice are also a boon. You need to ask for it when presenting your prescription.

Most pharmacists no longer give the instruction 'Take as directed', as this is recognised as being next-to-useless. Specific directions should be given on the label—the chemist can always get them from the doctor. Speaking of labels, you'll know they are sometimes so small that the print is almost impossible to read. Have you considered getting a magnifying glass and keeping it in your medicine cabinet?

Often, older people have said that uncertainty over whether or not they have taken their medications has led to problems. You can feel very anxious about not being able to remember, possibly miss altogether, or take double the prescribed amount as a result of uncertainty. Some medications, even some available without prescription, can cause memory loss, and some tranquillisers and tablets prescribed for high blood pressure can cause memory problems.

Using a memory aid can be a help. Many people simply use an egg carton to set out their pills, others use a reminder box or similar product which can be bought from chemists. These handy gadgets come in weekly or monthly sizes. The people who use them say that they work best when filling them is made a regular routine—Sunday evening seems to be a popular time. Certainly, some kind of system like this appears to avoid a good deal of anxiety and stress.

Many people believe it is sensible to look for alternatives to drugs for some problems (stress, sleeplessness or constipation for example). While drugs or pills will certainly help in the short term, you may like to consider whether you want to continue with them as a long-term solution.

Conditions such as stress and sleeplessness are usually a symptom, a warning even, that something in life is not right, and it may be helpful to look for that 'something' and try to put it right. Stress, for instance, can often be relieved by relaxation, meditation, talking with a friend, exercise, even perhaps simply by getting up earlier to give yourself more time to do the things you need to do. If you have sleeping problems, have you looked at what might be causing the problems? Similarly with constipation or diarrhoea—if you can find the cause. Sometimes modification of your diet is all that is needed.

Blood pressure lowering medicines

Some of the medicines that lower blood pressure make it more difficult to adjust when changing your body position from lying to sitting to standing. If you are being treated for high blood pressure or a heart condition, you will find it safer to change position slowly. For example, sit on the edge of the chair or bed for a moment or two before you stand up. Also take care when bending down to tie your shoelaces or pick up things from the floor.

Some examples of medicines which lower blood pressure are: Lasix, Moduretic, Aldomet, Inderal, Tenormin, Dyazide, Midamor, Betaloc, Adalat, and Minipress.

Medicines which induce sleep or reduce anxiety or stress

Many of the sedative-type medicines can accumulate over a few days in the body. This may make you feel a little groggy. If this is happening to you, you can discuss it with your doctor, as it may be possible to change your medicine. You may find that there are alternatives, such as relaxation techniques, counselling, exercise or herbal remedies.

taking medicine to help you sleep and you have to
room during the night you will realise that extra care

Some examples of medicines prescribed for sleeplessness, anxiety and stress are: Serepax, Murelax, Normison, Euhypnos,
Mogadon, Rohypnol, Ducene, Valium and Noctec.

Antidepressants

These drugs are normally prescribed if you have severe clinical
depression. They may also be prescribed as a means of assisting
you to control pain. The older so-called tricyclic antidepressants
were more likely to cause sedation and potential drops in blood
pressure—both potent contributors to increasing the risk of falls.

Examples of these older antidepressants include: Tryptanol,
Sinequan, Deptran, Surmontil, Allegron, Pertofran, Anafranil and
Prothiaden.

The newer antidepressants, Prozac, Aurorix, Aropax and Zoloft,
appear to be safer than the above, with reduced incidence of
sedation, dizziness or potentiation of falls. They are also safer if you
inadvisedly drink alcohol.

Antihistamines

Many of the older antihistamine preparations tend to make some
people feel sleepy or dizzy (there is usually a warning label to this
effect on the packet). If you use them it is safer to take them close
to retiring at night so that most of the side effects have worn off
by morning.

Examples of antihistamines prescribed for hayfever or sinusitis
are: Piriton, Dilosyn, Phenergan, Polaramine and Periactin.

Alcohol and drugs—a potent recipe for falls

All of the above drugs increase the risk of falls if taken together
with alcohol. If you drink alcohol, drink in moderation only and
not at all if you take any medication which has an effect on
concentration and coordination. Alcohol has a greater effect on our
balance as we get older. It may also impair our alertness and our
coordination.

Manage chronic conditions

The older people become, the more likelihood there is that some form of illness will develop. Some of these illnesses will be ones which cannot be completely cured or which continue over a long time—these are the illnesses or conditions referred to as 'chronic'. They result in problems which affect daily living and which may increase the possibility of falling. Some examples are chronic arthritis, Parkinson's disease, diabetes mellitus and some heart conditions.

This section deals with the way these chronic illnesses are related to falls and falls prevention. We can discuss this relationship only in a fairly general way because each of them affects individual people differently.

Nevertheless there are some tips that we can offer, knowing they have worked for other older people. You may want to consider some of them so that you can manage your condition rather than having it manage you.

Why do chronic illnesses increase the risk of falling?

First of all, there are those conditions which can affect consciousness by causing dizziness, light-headedness and/or a drop in blood pressure. These can sometimes result in a fall because of blacking out or fainting. Epileptic seizures, Ménière's disease, low or high blood sugar (diabetes) and blood vessel diseases which disturb blood flow to the brain are examples of these conditions.

Then there is a group of conditions including arthritis, rheumatism, Parkinson's disease, foot problems, spondylosis of the spine and paralysis due to stroke. These conditions can add to the risk of falling when they lead to symptoms such as stooped posture, muscle and joint stiffness, pain, shuffling, legs giving way or swaying of the body, because these symptoms can result in unsteadiness and poor balance. This not only increases the likelihood of a fall but means also that if you have a slip or trip, you are less able to save yourself from falling.

As well as the often distressing physical effects of chronic illness, we need to give attention to the equally distressing emotional effects. People who have a chronic condition or who know of or care for someone who has suffered chronic ill health for many years, will be well aware of the difficulties and heartaches that have to be worked through.

Some people may have a disfigurement or other change in their bodily appearance; others may have difficulties with their daily living and need to ask for help even though they would prefer to be fully independent; others may find it difficult to get out and about. If you have any of these changes in your life it is hardly surprising if at times you feel lonely, frustrated, angry or hurt. These are the times that you need to be especially careful.

If people experience loss of routines, or feelings of incompetence, or reduced amount of contact with friends or family, it is normal to feel a sense of grief or fear or anxiety. Many older people have reported that this is when they are most likely to become distracted. Chronic conditions can drain away energy and impair concentration, increasing the risk of a fall through lack of attention.

There are three main aims in managing chronic conditions:

- Preventing further deterioration, disability, injury or symptoms.
- Maintaining as much function and the highest level of wellbeing possible.
- If possible restoring some of the function that may previously have been lost.

Here are some suggestions on managing chronic conditions to avoid falls. Remember that where there is no cure, care becomes even more important.

A correct diagnosis is an important first step in knowing what to do. In general terms, the earlier a diagnosis is made, the earlier treatment can begin and the least amount of damage will be done.

Next, it is important to realise that if you have a long-term medical condition that affects your balance or causes dizziness, pain, light-headedness, foot numbness, stiffness or unsteadiness, you may be risking a fall unless you take precautions.

Find out everything you can about the condition that is affecting you. With information you can rely on your own judgement, wisdom, and ingenuity to control symptoms. Information empowers patients and, in your author's view, is particularly important with medical treatment. You should always be prepared to ask your medical practitioner for information on your condition and its proposed treatment.

Do you have enough information on:

- What the effects of the condition may be?
- What course the condition usually takes?
- How the progressive nature of the condition may be slowed or prevented—if this is possible?
- What treatments are available?
- What assistance is available?

- What are the signs and symptoms of a flare-up?
- What to do in the case of a flare-up?
- What action, specific to your condition, you can take to reduce the risk of a fall?

Take time to think about the problems that the physical disorder creates. Consider your needs and your knowledge of your own environment and then focus on possible approaches which may help you adjust to any limitation of your activities. Improving function is a realistic goal for some conditions. For other people a slowing-down of the illness or simply keeping it at a standstill might represent progress.

It is important to maintain the appropriate routine of exercise, meditation, rest, special diet, medication or other form of treatment, even during periods when you have no symptoms. Many people find that making these things a routine part of their day reduces the amount of disruption to their usual lifestyle. Reaching and maintaining your own highest possible level of wellness provides you with the best means of preventing a fall.

Make your home safer

As you get older you will find there are quite a number of things that you can do, or may already have done, to make your home safer. Many older people, when they speak of falling, tell of falls occurring on the street or in shopping centres or getting onto buses.

In fact, quite a large proportion of falls take place at home, particularly as people move into the over-75 age bracket. Since you are the person most familiar with your home and the way you use it, you are probably the person best placed to decide what safety measures to take. You can get information and advice on all aspects of home safety from occupational therapists, physiotherapists and community health nurses (contact them through your Community Health Centre).

When looking over your house to see how it could be made safer, you need to consider overall factors such as lighting, flooring and furniture placement as well as looking carefully at each individual room.

Lighting needs to be bright but not glary. Light switches should be easy to reach and as near to the doorway as possible. And can you turn on a light before you get out of bed? Do you keep a torch beside your bed? Would you think about putting a night-light on a stairway or in the corridor between bedroom and bathroom?

Floor coverings

Polished floors or tiles are surfaces to beware of and anything placed on them can act as a skateboard. Glazed ceramic tiles are particularly hazardous, especially in areas which may become wet. Unglazed ceramic tiles are less slippery, so you might consider them if new work is being done. With already-existing floor surfaces, however, there is the possibility of using some of the liquid products that can be applied by brush, roller or spray. Some of these achieve a non-slip effect by etching into the surface, others by adding tiny grit particles and others by reacting with the existing surface. More information on these products can be obtained from the Independent Living Centre or its equivalent in your nearest major city.

Where there are loose floor coverings often the edges begin to curl dangerously and can cause a trip. Have you thought about tacking them down? Sometimes people hide a worn patch with a small rug or mat and these too are best tacked down or given a non-slip backing.

Particularly dangerous are rugs placed on polished floors which can become a 'flying carpet', which can take you directly to the orthopaedic ward. Rugs which creep on carpets are also a falls hazard which can ripple enough to catch the smallest foot. Specialty floor coverings shops and some hardware suppliers sell add-on pieces of non-slip materials which can keep rugs from 'walking' over your carpets.

Arrange your furniture so that you can move freely about your house. It is particularly important to keep obstacles away from pathways you use a lot. Soft furnishings along the most regular paths through your rooms may prevent you from inadvertently bruising yourself or catching yourself off balance.

Your bedroom

Is your telephone in a place where you can reach it easily? Having it on a wall makes it difficult to reach if you should fall or are simply feeling unwell. If your phone point can't be placed next to your bed, make sure that any extension cords are securely stapled or fastened to the walls or floor—well away from your path to the bathroom or toilet.

Always get out of bed slowly, as you may still be drowsy. Standing up suddenly can cause dizziness. This is particularly dangerous when you are given medication which produces postural lowering of your blood pressure—known as postural hypotension. This includes commonly used blood pressure lowering drugs such as the fluid tablets given to decrease swelling in your ankles and some of those medications used to counter depression.

Your bathroom

In the bathroom consider having grab-rails installed in the bath, shower and near the toilet. An occupational therapist can advise you as to the correct position for these aids. They need to be installed properly so that they will take the weight of a person (ordinary towel rails will not take this kind of weight).

Many people use a slip-resistant rubber mat in the bath or shower, making sure there is good suction between the mat and the bath or shower surface. There are also textured strips available which can be stuck on the bathtub, the shower recess or bathroom floor to prevent slipping. (Good hardware stores can help, or you can contact the Independent Living Centre for information.) Shower seats which can be bolted into the wall of the shower recess and folded away when not in use are also available.

Toilet seats are sometimes uncomfortably low for older people— do you know that elevated seats are available? (Inquire about suppliers from the Independent Living Centre.)

Be careful not to hold your breath when you are using the toilet. This can cause you to pass out and fall when you stand due to a temporary fall in your blood pressure. This is more commonly seen when you strain to evacuate your bowel contents, particularly if you are afflicted with constipation. At times, this risk is increased when you stand quickly.

Electrical wiring is best run along beside walls, and cords to electrical appliances and phones should be kept clear of walk areas to avoid tripping.

Your kitchen

Keep your most-used items at waist level. Is it possible to have most of your shelves and cupboards at a comfortable level so you don't have to stretch or lean too far? Where tables and chairs are concerned, try to choose ones with four sturdy legs rather than three-legged stools or pedestal tables. Many people use a rubber mat near the sink area in case of spills—and of course spills need to be cleaned up as quickly as possible and the mat needs a non-slip backing or good suction.

Do not stand on chairs to reach into high cupboards. If you cannot avoid higher cupboards use a sturdy set of steps and try to have someone with you if you need to climb onto them.

Always close your cupboard doors or drawers after use to reduce the chances of tripping or knocking yourself off balance.

On the stairs

Non-skid treads can be attached to each step to act as a highlight in dark areas and for people with reduced vision. Firm handrails are a great help and are best placed on both sides of the stairs. Make sure lighting is adequate and provide switches at the top and bottom of the stairs.

Other cautions

As we get older we should always allow extra time to do any of our activities. Don't rush—one thing we should have is plenty of time to complete our activities. Be careful of small children and pets. Larger animals and children are capable of knocking you off balance and causing a fall. Smaller animals increase the chances of falls when they weave through your legs or get under your feet.

Even your author has suffered the indignity of falling flat on his face when tripped by the family pet one night on entering a darkened house. Fortunately, male bone density and some extra body cushioning prevented any serious consequences of my fall.

Good lighting

You should ensure adequate lighting on pathways to and around the house and in entry doorways. This will increase your safety in bad weather or at night. It might also be wise to keep shrubbery trimmed back so that pathways are clear.

Outside paths

Outside paths covered in leaves are particularly dangerous when wet. Outside steps and stairs often become slippery when wet and rails nearby are a good safeguard. They may also become mossy but there are products available to kill moss, fungi and lichen to make these areas less hazardous.

The world outside your home

This is the most difficult area in which to put forward suggestions. The world outside our own homes—the streets, the shops, the shopping centres, the railway stations—is an environment which many older people regard with apprehension and dismay. Many falls are caused by hazards in this environment—some of these hazards can only be 'managed', whereas others may possibly be 'changed'.

Footpaths

If possible avoid paths or walkways that have soft, loose or uneven surfaces such as gravel, cobblestones or brick. If the public foot-paths in your neighbourhood are pot-holed, bumpy and in need of repair, contact your local council or alderperson. This is something you might do either alone or in cooperation with your neighbours.

Roads

Here, too, if they need repair, contact your local council or alder-person. Perhaps when crossing roads you can allow yourself extra time, especially in bad weather.

Buses

The problem may be either that the bus stops too far from the kerb or starts off before you are safely seated. In either case, take your time. You are a paying customer! Having the fare ready can prevent you from losing your balance while fumbling for change. By not carrying too many packages you can keep one hand free to hold the handrail firmly as you get on the bus.

Remember to take a good look at each step before moving to the next. If you know that you are unsteady in the bus, it is your right to ask the driver to wait till you are safely seated before starting off. Getting on or off the bus can be a problem, especially if it has stopped some distance from the kerb, or other people are jostling. Again, take your time and hold firmly to the handrail.

Railway stations

Maybe rails are needed beside steps or perhaps a ramp is necessary. Acting in concert with others may be the way to get something done.

Shopping centres, supermarkets and shops

The common problems here are slippery floors, undefined changes in levels, spills not cleaned up quickly, scraps and rubbish left lying about. The owners or occupiers have a legal responsibility to take reasonable care to keep their premises safe. Shopping centre 'survival techniques' that have been suggested include: shopping at quiet times; using lifts rather than escalators; using a shopping buggy (good for carrying the shopping and providing some support at the same time); and making use of home delivery services.

Bicycles and skateboards

If these are being ridden on footpaths contact the local police, the local council and the local school. If your neighbourhood has 'beat police' they are probably the best place to start.

Driving

Age-related changes will probably impair your driving ability to some extent. Your eyes will be more sensitive to glare and slower to adapt to changes between light and dark, your coordination will not be as good as it once was and your reaction time will be slower. You can compensate for these changes in a variety of ways, possibly by driving more slowly, driving less at night and less during rush hours. If you need to drive long distances, maybe you could allow yourself more time and make more stops on the way.

Your driving comfort and therefore your concentration can be enhanced in a major way by using shaped and padded back supports or cushions. This is particularly important if you have significant back pain.

General points

- The outside world can be particularly dangerous if you are feeling rushed, distracted or not concentrating on what you are doing. Taking time and staying alert seem to be the best answers.

- You need to be aware not only of your own movements but also those of pets, small children, other pedestrians, joggers, cyclists, etc.

- If you use glasses or a hearing aid it is as well to go out wearing them.

- If you use a walking aid such as a stick, crutches or a frame, these need to be fitted individually and need regular maintenance. Here again, remember to take them with you when you go out.

- Wearing safe shoes will be a big help—they need to fit securely, have low, broad heels and slip-resistant soles (try to avoid smooth leather soles).

You may be interested to know also that if you do have a fall and need help with getting back to ordinary living, there are often small mobility groups available. These are organised by the occupational therapists of community centres and will help people return to doing their shopping, getting on buses, using walking aids correctly and so forth. It is not necessary to have had something as major as a hip replacement—after any fall you may feel somewhat anxious and lacking in confidence and there is help and support available to you.

Limit your alcohol intake

Heavy drinking can eventually cause permanent damage to the brain and central nervous system and so increase the likelihood of falling. Even moderate drinking can slow down brain activity and lessen mental alertness, judgement, physical coordination and reaction time, thus contributing to a higher risk of falling.

For older people, there are very real consequences associated with alcohol which suggest that it is wise to limit your intake:

- Even a small amount of alcohol can disturb already impaired balance and reflexes.

- Being a drug, it mixes unfavourably with many other drugs, both prescription and over-the-counter. As well, some prescription drugs may intensify the reaction to alcohol, leading to more rapid intoxication.

- Alcohol can dangerously slow down performance skills such as driving and walking and impair judgement.

- It can reduce alertness when taken with other drugs such as tranquillisers, barbiturates, pain-killers and antihistamines.

- It can produce exaggerated responses to other drugs as it can cause them to be metabolised more quickly—in particular, anticonvulsants, anticoagulants and antidiabetes drugs.

- Aspirin can sometimes cause bleeding in the stomach and

intestines—alcohol also irritates the stomach and may aggravate any bleeding if combined with aspirin.

• Alcohol and fluid tablets—diuretics—can combine in some people to reduce blood pressure, thus producing dizziness.

For all these reasons, if you drink, even moderately, it would be wise to check with your doctor or pharmacist about possible interactions with any medication you are taking.

What to do if you fall at home

There are two really important things to do if you have a fall at home:

• Stay quiet for a few moments to let the first shock pass so that you can think clearly.
• Remember to use a piece of furniture to help if you decide to try getting up.

It seems almost a natural instinct to try to get up, but it is worthwhile spending a few minutes being quiet and still before doing anything. You can then think out more carefully what your best course of action may be. If you have suffered an injury, you may decide you are better off calling and waiting for help rather than trying to get up.

If you live alone, calling may not be very effective, so instead of letting this be a worry you might consider getting a personal alarm system. This can be worn around the neck or at the waist, so that you can summon help in an emergency.

If after a fall you decide it is safe and sensible to try to get up, here are some suggestions as to how you could go about it. One method is to slide or shuffle along the floor to the nearest chair, sofa, bed or the like. Then manoeuvre yourself into a side-sitting position, then a kneeling one and then lever yourself up gradually onto the furniture. Another method is to roll onto your stomach, then raise yourself onto all fours and crawl to the nearest suitable piece of furniture. Place your hands on it and you will then be in the same kneeling position as above and you can raise yourself using the furniture for support.

In both cases, it is best to do everything slowly and carefully, remembering that, even if you are not hurt, you will have suffered a shock in falling.

It may be that neither of these methods will work for you—perhaps your knees are too painful for crawling on or your arms and shoulders not up to levering yourself onto a chair. So, if you decide not to try to get up, or are unable to, it is sensible to keep yourself warm and comfortable till help arrives. Maybe you can roll up in a carpet or pull a bedspread, coat or blanket over yourself. Maybe you can reach a cushion or pillow to put under your head or knees.

If you live alone and can't get up, you could try sliding along the floor and out your front door to summon help. While clearly this makes more sense than lying helplessly for hours waiting for help, there are potential risks involved with this course of action.

Summary

We have seen that as we get older and perhaps more frail there are a number of factors which are likely to increase the risk of falls. Understanding these factors should lead to appropriate remedies which will assist you to 'fall-proof' your home to the greatest possible extent. In turn, this will decrease the risk of osteoporotic fracture in those at greatest risk.

8

Treating osteoporosis

Twenty years ago, the treatments available to the family doctor for patients with osteoporosis were calcium, fluoride, and the anabolic steroid Decadurabolin. This anabolic steroid was thought to be useful to control the pain associated with the spinal fractures known to occur in patients with what was then called 'senile osteoporosis'. Strangely enough, a significant number of these women were in their late sixties and early seventies—giving the lie to the use of the word senile in the diagnosis.

As occurs at the present time, the use of Decadurabolin was restricted by the Australian Government to proven osteoporosis, and its administration was controlled by the Government placing limits as to how frequently medical practitioners could prescribe it.

The situation is much better and much more optimistic today. We now know many of the risk factors in women who may go on to develop the condition of postmenopausal osteoporosis. We now know how to reduce those risks which are preventable. As you have seen, the technologies are available today to diagnose the condition safely and reliably despite the fact that their usage is limited or heavily controlled by Government decree.

A whole spectrum of therapies has been developed to help the medical profession and the potential sufferers of this condition manage it, and hopefully prevent another generation of women and men from suffering from the ravages of the increased fracture risks and related medical problems associated with osteoporosis.

This chapter will focus on the treatments currently in use for the treatment and/or prevention of some aspects of osteoporosis. A description of each of the treatments, their availability, whether by prescription or over-the-counter, their benefits, possible side effects, contraindications and claimed successes will be covered in the following pages.

Treatment

The objectives of treatment in established osteoporosis are to prevent further bone loss and to replace bone already lost. Several agents are currently undergoing clinical trials, used singly or in combination. Some have been shown to increase the density of bone, but there is still uncertainty whether this increase in bone density necessarily means that fractures will be reduced.

Calcium

Despite controversy about the role of calcium in the management of osteoporosis, it is widely recommended (as dairy products or calcium tablets) by specialists. Calcium supplements are certainly advisable for patients who avoid dairy products. Some authorities favour administration of calcium in the evening to offset the obligatory loss of calcium which occurs during the night.

Sex hormones

The use of oestrogen replacement therapy or—as it is more commonly referred to—hormone replacement therapy (HRT) has been widely documented in the medical and lay literature. Popular books on the subject have appeared in the literature both in favour[1] and against[2] in recent years. The subject of HRT has achieved such a degree of controversy that it will be dealt with separately in this book.

The male sex hormone, testosterone, is occasionally of use in women to enhance the libido, but is more likely to be of use in men with osteoporosis due to failure of production of the male hormone. This decrease in testosterone occurs in men for a variety of reasons, some of which will be dealt with separately in this book.

Anabolic steroids

Anabolic steroids have long been used in the treatment of women with osteoporosis and have now been shown to increase bone mass. The injections of Decadurabolin and Durabolin are thick oily preparations which are given by deep intramuscular injection every three to six weeks. Advocates of this treatment favour intermittent courses of six to nine months' duration to minimise side effects, the principal ones being huskiness of the voice and facial hair growth. There is also some question as to the possibility of liver damage with some of the preparations available to be taken by mouth.

Fluoride

This substance has in the past been mainly used for severe osteoporosis of the spine, since this is the major area in which fluoride has been shown to be effective. While fluoride can have a sustained action in promoting bone formation, up to one-third of patients do not respond and there are a number of side effects of treatment. Importantly, recent evidence indicates fluoride treatment, while increasing bone density of the spine, may not protect against spinal fractures, and may increase risk of fracture of other bones.

Vitamin D

Vitamin D has until recently been considered a vitamin which is essential for life, particularly for the formation of good bones, and the efficient absorption of calcium from the gut into the bloodstream. However, vitamin D is now considered by most experts to act more as a hormone than as a vitamin.

Vitamin D fulfils the requirements of a hormone, as it is produced by one organ—the skin—and acts on distant organs or tissues, including your bones. More than 90% of vitamin D is produced in your skin, therefore you probably do not need to take vitamin D supplements, particularly in a usually sunny country such as Australia.

The possibility of making an excessive amount of vitamin D is reduced because there is a balance of vitamin D made by the skin and the amount circulating throughout your bloodstream. Your skin will stop making vitamin D when there is a likelihood of an excess occurring.

Over-the-counter vitamin D is not as safe, because excessive amounts are stored in your liver. Even in an Australian winter, the amount of ultraviolet light from the sun is adequate for your average needs.

In some societies or ethnic groups it is common for the skin to be totally covered and often in all-black clothing. This leads to a potential lack of circulating vitamin D. People who are confined indoors because of chronic illness or elderly people who are institutionalised are particularly at risk of being low in vitamin D.

Where vitamin D deficiency is possible, it can prevented by taking the safe dosage of 400 units of calciferol daily. Larger doses of vitamin D can be harmful and should be taken only under medical supervision for special reasons. For those who may require additional vitamin D, combination vitamin and mineral preparations such as 'All in One' capsules may be an acceptable supplement.

Vitamin D is available as fish oil capsules. These oils are activated in the liver and kidneys into the final essential form. Most vitamin preparations are measured in International Units.

Whether vitamin D or its metabolites are of benefit in preventing further bone loss in patients with osteoporosis is not established. There have been a number of studies[3] which suggest bone density is not increased, but bone breakdown may be prevented.

Calcitriol

Calcitriol, marketed in Australia by the pharmaceutical company Roche and available as Rocatrol capsules, is an active form of natural vitamin D_3. It is said to increase calcium absorption and to regulate bone modelling, yet at the same time it prevents bone loss. According to Professor Philip Sambrook of the Garvan Institute of Medical Research, St Vincent's Hospital, Sydney,[4] 'calcitriol is classified as an anti-resorptive [preventing further bone loss] because it enhances the . . . absorption of calcium [from the stomach and gut].' He goes on to state that calcitriol reduces the bone resorption or loss stimulated by the parathyroid hormone.

Calcitriol is claimed to reduce the incidence of vertebral fractures in established osteoporosis and also to reduce the incidence of those fractures which occur in the limbs, that is, those that occur in the wrists and ankles, hands and feet.

A recent study by Professor Murray Tilyard in New Zealand and published in the prestigious *New England Journal of Medicine*[5] covered a three-year investigation into over 600 patients with osteoporosis. It was conducted under the auspices of the Royal New Zealand College of General Practitioners, and compared the safety and effectiveness of 0.25 micrograms calcitriol twice daily against 1000 mg of calcium taken daily.

To be included, the participants in the study had to have X-ray evidence of at least one compression fracture in the spinal vertebras. A fracture in this study was defined as the loss of height of the

115

front of the vertebra of 20% compared with the height of the back of the vertebra.

The study showed a major difference between those treated with calcium and those given calcitriol. There were only one-third of the number of fractures recorded in the three-year period in those treated with calcitriol compared with the calcium-treated group. This represented a 70% reduction in the number of new vertebral fractures in the calcitriol-treated group. Importantly, there were no serious side effects in the group treated with calcitriol.

The beneficial effects of the calcitriol were not seen until the patients had taken the medication for two years, and were seen only in those women with 'mild to moderate osteoporosis (i.e. five or fewer fractures)' at the beginning of the study.

The explanation given for the effectiveness of calcitriol was that it improved the intestinal absorption of calcium and also controlled the balance of calcium at other sites in the body.

Other studies[6] had shown that calcitriol was able to increase bone mineral density in osteoporotic women with previously lowered bone calcium levels, with consequent decrease in new vertebral fractures, reduction in pain and improvement in mobility. These studies support the safety of calcitriol in the treatment of patients with osteoporosis.

The Tilyard study concluded '. . . Three years of calcitriol therapy in women with postmenopausal osteoporosis significantly reduced the incidence of new vertebral fractures as compared to calcium . . . supplementation'.

The report finished by stating 'These results suggest that calcitriol is an important therapeutic option in the treatment of women with postmenopausal osteoporosis'.

In Australia, the authorities responsible for determining the listing of drugs on the Prescribers Benefits Schedule, 'the yellow book' of drugs which are sometimes heavily subsidised by the Federal Government, have determined that the only patients entitled to a reduced price for calcitriol are those with 'established postmenopausal osteoporosis with one or more non-traumatic vertebral compression fractures on X-ray'.

However, Australian experts in the treatment of osteoporosis, including Professor Sambrook, have suggested that calcitriol should be made available for women with significant osteopoenia, that is, bone mineral loss (without fracture), in the same manner as the treatment of patients with high blood pressure before the occurrence of strokes in those patients. However, this raises the difficult problem of bone mineral density scanning and its availability (discussed elsewhere in this book).

Sambrook has also stated that calcitriol's place in the treatment of established postmenopausal osteoporosis probably comes after the use of oestrogen replacement therapy and the use of anabolic steroids or when patients are not able to tolerate these therapies.

Calcitriol has recently been found to be effective in the treatment of steroid-induced osteoporosis[7] in clinical studies, but is not available for these patients under Australia's subsidised drug scheme. Women most likely to be taking these cortisone-like substances, such as prednisolone and Decadron, are those who have chronic illnesses responsive to these drugs. These conditions include chronic asthmatics, sufferers from rheumatoid arthritis, and the auto-immune diseases such as systemic lupus erythematosus (SLE).

Calcitriol is also being used in the treatment of New Zealand men with osteoporosis, according to Tilyard in a recent video-conference for Australian GPs.

Calcitriol should be avoided in those who are routinely taking calcium or vitamin D supplements, owing to the possible toxicity of increased serum levels of both calcitriol and calcium. The most common of the uncommon reactions to calcitriol treatment are excessive blood levels of calcium leading to drowsiness, headache, nausea, vomiting, weakness and constipation. Muscle pain, bone pain and a metallic taste in your mouth may also be indications of excessive blood levels of calcium.

Your doctor will need to monitor your calcium levels and kidney function with blood testing on a regular basis while you are taking the medication. You may be asked to have review spinal X-rays after twelve months or so and perhaps repeat bone density scanning.

Despite the potential for side effects it must be said that calcitriol is well tolerated at the recommended dose of one gelatin capsule of 0.25 micrograms twice daily by mouth.

Calcitonin

The hormone calcitonin was discovered as recently as 1961, when experiments on the tiny parathyroid glands revealed the presence of a chemical substance which lowered the calcium levels in the blood. The name calcitonin was given to this substance because it appeared to modulate the 'tone' of calcium in body fluids.

It has been subsequently discovered that any tendency to increase the amount of calcium in the blood causes the body to release calcitonin. The hormone acts to prevent the breakdown or resorption of bone by targeting the cells which break down bone—the osteoclasts. Calcitonin appears to work only in the presence of increased calcium levels, as in osteoporosis and other diseases, and not in normal people.

Calcitonin also appears to stop an excess in blood levels of calcium after calcium-rich meals, and it protects against the loss of your body's calcium stores in those conditions in which the body is at risk of losing calcium. These include pregnancy, lactation, growth, and prolonged low dietary intake of calcium.

Other important effects of calcitonin outside of the bones have also been described in the medical literature[8]. These include an ability to increase the amount of sodium in the urine and an increased flow of urine in patients taking the calcitonin. It prevents or reduces the release of other hormones in the body, including prolactin, growth hormone and insulin.

Several calcitonins may in the future be available for use in the prevention of postmenopausal osteoporosis—mainly developed from salmon, pigs and humans. The most potent, and therefore most commonly used, is the salmon calcitonin. Most of these are given by injection, although nasal sprays offer the possibility of a safe and convenient method of administration. Studies[9] have shown the intranasal preparation appears to slow the bone loss in post-menopausal women.

There appear to be few side effects of these preparations, with the exception of local pain at the site of the injection.

At present, there is no listing in the Australian Schedule of Pharmaceutical Benefits for the use of calcitonin in osteoporosis. The only condition these preparations are likely to be used for is Paget's disease of bone. Therefore, it is likely that the cost of the injections of between $100–200 for a pack of five to ten pre-loaded syringes is likely to militate against their widespread usage.

Calcitonins available in Australia include Calcitare, which is derived from pigs and produced as ampoules of 160 IU at a cost of $250 per ten ampoules or as a subsidised pharmaceutical benefit for patients with Paget's disease. Also available is Calsynar or salmon calcitonin—100 or 200 IU ampoules cost $55 for five pre-filled syringes. Miacalcic is another salmon calcitonin, and Cibacalcin is derived from human sources. At the present time these medications are severely restricted by the Australian health authorities to the treatment of 'proven Paget's disease or hypercalcemia'.

The bisphosphonates or disphosphonates

These drugs were developed from research into the water-softening agents added to washing-machine powders. They have a double action on bone mineral crystals: they are able to stop small crystals from forming, and they can protect the larger crystals from being dissolved. The action which occurs depends on the chemical composition of the bisphosphonate and on the dose.

The bisphosphonates appear to be taken up very rapidly by bone and are taken up by and attach to the bone surface, particularly when the remodelling of bone occurs. They appear to prevent bone breakdown by stopping the cells which break down bone—the osteoclasts—from acting on the bone.

Bisphosphonates are not readily absorbed from the gastrointestinal tract and should be taken on an empty stomach. They are poorly taken up when food contains calcium. Studies have shown up to 20–40% of the drug retained by the bone; the rest is excreted in the urine.

One of these bisphosphonate drugs, etidronate, has recently been licensed in Australia for treating established osteoporosis. It is anticipated that it will be available in Australia at the time of publication of this book. Approval for the Australian marketing of the drug for the treatment of postmenopausal osteoporosis was granted to the manufacturers early in 1993. In Australia the preparation is known as Didrocal.

Several scientific trials have shown the ability of this drug to increase bone mass in the spine and to lead to a significant reduction in bone fracture.

A study by Watts[10] showed intermittent cycles of treatment with an oral salt of etidronate appears to result in small, significant increases in the calcium content of the vertebral bones. Etidronate has been described as a minimally toxic compound active against bone breakdown and has been mainly used up to now in the treatment of Paget's disease of the bone. The authors of the research paper claimed that after treatment for one year, a significant decrease in the rate of new vertebral fractures was shown. The study was a scientifically verified double-blind study of the active agent etidronate compared with an inactive placebo and was carried out in the United States.

The study group was composed of 429 postmenopausal women of an average age of 65 years with osteoporosis and with one to three compression fractures of the spine. For three years the subjects of this trial were given two weeks on etidronate followed by supplemental calcium for the rest of the three-month cycle of either the active drug Didronel or the placebo. This was carried out over ten complete cycles or approximately three years.

In the group undergoing the active treatment, average vertebral bone content or bone density increased significantly compared with a decrease in the placebo group. They also noted a significantly lower rate of new vertebral bone fractures in the treated group, beginning in the second year of treatment. An increase in bone density was not seen in the bones of the wrist, showing that the increase in bone density of the spinal vertebras was not at the expense of the other long bones of the body.

The investigators claimed that few side effects were seen in this group of patients. They found no ill effects on those bones not affected by the osteoporosis.

The study was carried out over a three-year period. Importantly, significant increases in bone mineral density were observed after eighteen and 24 months in all etidronic acid recipients compared to those who received either phosphate or calcium. Significantly fewer fractures in the spinal vertebras occurred in the group taking the drug (known overseas as Didronel).

Another of the most widely quoted studies into cyclical etidronate therapy as a part of the same multi-centre trial was performed by the Danish investigator Dr Tommy Storm and his colleagues.[11] They investigated 66 women in a double-blind study in which neither the investigator nor the patient was aware of whether they were receiving the active etidronate or an inactive placebo. The patients were randomly assigned in equal numbers to receive oral etidronate (400 mg per day) or placebo for two weeks, followed by a thirteen-week period in which no drugs were given.

The sequence was repeated ten times for a total of 150 weeks. Daily oral supplements of calcium and vitamin D were given during the study into both groups. At the end of the study the investigators claimed significant increases in bone mineral density content. They also claimed that after approximately one year of treatment there was a significant decrease in the rate of new fractures.

The most recent study to be published on etidronate in this review was that of Harris and his associates.[12] This study was again part of the same multicentre trial and was published in the *American Journal of Medicine* in December 1993. It confirmed the above positive results. The paper concluded:

> Our extended experience with intermittent cyclic etidronate therapy demonstrated beneficial effects on bone mass of the spine and hip, with a significant reduction in the rate of vertebral fractures in those

patients at highest risk of fracture. Etidronate therapy appears to be safe and effective for the treatment of postmenopausal osteoporosis.

Thus, a number of experts in the field of postmenopausal osteoporosis have declared etidronic acid or Didrocal to be another welcome option for osteoporosis therapy.[13]

Despite their enthusiasm, researchers into the use of the drugs which prevent the breakdown of bone after menopause believe that study must continue to assess how long the increase in bone density observed with Didrocal can be maintained. They also stress the need to monitor any possible adverse effects of the drug on bone cell activity and bone strength.

Didrocal is given in a cyclical manner, with the patient taking the drug for two weeks and then having a break for the next eight to eleven weeks, during which calcium is taken. The treatment is recommended for about three years only.

The major use for Didrocal is that of a non-hormonal alternative to oestrogen replacement therapy. It may have particular application in the older osteoporotic woman or when HRT is unsuitable—after cancer of the breast or following hormone suppression therapy of endometriosis.

Didrocal is currently not listed in the Australian Schedule of Pharmaceutical Benefits. Its manufacturers (Procter & Gamble) hope that Didrocal will be made a subsidised benefit by the time this book is published.

Summary

This chapter has covered the medical treatments available to prevent either worsening of already present osteoporosis or to prevent the unpleasant consequences of osteoporotic fracture. We have seen there is now a wider choice of drugs to prevent the occurrence of fractures than in previous times.

The major drugs available to prevent the further loss of bone mass include calcitriol—classified as a non-hormonal agent (as opposed to oestrogen replacement therapy), which has been approved as a subsidised pharmaceutical benefit by the health authorities for use in patients with previous spinal fractures. The other promising drug to be released in Australia, in the near future, is Didrocal, which is another non-hormonal bone-conserving drug which offers hope to many postmenopausal women in the battle against osteoporosis.

HRT is covered in Chapter 10 and calcium therapy and supplementation are covered in Chapter 9.

9

Nutrition and osteoporosis

Postmenopausal bone loss is an important medical problem. As we have already seen, the cost of hip fractures alone is estimated at more than $100 million per year in Australia. Other important statistics suggest serious fractures will occur in more than 30% of women during their lifetime. Up to three-quarters of these fractures occur in patients whose bone densities are much lower than that of the average younger woman. It makes a great deal of sense to use a cheap and effective method of preventing or slowing bone loss without causing side effects. Despite having many outspoken critics, calcium supplementation is still widespread. Recent reports have led to its increasing acceptance by workers in the field of osteoporosis.

Calcium is one of the three key requirements for helping prevent or manage osteoporosis because of its major role in building bones. It is very important to understand that having adequate calcium, on its own, will not prevent or minimise osteoporosis. You must also be getting adequate regular weight-bearing exercise (exercise on your feet) and have an adequate level of sex hormones (particularly oestrogen) circulating in your body.

Surveys of dietary intake have shown that many Australians do not consume enough calcium. Many women and adolescent girls are consuming less than half of what is recommended for growth and maintenance of bone.

Our calcium 'bone bank'

Every day you excrete some calcium from your body. This loss mainly occurs in your urine and faeces and has to be made up for by consuming adequate amounts of calcium. This counteracts the effects of the parathormone which is released into your bloodstream by the parathyroid glands. This hormone is partially responsible for the bone-robbing activity which is going on constantly in your bones.

If the amount of calcium in the blood falls below normal, the body will take from your bones what it needs for other important functions of the heart, muscles, blood and nerves. The bones act as a storage site or 'bank' for calcium. If you are not consuming enough calcium and therefore making adequate deposits into the 'bone bank', then the 'withdrawals' of calcium from the bank will be greater than those deposits, and your bones will begin to weaken.

Parathormone is largely produced and released during the night, so taking your calcium at night will help to reduce the excessive activity of this hormone.

There is constant and unavoidable loss of calcium into the urine and faeces every day. As a result, the daily requirement for calcium is considerably greater than for the other minerals distributed throughout your body. Careful studies of the balance of calcium in the body indicate that the normal daily requirement for calcium is 500–600 mg if you are a woman who is premenopausal and at least 600–800 mg daily if you are postmenopausal. The recommended daily allowances of calcium of 800 and 1000 mg respectively, have been set from this information. However, these figures probably underestimate the daily needs because the loss of calcium in your sweat is not allowed for in these calculations.

There has been a great deal of support for these figures and the benefits of calcium supplementation have been shown in a number of recent studies of changes in bone mass in women on different calcium intakes.

Premenopausal women

In one study[1] of dairy-based calcium supplements in premenopausal women, a beneficial effect of calcium on bone mass was observed after two years. The treated subjects had a 2% greater bone density at the end of this time than the control group who were not given the supplements.

Postmenopausal women

Calcium supplements lower the high urinary hydroxyproline of postmenopausal women, showing a decrease in the bone-robbing effects of bone resorption. The calcium supplements appear to work by suppressing the effects of the parathyroid hormone. Calcium is often recommended at night to counter the increased amounts of parathormone which are released into the bloodstream at night.

Most studies of calcium supplementation in postmenopausal women show a reduction in the rate of bone loss. A recent detailed analysis of a large number of these studies has shown overwhelming evidence for such a beneficial effect. In twelve lengthy studies of calcium therapy in postmenopausal women, a positive effect on bone loss was found in eleven.

One exception to this rule may be the inner more delicate trabecular bone in the spine which appears not to respond to calcium in the first five years after the menopause. However, in older women and, importantly, in osteoporotic women, calcium supplementation does have a protective effect at this site.

Osteoporotic women

There is evidence that calcium can prevent further bone loss in women who already have osteoporosis. The calcium-supplemented 'controls' in the recent calcitriol and fluoride treatment trials did not lose bone. Australian researchers Need and Nordin have investigated a number of osteoporotic women with normal calcium absorption from calcium to no calcium or the reverse, and they have found it is quite clear that calcium has a therapeutic effect.[2]

Fracture prevention

There is strong evidence now available to suggest calcium supplements reduce fracture rates in postmenopausal women. A reduction in vertebral and hip fracture rates has been shown in a number of studies. There has been no evidence that calcium has caused any damage to the bone of the women treated in this way. This strongly supports the theory that calcium supplements merely control excessive parathormone levels—thus preventing increased bone loss.

Recommended daily calcium intake

Category	Age	Calcium (mg)
Children	1–3 years	700
	4–7 years	800
Boys	8–11 years	800
	12–15 years	1200
	16–18 years	1000
Girls	8–11 years	900
	12–15 years	1000
	16–18 years	800
Men	19–64 years	800
	64+ years	800
Women	19–54 years	800
	54+ years	1000
Pregnant, last 3 months	–	1100
Lactating	–	1200

Source: National Health and Medical Research Council of Australia

Food sources of calcium

In most cases dairy foods are the easiest way for you to obtain adequate calcium. This is because, as you will see from the following charts, dairy foods are particularly high in calcium. Also, calcium in dairy foods is far more easily absorbed into the body than it is from other foods.

In most cases you should aim to get at least half your daily intake of calcium from dairy foods. The drop in consumption of dairy foods seen in recent decades has stemmed from the largely mistaken belief that dairy foods are contributors to heart disease and obesity.

Milk

Recent advertising campaigns from the Australian Dairy Corporation have stressed the low fat content of milk—4%. These figures were supported by figures published by health authorities. You can now buy a wide variety of low- to very low-fat dairy products. Low-fat milk, yoghurt and cheese are now available through most food and dairy outlets. Anyone concerned about their weight or risk of heart disease should choose such low-fat products. Calcium-enriched low-fat dairy products mean you should be able to obtain optimal calcium levels plus the low-fat benefits for your health.

Misconceptions about dairy foods

Many believe dairy foods contribute to the occurrence of the common cold or make it worse, despite the lack of supporting scientific evidence. In fact, dairy foods are an excellent readily digestible source of nourishment when you are unwell.

It is also popular to claim that dairy foods stimulate the formation of excessive mucus. Some people, especially those with nasal or respiratory problems, may produce excess mucus after consuming any type of fluid, especially in the morning. Milk cannot be singled out as the only fluid that produces such a reaction. Most people will not experience this effect.

Lactose intolerance is said to be common. Most people in our community, however, do not have a true lactose intolerance. It is more common among people of Asian or Mediterranean origin than among people of Anglo-Saxon origin. Where there is lactose intolerance, measures can be taken to deal with it or people may prefer to obtain calcium from other sources.

Some individuals do not have a genuine intolerance to lactose. Rather, due to the exclusion of dairy products from their diet for some years, their ability to produce the enzyme lactase (which breaks down lactose) is decreased. The ability to produce this enzyme is recovered over time when dairy products are re-introduced into the diet. Some degree of lactose intolerance may be a problem with advancing age.

If you are concerned about lactose intolerance, discuss this with your doctor or a dietitian.

Fish

Canned fish with bones—particularly salmon and sardines—is a good source of calcium. When eating canned fish don't forget to eat the bones. When buying, check the labels and choose those products that are low in salt. This is because salt interferes with our absorption of calcium. Prawns and crab meat are other relatively high sources of calcium.

Other foods

Calcium occurs in a large number of foods but often in only small amounts, so it is important to eat a balanced diet from a wide variety of foods.

In some foods, such as some nuts and vegetables, calcium occurs in relatively large amounts. However, the calcium may not be absorbed efficiently by the body due to the presence of other substances. An example is spinach, where the calcium is poorly absorbed because of the oxalic acid in the spinach.

What foods are the best sources of calcium?

Following is a calcium chart which you can use as a guide to your eating habits to obtain adequate calcium.

The chart below includes non-dairy sources which are relatively high in calcium. Remember, however, that the calcium from vege-

Calcium content of foods

Food	Serving size	Calcium (mg)	Kilojoules (kJ)
Milk: regular	250 ml	310	707
skim	250 ml	340	369
reduced fat	250 ml	350	606
low fat	250 ml	380	382
Yoghurt: plain	1 tub (250 g)	330	650
plain, low fat	1 tub (200 g)	360	442
fruit	1 tub (200 g)	330	826
Cheese: Cheddar	35 g	275	589
Edam	35 g	300	526
Parmesan	35 g	380	621
Icecream	100 g	140	704
Meat			
Beef, steak, grilled/flamed	100 g	13	803
Lamb chop, mid loin, grilled	100 g	8	1529
Chicken: roasted/skin	100 g	10	913
roasted/no skin	100 g	16	783
Salmon, canned	100 g	95	649
Eggs, boiled	1 large	30	318
Broccoli	100 g	29	101
Apricots, dried	50 g	46	388
Almonds	50 g	125	1168
Baked beans	50 g	25	135
Spinach/silverbeet	100 g	50	78
Apples	1 medium	5	196
Oranges	1 medium	45	234
Bread, wholemeal	1 slice	15	244

Source: Australian Dairy Corporation

tables, nuts and fruits may not be absorbed as efficiently by the body as it is from dairy products. Therefore, for most of you, trying to obtain adequate calcium from this section alone without the dairy or fish sources would be difficult.

Ways to increase calcium in your diet

Dairy foods

Aim to get at least half your daily intake from dairy foods. This will make it easier to get your daily requirement because dairy foods are high in calcium and calcium is more easily absorbed from dairy products than from other foods.

Aim for two serves daily, for example two glasses of low-fat milk or one glass of low-fat milk and 35 g of hard cheese. Use calcium-enriched dairy products.

Try different ways of using dairy products. Add milk or skim milk powder to soups, stews, casseroles. Use yoghurt instead of cream. (Cream is not only high in fat, but extremely low in calcium.) Add yoghurt to soups, desserts, salads.

Eat calcium-rich fish

Eat more canned fish with bones, especially canned salmon and sardines. Don't forget to eat the bones—this is where most of the calcium is concentrated.

New recipes

There are many tempting ideas available for the use of dairy products. These are produced in great variety by the Australian Dairy Corporation or other dairy authorities. For those who for cultural or medical reasons do not eat or drink dairy products there are many alternatives included in these excellent brochures and publications.

Distribute your daily calcium over the whole day

Consume some of your daily calcium between meals and before going to bed at night. Include dairy products or soft-bone fish as a mid-morning or mid-afternoon snack. For example, have a milk drink or a biscuit with cheese for a mid-morning snack. Have a salmon or tuna snack and take your calcium supplement at bedtime.

Our bodies lose some calcium all the time. This is a natural process—we are constantly losing calcium in our urine, faeces and sweat. However, more calcium is lost at night. Therefore it is a good idea to take some calcium in the evening, e.g. a glass of milk before bed. This appears to reduce the release of the bone-robbing parathormone. It may also help you get a good night's sleep!

Use a calcium guide chart

As a guide and reminder you may wish to put a chart of foods with their calcium content on the refrigerator door or other prominent place in the kitchen. Here is a quick guide to give you a comparison of the amounts of various foods you can choose from to give you 300 mg of calcium.

Calcium comparisons of food

Food	Quantity
Milk: regular	1 glass (250 ml)
skim	1 glass (250 ml)
reduced fat	1 glass (250 ml)
low-fat	1 glass (250 ml)
Yoghurt: plain, low-fat, fruit	1 tub (200 g)
Cheese: cheddar, Edam, Parmesan	35 g
Icecream	200 g
Meat: beef, steak, grilled/trimmed	2.5 kg
Lamb chop, midloin, grilled	3.7 kg
Chicken: roasted/skin	3.0 kg
roasted/no skin	2.0 kg
Salmon, canned	320 g
Eggs, boiled	10
Broccoli	1.0 kg
Apricots, dried	326 g
Almonds	120 g
Baked beans	652 g
Spinach/silverbeet	600 g
Apples	7.5 kg
Oranges	1.0 kg
Bread, wholemeal	20 slices

Source: Australian Dairy Corporation

Have variety in your diet

Plan your meals and eating habits to have a variety of foods rich in calcium. This will help make your goal of regular adequate calcium intake more interesting and enjoyable. If you haven't done so already, you may wish to try foods other than the dairy and fish sources. For example, soya bean products such as tofu (soya bean curd) can add a new dimension to your diet.

I don't like dairy products. What can I do to ensure I get enough calcium? Some of you may have a personal dislike of dairy foods, or you may have a cultural background in which dairy foods are not part of the traditional diet.

However, before you decide that dairy foods aren't for you, consider the following points:

- You may not have tried some of the vast range of products on the market and it may just be that there is something you could develop a taste for. There is a large variety of low-fat yoghurts and one of these may be the answer to your problems. Use your sense of adventure and sample the large range which is available.
- Remember there are ways of disguising the taste of some dairy products. The taste of skim milk powder in savoury dishes for example is completely undetectable.
- The Australian Dairy Corporation publishes numerous books and publications with tasty and varied recipes—suitable for those who are prepared to eat dairy foods. They also produce menus for those of a vegetarian leaning.

I can't tolerate lactose (milk sugar). Do you have any suggestions? If you think you have an intolerance to milk then consider the following before you rule out dairy foods.

Lactose intolerance is another phenomenon which appears to have grown over the past decade or so. It was seldom encountered when this author was in general practice.

If you think you have lactose intolerance you should check with your family doctor or dietitian to see whether you really do have an intolerance. Many people feel they must have such an intolerance because they misinterperet stomach upsets or symptoms such as flatulence or constipation.

If you do have true lactose intolerance it can be handled by a product on the market called Lactaid that contains the enzyme lactase which breaks down the lactose. A liquid form is simply added to milk or a tablet form is taken with solid dairy foods. You should speak to your doctor, dietitian or other health professional before commencing self-treatment.

At times an apparent lactose intolerance develops due to the avoidance of dairy products in the diet over a considerable period of time. The ability to break down the lactose redevelops as you gradually reintroduce dairy foods into your diet.

Calcium supplements

Calcium supplements have received so much publicity that some people believe if they take them then osteoporosis will be avoided. Unfortunately it's not so simple! First, it is best to obtain adequate calcium from the diet and to ensure that you are having a balanced diet from which you get adequate supplies of all nutrients including vitamins and minerals. Second, you need an overall healthy lifestyle, including adequate weight-bearing exercise, to protect against osteoporosis.

If it is difficult for one reason or another to obtain adequate calcium from the diet, then you need to consider calcium supplements. If this is the case then discuss supplements with your doctor. The amount you take will depend on how much calcium you are consuming from food sources.

When taking calcium supplements you need to check the bottle labels to see how much elemental calcium they contain. 'Elemental calcium' means the amount of calcium contained in the preparation. Many products now state the amount of elemental calcium they contain. If they don't, use the following guide.

Elemental calcium guide

Type	Elemental calcium content
Calcium carbonate	40%
Calcium chloride	36%
Calcium lactate	13%
Calcium gluconate	9%

This chart illustrates the fact that a variety of calcium preparations are available and can be mixed to suit your needs.

Calcium preparations available in Australia have differing levels of calcium and contain vitamin D along with other nutritional supplements. Most experts would advise you to take only those preparations which supply calcium on its own.

Many of these preparations are available on the Pharmaceutical Benefits Schedule in Australia, providing you have osteoporosis, kidney failure, lowered blood calcium levels or proven poor absorption from your gut.

What calcium supplements are available?

Among the preparations available from your chemist both as over-the-counter preparations or by your doctor's prescription are the following: Calcimax, Caltrate, Effercal–600, Sandocal 1000 and Vita–Valu Calcium Gluconate. There are a number of 'compound' over-the-counter products which contain vitamin D derivatives. Most of these will be unnecessary for people who do not have vitamin D deficiency.

You must not use calcium supplements if you are prescribed calcitriol. If you are taking Rocaltrol or calcitriol for prevention of postmenopausal osteoporosis, calcium tablets or supplements are definitely not to be taken, because combined they may cause a serious rise in the blood levels of calcium.

Are there dangers in taking calcium supplements?

Misconceptions about the effects of calcium supplements on the body have entered the folklore of nutrition. Among these are the claims that calcium increases your chances of developing bone spurs. However, spurs are usually caused as a result of tension of muscles and tendons on their bony attachments. Bone spurs are not the result of eating or ingesting excessive calcium-containing foods.

Another claim is that taking calcium supplements causes kidney stones. There is little evidence to support this claim with intakes of calcium below 1500 mg per day—the maximum usually recommended to prevent the development of osteoporosis. However, if you have had kidney stones in the past, you should check with your doctor before starting a calcium supplement.

Just be sure to drink plenty of fluids whenever you take a calcium tablet. It is very important to maintain an adequate intake of fluids as one of the means of preventing dehydration—in itself a cause of kidney stones.

Large doses of certain calcium supplements appear to cause constipation in some people. Maintaining adequate fluids and fibre should help to overcome this problem.

Some calcium supplements contain salt (sodium). These are the effervescent supplements. You should always check the label or ask your chemist whether the calcium preparation contains salt or not. If you should develop stomach upset and diarrhoea you should avoid them. If you have high blood pressure and loss of calcium, you should avoid these supplements.

Be wary of calcium supplements containing vitamin D. Excessive doses of vitamin D can be toxic. Mega-doses of vitamin D should also be avoided.

The vegetarian lifestyle

Interest in vegetarian diets has been increasing over the past decades. Many people have chosen to avoid animal products because of an interest in the associated philosophy of not harming animals in any way. Others have taken up the lifestyle in the belief that animal fats and products are harmful.

The major emphasis on decreasing animal fats to reduce cardio-vascular disease from health authorities and the popularity of diets advocated by US nutritionist Nathan Pritikin have also contributed to the popularity of vegetarianism.

With such an abundance of exotic fruits, vegetables, cereals and other fresh foods, it's not surprising that many Australians are adopting a vegetarian lifestyle, or at least including a vegetarian meal or two in their weekly diet. And while vegetarian meals are generally regarded as healthy, it is just as important to balance a vegetarian diet as it is a meat-containing diet.

A balanced diet is simply adequate nutrition based on a wide variety of foods, providing energy, nutrients, dietary fibre and fluids in amounts appropriate for good health.

Associated with the increased interest in the prevention of osteoporosis there has been a great emphasis in some quarters on the use of dairy products to give much of the needed intake of calcium. This is logical since dairy products, as we have already seen, are the richest sources of dietary calcium, along with soft-boned fish.

The major precaution with any diet which avoids dairy food or fish is the potential for that diet to produce an increased risk of nutritional problems, including osteoporosis.

So what is a vegetarian?

'Vegetarian' is a term used as a broad description of people who avoid flesh foods such as meat, fish and poultry. Instead, a vegetarian relies on plant foods such as fruit, nuts, cereals and vegetables to meet nutritional requirements. Among vegetarians, however, there are three broad groups:

- Vegans: strict vegetarians who do not include flesh foods, dairy products or eggs in their diet.

- Lacto-vegetarians: do not eat eggs, but consume all dairy foods in addition to foods of plant origin.
- Lacto-ovo-vegetarians: consume dairy products and eggs in addition to foods of plant origin.

A balanced vegetarian diet can provide a number of benefits because it is lower in total fats, high in fibre, satisfying and generally more economical. But a strict vegetarian diet, unless carefully planned, can lead to a deficiency in certain proteins, vitamins and minerals. The best way to ensure a balanced diet is to combine a variety of foods from each of what nutritionists call the 'five food groups'. Each of the groups has a special role in nutrition and health. Eating too much of one or too little of another can lead to health problems. That's why it's called a 'balanced diet'. Eggs and dairy produce make balancing a little easier.

Lacto-ovo-vegetarian diets make the task of balancing meals a little easier and lessen the likelihood of nutritional shortages. Dairy foods and eggs are good sources of calcium, riboflavin and vitamins A, D and B_2. Such an eating pattern also ensures the intake of high quality proteins, which may be lacking in meals restricted to food of plant origin.

The importance of protein—quality and quantity

Proteins are made up of smaller units called amino acids. To perform their unique function of building and maintaining muscle and tissue, proteins must supply all the essential amino acids in the proper amounts and proportions. Animal and vegetable proteins differ in quality, that is, in the kind and amounts of amino acids they contain.

Although vegetarian diets provide an adequate quantity of protein, care must be taken to ensure a sufficient supply of high-quality protein. This can be achieved in several ways. One way is to combine, in each meal, proteins that complement one another, for example, combining animal protein with cereal and vegetable proteins, such as milk with cereal, or cheese with macaroni. Alternatively, combine the high-quality proteins of legumes, such as dried beans, peas or soya beans with cereals. Or try and use vegetables in which the protein content is fairly high, for example, soya beans and chickpeas. The selection of foods for any meal can be as varied as your imagination. The following provides information on the five food groups adapted for lacto-ovo-vegetarian requirements.

If weight loss is not desirable, add foods from the basic food groups, rather than refined sugars or extra fats. Cooked as well as

The five food groups for lacto-ovo-vegetarians

1	2	3	4	5
Breads and cereals	Fruit and vegetables	Meat alternatives	Milk and dairy products	Butter and margarine
Eat according to energy needs but select at least 4 serves daily and choose wholemeal products wherever possible. 1 serve = 1 slice bread or 1/2 cup of cooked rice or pasta.	Eat at least 4–5 servings daily, especially citrus fruits (like oranges, grapefruit), tomatoes, leafy green vegetables, potatoes, and some raw fruit and vegetables.	1–2 serves daily, select from eggs, legumes (e.g. dried beans, peas and lentils), nuts, seeds, meat analogs e.g. Textured Vegetable Protein (TVP). 1 serve = 2 eggs or 1 cup of cooked legumes or 60 grams of nuts (preferably ground).	600ml of milk for children and adults. 600ml –1 litre for teenagers, pregnant and nursing mothers. If you like, you can substitute regular milk with slim or fat-reduced milk. 250ml of milk may be substituted with 3cm cube (35g) of firm cheese or a 200 g tub of yoghurt.	Up to 20g (1 tablespoon) daily on bread and in cooking.
This group provides most of our energy needs, plus fibre, protein, vitamins and some minerals.	Fruit and vegetables provide lots of fibre, minerals and vitamins, especially vitamin C, vitamin A, some iron and calcium.	This is one of our major sources of body-building protein, and is a rich source of some vitamins and minerals.	Milk and dairy foods are our most abundant source of calcium which is essential for bone and teeth building. They also provide lots of protein, energy, and vitamins A and D, thiamine, riboflavin and niacin.	This group provides energy and vitamins A and D.

Source: Australian Dairy Corporation

raw fruits and vegetables should be used, because cooking improves the availability of some nutrients in some vegetables. Similarly, chopped or crushed nuts can be more beneficial than whole ones.

Try not to rely on single plant sources, as this can lead to deficiencies in vitamins, minerals and a restriction in the intake of high-quality proteins. Grains are a good source of carbohydrates, proteins, thiamine, iron and trace minerals. Nuts and other seeds contribute fat, protein, vitamins, and iron. Dark-green leafy vegetables are sources of calcium, riboflavin, iron and vitamin A. Plant foods contain minimal vitamin B_2, but milk and eggs are satisfactory sources.

Women and children need special consideration. Women on vegetarian diets, particularly during their child-bearing years, may have difficulties in obtaining sufficient iron to meet their daily needs. Including eggs in the diet will help overcome this problem.

It's difficult to provide the quality and quantity of protein needed by young children from foods of plant origin alone. It is recommended that milk and eggs be included to ensure that both protein and calcium needs are met.

Many of the plant foods are high in bulk and therefore very filling, so it is important to make sure that energy needs are fulfilled. More than three meals per day may be required.

Other hints for healthy eating

Eating a variety of foods is just one aspect of overall good health; here are some more ideas.

- Prevent and control obesity. A decrease in energy intake combined with increased physical activity may be necessary if you're overweight. Reduction of fat, sugar and alcohol consumption will all assist in reducing overall energy intake.
- Decrease total fat consumption. The average Australian diet is high in fat. To maintain good health, a more moderate fat intake is recommended; ideally, no more than 35% of total energy should be provided by fat in the diet.
- Increase consumption of complex carbohydrates and dietary fibre. Varieties of bread and cereals (especially wholegrain cereals), fruit and vegetables are foods which provide dietary fibre and a variety of nutrients. They're the best foods to replace those high in fat and sugar.
- Reduce your sodium intake. Excessive sodium intake is believed to contribute to hypertension. Table salt is the most common form of sodium consumed by Australians. Try to reduce salt in cooking and at the table. Use sparingly.
- Drink plenty of water. Water is important for good health. It helps get rid of waste products from digestion and metabolism and prevents constipation. Try and drink 1.5 L (eight glasses) a day, either as plain water or as tea, coffee, fruit juice or unthickened soups.
- Decrease your consumption of sugars. Added sugars are solely

an energy source in the diet and are devoid of other significant nutrients. They are one factor in dental caries and may contribute to obesity.

- Limit excessive alcohol consumption. Excessive alcohol intake has contributed to the nutritional problems of many Australians, including obesity and alcoholism. Be moderate.

Summary

It is widely recognised that calcium intake in Australian postmenopausal women (about 800 mg/day) is well below the recommended daily allowance (1000 mg/day). Increasing the intake of the large numbers of women taking less than the recommended amount should do much to stem the rising tide of hip fractures now facing healthcare providers in Australia. A wide variety of calcium supplementation is now available, whether through increased intake of dairy foods and soft-boned fish or calcium-containing medication.

Directing our efforts to women found to have a low bone density at the menopause may be especially rewarding. Many believe it is time that this was done.

Some have suggested calcium absorption is enhanced in the presence of HRT and other experts have stated that HRT is unnecessary. You should remember that three essential elements are necessary to promote optimal bone density and therefore bone strength. These three pillars that support your bones are calcium, oestrogen and weight-bearing exercise.

Calcium therapy in women who have already developed osteoporosis may also be helpful in preventing further deterioration in the spine and a further increase in the number of fractures.

Later in this book the other measures found to be helpful in preserving bone health into your old age will be explored. Measures to reduce calcium loss after the menopause will be detailed.

10

The HRT controversy

Dr Elizabeth Farrell, menopause expert and author of the *HRT Handbook*, was recently quoted in the Melbourne *Age* newspaper as follows:

> Five years ago, a lot of doctors were very keen on universal HRT, we have moved away from that. It is now very much an individual woman's decision, and there is an acceptance that there are women who are low risk in all areas and who don't need HRT. There has been a rationalisation of the view that women benefit from HRT.[1]

The supporters of HRT claim the treatment, given under the correct circumstances, is a safe and effective method of controlling many of the unpleasant or unwanted effects of the menopause. They support HRT both as a treatment for postmenopausal women, and also for those with premature menopause.

HRT at the menopause reduces the symptoms of the menopause and has the potential to improve quality of life. HRT is also claimed to aid in the prevention of osteoporosis and fractures, and to reduce ischaemic heart disease[2] (due to blockage of the heart's arteries and those of the rest of the body) and strokes. It is widely recognised that HRT reduces the incidence of mortality due to heart disease and strokes.

Many gynaecologists and GPs will raise these as positive reasons for you to begin HRT. These reasons should be carefully weighed against the disadvantages to be discussed later in this chapter, such as the possibility of increasing the risk of cancer of the endometrium (lining of the uterus), higher blood pressure, alteration in blood clotting, breast tenderness, nausea and increased incidence of gall bladder disease. A more recent complication is the development of skin irritation from the oestrogen skin patches.

You need to weigh the reported advantages against the disadvantages in deciding whether you should start long-term HRT.

Some readers may have been concerned by the recent passionate debate on both sides of the Tasman. On one side of the debate, the proponents of HRT see it as a rational and convenient way to assist menopausal women reduce the unpleasant aspects of the menopause. At the same time they feel they are protecting the same women against the known problems that are present in increased frequency after the menopause.

To its sometimes strident critics, HRT is yet another attempt by a male-dominated medical profession to impose its will on a largely unsuspecting female population. These critics also condemn bone density scanning and even mass breast screening as science gone mad—women being sacrificial victims to the God of Science.

Contrast the statement attributed to Dr Farrell at the beginning of this chapter with that of Sandra Coney, a recognised women's health activist and author of *The Menopause Industry*, who recently stated during a feminist forum on HRT:

> The woman who must take oestrogen tablets every day is consistently giving herself a message that in her 'natural state' she is inadequate, and that only by taking her medicine will she be a normal human being.
>
> In addition, she must constantly visit the doctor, and attend for additional tests such as mammography, blood pressure tests and sometimes endometrial biopsies. She is locked into dependence on the medical system.[3]

Coney was not finished with the subject and went on to conclude her address in the following manner:

> Women should resist an ideology which seeks to undermine these advantages and brainwash women into a narcissistic preoccupation with lines and wrinkles. They should insist on the normality of menopause, and demand the right to age gracefully, as self reliant women, not poppers of pills and potions. They can best do this by rejecting passive dependency on medical messiahs with their miracle nostrums, and by asserting their right to be active players in the world.[4]

Supporting the voice of the moderates in this debate was Dr Susan Silberberg, an endocrinologist at Melbourne's Monash Medical Centre, who was speaking at the same feminist seminar as Sandra Coney. Dr Silberberg concluded her presentation as follows:

There is clear evidence that HRT is effective in the treatment of hot flushes and associated symptoms, vaginal dryness and certain urinary symptoms. There is excellent evidence that HRT will markedly reduce bone loss and subsequent fractures; ideally the at-risk groups should be identified so that lifestyle measures and HRT can be better targeted.

There is strong epidemiological evidence, and increasing evidence from prospective studies that oestrogen therapy reduces the risk of cardiovascular disease, heart attacks etc. by about 50%. This almost certainly applies to cyclical HRT, and there is encouraging evidence that continuous combined HRT will have the same protective effect.

I and my colleagues believe that every woman at the time of menopause should evaluate her lifestyle, her personal risk factors particularly for osteoporosis and cardiovascular disease. She should then weigh up, with the help of her doctor the pros and cons of HRT as they apply to her. It is her choice, and it is our role to make sure that it is an informed one.[5]

A recent letter to the editor of the *Sunday Herald-Sun* newspaper from Dr Susan Davis of the Jean Hailes Menopause Foundation concludes this brief survey of the attitudes of the moderate experts on HRT.[6] Her letter states:

Just as women's physical and emotional responses to pregnancy and childbirth differ in the extreme, so do their transitions through menopause . . . Women who chose to take oestrogen shouldn't be made to feel guilty or be told they are being manipulated by male-dominated powers.

Dr Davis goes on to write:

To describe such women as being in an 'anxious and powerless state of hypochondria' shows complete lack of compassion. The needs and choices of the individual are paramount.

Dr Davis was writing in response to an earlier article in the same newspaper by one of the more vocal critics of HRT. Dr Davis's was not the only letter written by the often silent and significant body of women who have freely chosen to use HRT.

They have made this choice as what they believe to be a counter to the unpleasant results of menopause. They and their medical advisers realise menopause is a natural event in the life of every woman, part of the natural progression of female life. Menopause is not a disease state nor should it be regarded us such. Most supporters of HRT believe it provides many women with a largely safe method of easing their way through 'the change'. At the same time HRT protects them against the cardiac and skeletal ravages of oestrogen depletion.

What is the menopause and how will it affect you?

Before any further discussion of HRT, it is important that we consider the menopause or—as it is also known—the climacteric. This is the stage of life in which women make the transition from decades of fertility to the later years of life in which the ovaries have largely ceased their functions of producing egg cells and hormones. Women are now spending more than one-third of their lives in this postmenopausal stage.

Menopause may be defined as the cessation of your menstrual cycle and of your monthly periods, due to the decrease or cessation of the activity of the follicles of the ovaries. The follicles are the sites where monthly production of your ova (egg cells) occurs and where the female sex hormone oestrogen is produced from the time of onset of your periods—the menarche—to your menopause.

The average age at which menopause occurs is 50 years. Doctors hold the convention that the occurrence of the menopause before 40 years of age should be called premature ovarian failure.

Your menstrual periods may stop suddenly or there may be menstrual irregularity for some years, during which time many women may have menopausal symptoms. At this time, the number of ovarian follicles falls steeply and the levels of the follicle stimulating hormone (FSH) levels rise. The development of the ovarian follicles becomes unpredictable, oestrogen production fluctuates and anovulatory cycles—cycles which do not lead to the production of egg cells—become more frequent.

Despite the cessation of your periods, your ovaries may still function at a reduced level for up to five years. The oestrogens produced by the ovary may still be enough to cause a breakthrough bleed occasionally.

After menopause, the ovaries and the small adrenal glands (which sit on top of your kidneys) may still produce the male hormone androgen, which is converted in your fatty tissues to oestrogen to supplement the reduced amount of oestrogen produced by the ovaries. This may be necessary to assist in maintaining bone mass and general wellbeing. The young woman who has lost her ovarian function due to surgical removal or medical treatment (for endometriosis or cancer) is particularly likely to experience the effects of hormone deficiency.

How can your menopause specialist help?

Before any consideration of the need for HRT you will need to have a full assessment by the doctor of your choice. Whether you choose to be referred to one of the specialist menopause clinics such as those listed in this book or a private GP or specialist, the assessment process will probably follow these lines.

Your doctor will need to take a full medical history, taking special note of any symptoms of oestrogen deficiency. These symptoms may include the development of flushes, menstrual irregularity or cessation, mood swings and decreased libido or sex drive. You will need to report any recommencement of vaginal bleeding, particularly if this occurs some time after the previous apparent cessation of your periods. This may simply be related to intermittent production of hormone levels sufficient to cause a build-up of the uterine lining, or it may be caused by a growth in the uterus.

You will be asked if you have had a history of breast cancer, blood clotting or thrombosis, heart attacks or coronary heart disease, and/or recent or past fractures of the spine or extremities. Particularly important to your doctor will be a family history of breast cancer and of osteoporosis, since there are strong links between these diseases and members of the same family. The assessment will also need to take note of your social history and whether there has been any change in your financial or emotional wellbeing. If you are still menstruating you will be asked questions about your preferred method of contraception.

You will be asked more general questions about whether you drink alcohol or coffee, whether you smoke and whether you exercise and what form this exercise takes. As you have seen, some of these questions relate to the menopause in general and some to the risk factors in the development of postmenopausal osteoporosis.

The physical examination

Measurement of your blood pressure, weight and height will need to be obtained. You will most probably have your chest listened to and your heart assessed. Your breasts will be examined and you will be taught breast self-examination if you have not previously been taught this. Your abdomen will be examined to assess the abdominal organs and to exclude the presence of any lumps or masses. Following this your doctor will carry out a vaginal examination and a pelvic examination. A Pap smear will be taken if this is indicated.

Additional assessments

Many experts now believe that all women over the age of 40 should have a mammography study carried out every two years. This may be advised on an annual basis for those women who have an increased risk of breast cancer (breast cancer in sisters or mother, no breastfeeding etc.). It should not be necessary for a pathological examination or biopsy of the uterine lining unless there is undiagnosed vaginal bleeding.

The levels of the female sex hormones or those involved in stimulating the ovaries may be checked in a young patient (e.g. under 45 years) whose periods have ceased—amenorrhoea—to see if she is menopausal. Occasionally this measurement is necessary in women who have had a hysterectomy and in whom the hormonal status is in doubt.

It is normal for some women around the time of the menopause to have irregular menstrual cycles with erratic hormone patterns. In these women blood tests of hormone levels are of little help in predicting the progress of the menopause.

Therefore the decision for, and the effect of, oestrogen replacement therapy is based predominantly on the clinical history and examination of you—the individual patient. Depending on the results of this detailed assessment, and after full discussion of the advantages and disadvantages of HRT, its strengths and possible weaknesses, a range of treatment options are available. These will be discussed later in this chapter.

HRT—advantages and disadvantages

With the onset of menopause there is a subsequent decrease in the secretion of the female sex hormone—oestrogen. Menopause experts now advocate oestrogen replacement medication for a period of eight to ten years. This should be commenced as soon as possible after the start of the menopause.

The use of HRT was fairly restricted until recently, as doctors feared an associated increase in the risk of cancer of the endometrium (the lining of the uterus) and breast cancer. Oestrogen is now combined with progestogens (female hormones which are used in contraception to thicken the lining of the uterus) when the lining of the uterus is intact. Extensive scientific studies appear to have ruled out any association of HRT with these cancers.

However, the actual presence of these types of cancers provide some of the absolute contraindications for HRT. Contraindications are the medical reasons for not giving a particular treatment to a particular patient. Such reasons for not using HRT are covered later in this chapter.

In addition to the support for HRT, recent studies reported in Australia by the late Professor R. Shearman and others have now supported the use of oral contraceptives up to the age of 50—provided those who use them do not smoke, and other contraindications are followed. It is further claimed that the use of oral hormonal contraception may play a positive role in the maintenance of bone mass in a large number of women exposed to some of the other risk factors for postmenopausal osteoporosis, such as smoking and alcohol intake.

Figures claimed to be the first on a sample Australian population have recently been published.[7] These were part of a study of the prevalence of oestrogen replacement therapy in a representative population sample of Australians. The study excluded premenopausal women taking oestrogen progestogen combinations for contraceptive reasons only and women on progestogen therapy alone for menstrual control. Thus, this survey was primarily concerned with oestrogen replacement therapy, although it is commonly accepted that most Australian women with a uterus usually take progestogen therapy in conjunction with oestrogen therapy.

Recent statistics had suggested that there was up to a sevenfold increase in women taking Premarin between 1978 and 1981. The article by Alistair McLennan and his co-workers suggest that oestrogen use had increased from a prevalence of approximately 2–3% to 13.6% at the end of 1991.

Studies overseas had suggested that half of the initial users of HRT had stopped the medication, most of them because of the development of minor side effects. Other workers in Australia have confirmed that up to 50% of women on a combination of Premarin and intermittent Provera experience side effects in the early stages of therapy. These side effects can be controlled by minor modifications in the dosage in many cases.

This appears to support the importance of allowing individualisation of HRT to improve compliance.

One of the more common reasons for ceasing HRT or for not ever taking it was a belief that long-term therapy was unnecessary or unlikely to be beneficial. Few users of HRT in the Australian study seemed aware of the protection given by long-term oestrogen therapy from osteoporosis, cardiovascular and cerebrovascular disease.

More than 12% of the non-users of HRT in this study did not know enough about oestrogen or had been dissuaded by friends, family, doctors or the media from continuing or ever starting treatment. The authors of the study emphasise the need for further education of the public, the media and the medical profession.

There is clearly a need for modern health information on the menopause and the option of information about HRT to be made available in languages other than English. Women from an Australian or British background are more likely to be users of HRT. Information not only should be available in a variety of languages, it should also be produced with sensitivity to specific cultural attitudes to the menopause.

The fact that more than three times the number of women who have had hysterectomies are likely to use HRT appears related to the advice of the gynaecologist performing the surgery. It has also been related to the frequency of removal of the ovaries at the time of the hysterectomy, making the woman vulnerable to acute reduction of oestrogens and the increased likelihood of osteoporosis.

Women who have had hysterectomy and removal of the ovaries are less likely to need the combination of oestrogen and progestogen. Taking oestrogen on its own is likely to be associated with a consequent reduction in possible side effects.

The Australian study found low income earners and less educated women were the least likely to be current or past users of therapy, perhaps reflecting inadequate health education of these groups, less access to informed medical care and the cost of therapy.

It is now recognised that women are living many more years after the menopause than in past generations. The life expectancy of women is expected to be 86 years by the early part of the 21st century.[8]

Reduced oestrogen production is now a feature of more than one-third of most women's lives, increasing the risk of osteoporotic fractures, heart disease and stroke. It is predicted that reduced oestrogen levels will continue to be a major detrimental influence on the overall quality of life for many women.

McLennan states in the conclusion to his study:

The future health of our rapidly ageing female population will probably be greatly influenced by the prevalence of hormone replacement therapy and it will be useful to continue monitoring the use and the effects of these therapies together with the knowledge of the population and its attitude to therapy.

Contraindications of HRT

You should not take HRT if the following apply to you:

- history of breast cancer;
- a past history of abnormal blood clotting (thromboembolism);
- diabetes; or
- high blood pressure.

Less definite reasons for you to avoid HRT include:

- a history of fibrocystic disease of the breasts (lumps in the breast tissue);
- a family history of cancer of the cervix; or
- a history of gall bladder disease.

Benefits of oestrogen therapy

The known or recognised benefits of oestrogen therapy are both short- and long-term. The short-term benefits include the relief of hot flushes and sweats (which commonly interfere with sleep). HRT also helps stop formication (the sensation of ants crawling over the skin), muscle and joint aches and pains of which many menopausal women complain.

One in five women have flushes whilst still menstruating regularly; one in three still have them five to ten years after the menopause. This symptom complex is a greater disturbance than most doctors have recognised in the past.

Oestrogen therapy may also assist with the acute psychological problems experienced by many women. These include feelings of depression, loss of confidence or self-esteem, forgetfulness, anxiety, dizziness, headaches, emotional fragility and feelings of panic. Many menopausal women have been to their medical practitioners with these complaints and have taken the offered tranquillisers and antidepressants without beneficial effects. Many women fail to report to their doctors a decrease in their sex drive or libido.

Can HRT improve your sex life?

Oestrogen therapy may help you to regain your libido—if other factors are also considered and corrected. While oestrogen, and perhaps even the male sex hormone testosterone, may help in relieving this symptom, other factors such as the compatibility and health of the male partner, medications and the presence of depression must also be assessed.

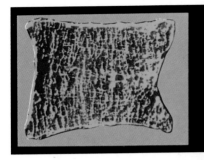

As calcium is lost from the bone, the fine internal structure literally collapses under the body's weight. The photograph on the left shows the normal bone in a cross-section of spinal vertebra; on the right the deterioration is clearly visible and has resulted in a crush fracture.

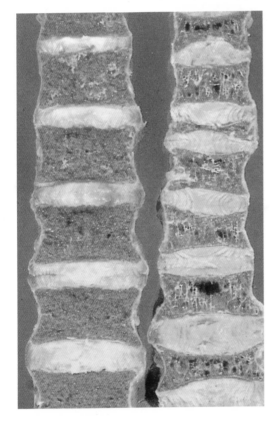

Left, a normal spine; right, this picture illustrates clearly how height and spine strength are lost as a result of osteoporosis.

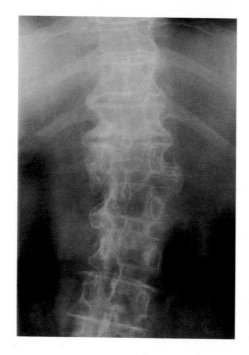

An X-ray of the lower (lumbar) spine, showing typical osteoporotic distortion of vertebrae with compression fractures and severe curvature.

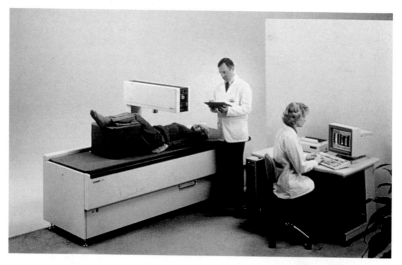

A bone density scanner, Lunar DPX. The patient lies on their back with their legs elevated on a cushion to flatten the lower spine. The technician reads the scan from the computer screen, and can print out results for interpretation and forwarding to the patient's doctor.

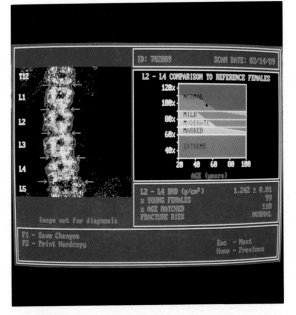

Bone density scans. In the scan above, the position of the asterisk on the graph shows a normal reading for a low fracture risk. The scan below indicates a reading in the extreme fracture risk region.

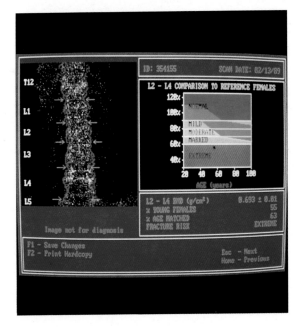

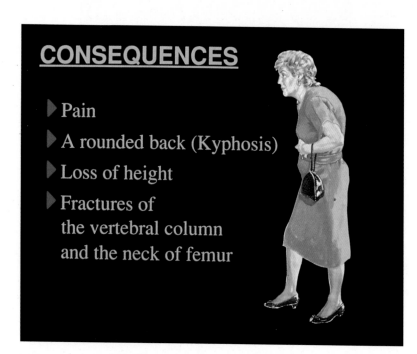

CONSEQUENCES

▶ Pain

▶ A rounded back (Kyphosis)

▶ Loss of height

▶ Fractures of
the vertebral column
and the neck of femur

Unless the importance of calcium and exercise is recognised and responded to early in life, one in five women over the age of 50 will suffer from osteoporosis as a result of bone loss following menopause.

Oestrogen therapy also helps reduce problems of your urinary system and genital tract. With menopause and the reduction of oestrogen the specialised skin lining of the vagina and vulva becomes thin, dry and inelastic, causing burning, itching, painful intercourse, and sometimes bleeding from the thinned tissues.

During the menopause the capacity of the urinary bladder falls. This causes many women to experience an increased frequency of the passage of urine—micturition—and there is an increased incidence of urinary incontinence. Oestrogen by any route appears to improve these symptoms.

What are the long-term benefits of HRT?

Prevention of osteoporosis and fractures As you have seen in early chapters of this book, bone density, which is related to fracture risk, is determined by the peak bone mass a woman achieves in her youth and the rate and the length of time during which subsequent bone loss occurs.

Bone loss is most rapid in the first five years after the menopause and up to 15% of bone mass may be lost at this time with a subsequent loss of 1–3% per year. Over one-third of women who are not treated with hormones will have osteoporotic fractures in later life. Oestrogen therapy is believed to arrest or retard bone loss if begun shortly after the menopause. This effect continues for at least ten years and it also reduces the incidence of fracture at all studied sites.

Dr Elizabeth Farrell, author of the recently published *HRT Handbook*, recently stated:

> The most important established long-term benefit of hormone replacement therapy is the prevention of bone [density] loss, particularly of the hip, wrist and spine, and hence a reduction in the risk of fractures in elderly women.[9]

Protection against heart disease Before the age of 55, a man has a five- to ten-fold greater chance of dying from a heart attack than a woman. However, this protective factor decreases rapidly in the ten years after the menopause if no HRT is used. Most recent large studies suggest that postmenopausal oestrogen use is associated with a 50% or greater reduction in ischaemic heart disease, and that the risk of dying following a myocardial infarction if a woman is on oestrogen is similarly reduced. Comparable effects have now been shown for strokes. It is suggested that the effect of oestrogen is substantially mediated through increased blood levels of high density lipoprotein (HDL).

However, recent animal studies described at an FDA advisory panel meeting suggest oestrogen may also have a direct protective effect on the arterial walls. It is suggested oestrogen assists in reducing cholesterol deposits from the blood vessel walls.

Although oestrogens appear to increase the blood levels of HDL, the other hormones commonly used in combination with them in treating the symptoms of the menopause, the progestogens, weaken the rise in HDL. This is particularly seen with higher doses of the more masculinising progestogens, such as norgestrel and norethisterone.

There are suspicions, not yet proven, that these progestogen-induced changes are undesirable. It therefore makes sense to suggest progestogens should be given in the smallest effective doses to prevent excess thickening of the lining of the uterus, and it may be prudent to use preparations such as medroxyprogesterone acetate—Provera—which have less androgenic properties.

What preparations are used for HRT?

Oral oestrogens

Oral oestrogens are a satisfactory choice for most women, according to Australian menopause expert Dr Suzanne Abraham. She favours the use of hormones called 'natural oestrogens' because they are used and broken down in the same manner and as rapidly as the naturally produced hormone, oestradiol.

The drug ethinyloestradiol is very potent because it is broken down poorly in the body, and is more likely to produce more marked effects on your liver. These potential liver problems include increased levels of a variety of substances which may have an adverse effect on your health. These include blood clotting factors and proteins which interfere with the action of natural steroid substances and the thyroid hormones. Dr Abraham and her colleagues have found ethinyloestradiol may not be well tolerated by some postmenopausal women.

Many believe there is no need to stop oestrogen therapy for even one week and that continuous therapy should be recommended. Oestrogen doses should be always be adequate to protect against bone loss. A lower dose of oestrogen will usually be prescribed if you have been without oestrogen for a long time, to minimise possible breast tenderness. The dose can then increase according to control of your symptoms. The range of doses that may be used are set out in the table below.

Natural hormones The following equivalent doses protect against bone loss in most women. The first four listed are 'natural oestrogens'. These oestrogens are laboratory-made copies of the natural hormones your body makes or, in the case of Premarin, are hormones produced from the urine of pregnant mares.

Premarin is an extremely potent combination of human-like and equine hormones which may cause liver damage in women at risk. Its potency—related to the horse's hormones—means Premarin may not be suitable for you if you are overweight, have high blood pressure, a history of liver trouble, or if you smoke.

Synthetic hormones Ethinyloestradiol is a synthetic hormone said to be up to 30 times more potent than the natural hormones. Synthetic hormones are more difficult for the body to break down and therefore last longer in your body. These hormones are more likely to be toxic as far as your liver function is concerned. The warnings about Premarin are even stronger if you have these problems and are to be given synthetic hormones.

Oestrogen preparations

Generic name and dose	Trade name
Oestradiol Valerate 2 mg	Progynova
Piperazine Oestrone Sulphate 1.25 mg	Ogen
Conjugated Equine Oestrogen 0.625 mg	Premarin
Oestradiol—micronised	Trisequens
Ethinyloestradiol 0.02 mg	Estigyn

Oral oestrogen preparations and their strengths currently available in Australia include:

Generic name	Trade name and dose
Oestradiol valerate	Progynova 1–4 mg
Piperazine oestrone sulphate	Ogen 0.625–2.5 mg
Conjugated equine oestrogen	Premarin 0.3–1.25 mg
Oestradiol—micronised	Trisequens 2 mg and 1 mg
	Trisequens Forte 4 mg and 1 mg
Ethinyloestradiol	Estigyn 0.01–0.03 mg
	Primogyn C 0.01–0.03 mg
Oestriol	Ovestin 1–4 mg

When should oestrogen be administered by a route other than by mouth?

There are alternative methods to administer oestrogens to the meno-pausal or postmenopausal woman. These include vaginal creams and pessaries, the newly introduced skin patches and hormonal implants which are inserted under the skin and allow the release of oestrogen slowly through the tissues.

Alternative routes to the mouth will normally be considered if oral forms give unsatisfactory control of symptoms or gastric upset. The alternative methods of hormone administration will also be considered in cases of unusual increases in blood pressure as reaction to oestrogens. These have been found to occur in 5% of patients on Premarin.

They will also be considered in those women who have a history of mild liver disease to avoid oestrogen-induced changes in the manufacture of proteins by the liver. Alternative routes also need to be used in women who have a history of blood clotting (thrombosis). This is particularly important after a long period of immobilisation.

Vaginal creams

If the major symptoms are urogenital, then vaginal creams can be used. Vaginal oestrogen creams include Dienoestrol cream used in a dosage of half an applicator nightly for one to two weeks, then two to three times per week, or Ovestin cream, one applicator nightly. The applicators are clearly marked so that dosage can be accurately delivered. The Dienoestrol cream is well absorbed and may cause a build-up of the lining of the uterus with prolonged use. Therefore it is common for your doctor to order a twelve-day course of progestogen to be taken every three months.

Implants of oestradiol—long-term continuous therapy

Implants of oestrogen can be used for all the reasons given above and also for those women who prefer not to take daily tablets. Implants can be used in those who also require the male sex hormone testosterone (as an implant) for decreased sex drive or libido. Many menopause experts claim hormone implants are very effective in the young postmenopausal patient. Effective levels of oestrogen can be obtained for about six months.

The oestrogen implants are usually inserted through a small incision in the fatty tissues below the skin of the abdomen or buttock. The procedure is usually performed under local anaesthesia using a specially designed wide-bore instrument to place the pellet beneath the skin. If you still have your uterus it will probably be necessary to use cyclical progestogens. You will be asked to return for the next implant when unpleasant symptoms start to return.

Transdermal skin patches

Oestrogen-containing adhesive patches with the trade name Estraderm are now available to Australian women in three strengths, 25, 50 and 100 mg. They are available as a subsidised benefit for women who are unable to tolerate oral oestrogens.

The plastic-covered patches, containing the natural hormone oestradiol, are applied twice a week on the skin of the lower abdomen or buttocks. The hormone passes from the patch through a special membrane which controls the rate and amount of hormone passing into the skin and thence to the bloodstream. This form of hormone delivery has been shown to slow bone loss and to increase the levels of the HDL shown to be beneficial in protecting you against heart disease.

Progestogens?

Oral administration

A progestogen is a hormone preparation which is designed to mimic the naturally occurring hormone progesterone. It is used in combination with oestrogen in HRT to ensure regular shedding of the intact uterus lining.

Most experts agree on the necessity of using progestogens in those women with an intact uterus who require oestrogen supplementation. There is weak evidence the progestogens counteract any harmful effects of oestrogen on the breast. Therefore, progestogens are not routinely prescribed in women who have had a hysterectomy, except where there is a strong family history of breast cancer or a history of benign breast disease.

Progestogen preparations at times cause premenstrual-type symptoms, nausea, breast tenderness and bloating. This often requires the trial of a number of different preparations before success is achieved with minimal or no side-effects. A common choice to begin with might be Provera 10 mg or Primolut N 1.25 mg for twelve days a month.

A typical range of doses used is listed below. It is common for a withdrawal bleed to occur two days or so after the course finishes. If you bleed before the end of the progestogen course it should suggest to your treating doctor that an inadequate dose of progestogen is being used.

Progestogens on their own have a beneficial effect on hot flushes, e.g., Provera 10–20 mg daily. There is some possibility they may help to reduce osteoporosis but the vaginal skin remains wasted, thinned and dry.

Oral progestogen preparations

Generic name	Trade name	Dose range/day (twelve-day course)
Medroxyprogesterone acetate	Provera	5–10 mg
Norethisterone	Primolut-N	1.25 mg (¼ of 5 mg tablet)
Norethisterone	Micronor	0.70–1.05 mg
	Noriday	
Dydrogesterone	Duphaston	10–20 mg

To the progestogen preparations listed above can be added Trisequens and Trisequens Forte which contain cyclical courses of hormones which include norethisterone acetate 1 mg together with oestradiol 1 mg. In addition, each course consists of twelve tablets of either 2 mg or 4 mg, and six tablets of oestradiol 1 mg.

Combination therapy

Recent additions to the range of HRT preparations combine two of the more common oestrogen and progestogen preparations. Premarin and Provera have been combined by two pharmaceutical companies in a single 'convenience pack'. Menoprem and Provelle–14 are produced by Ayerst and Upjohn respectively. Ciba–Geigy has recently relaunched its own version of the convenience pack, known as Estrapak, combining oestrogen patches with fourteen days of oral progestogen.

Testosterone

The male sex hormone testosterone in the form of an implant together with oestradiol may be offered to those women who do not have a complete return to wellbeing or libido on combined oestrogen and progestogen therapy. The dosage used is less than 10% of the male dose, and gives serum levels within or just above the normal range for females. At this dose, it is unlikely to produce excess facial or body hair, hoarseness of the voice, or significant changes in blood fats.

Who should not take oestrogens?

HRT should not be used by any woman who has a history of oestrogen-sensitive cancers such as breast cancer or cancer of the lining of the uterus. HRT should be avoided in those with undiagnosed vaginal bleeding or active liver disease.

What are the potential disadvantages and side effects of oestrogens?

Excessive thickening of the lining of the uterus and cancer

The incidence of cancer of the lining of the womb in postmenopausal women not on HRT is just over one in 1000. The use of oestrogen on its own for greater than five years increases the incidence of this type of cancer to one woman in 200. However, the combination of oestrogen and progestogen when used in an adequate dose and for an appropriate time will cause the incidence to fall to one in 1000 or less.

The tumours that are detected while women are on HRT are generally at an early curable stage because women on HRT are under surveillance and are told to report abnormal bleeding. There is no increased risk of cancer of the cervix.

In the *Menopause & Osteoporosis Therapy—GP Manual* produced by the National Osteoporosis Society in the United Kingdom, the authors note: 'Some women with endometrial cancer may choose to take HRT at their own risk to improve quality of life. They should be referred to a hospital specialist or a menopause clinic for individual counselling'.[10]

Hypertension

Occasionally, high blood pressure develops in women treated with natural oestrogens in hormone replacement doses. However, there is usually a small decline in blood pressure. Women may show a rise in blood pressure on some of the hormones such as ethinyloestradiol or conjugated oestrogens. If this should happen, you would be changed over to another preparation. Despite this, there is no reason to avoid treating postmenopausal women on antihypertensive medication with oestrogen.

Blood clotting problems

High doses of hormones such as ethinyloestradiol and conjugated oestrogens unfavourably alter blood clotting factors. However, these changes are not seen with the doses of HRT used for menopausal women. More importantly, there is no evidence of increased blood clotting in the veins of women on HRT. If there has been a history of thrombosis or certain family history of a clotting tendency, then it is likely that you would be offered an injectable oestrogen preparation. These avoid high concentrations of hormones passing through the liver. Your doctor will check the blood levels of various clotting elements in your blood before therapy and after you have been on therapy three months.

Gloria's story

Gloria is a 44-year-old woman who had her polycystic ovaries removed several years ago after a number of earlier operations to control frequent ovarian cysts. Her physician was concerned about the early development of osteoporosis after Gloria's surgical and premature menopause, so he suggested HRT. Gloria still had an intact uterus and so was placed on a combination of oestrogen and progestogen—in this case Premarin and Provera.

All went well for the first few months, until Gloria noticed painful swelling of one of her legs. She reported this to her GP, who carefully examined her for the presence of a deep vein thrombosis—clotting of one of the deep veins of the leg which cause obstruction to the circulation. At this visit her circulation was checked most carefully but no evidence of thrombosis was obvious. Gloria was sent home on anti-inflammatory medication and the swelling settled down within a few days.

Three months later, Gloria developed sudden chest pain and started coughing. She became very alarmed when she coughed up a blood clot and rapidly developed shortness of breath. She was rushed to hospital, where X-rays and other tests confirmed the presence of a pulmonary embolus—a clot of blood in the lung. Almost certainly this had developed as a result of the unrecognised thrombosis in her leg several months previously.

154

Emergency treatment was immediately instituted, as this was recognised as an emergency situation. She was given intravenous anticoagulants or blood-thinning agents and after a few days was well enough to be placed on oral medication which she will have to remain on for an indefinite period. Her HRT was immediately ceased and will not be recommenced. In the absence of any other obvious cause it is most likely that Gloria was unfortunate enough to be one of the very few women to develop a blood clot as a direct result of her HRT.

Gall bladder disease

A slight increase in the frequency of gall bladder disease has been reported to result from taking HRT.

Some common problems

Breakthrough bleeding Any woman on HRT who bleeds, other than at the end of each progestogen course, requires a full pathological assessment of the uterine lining. Fortunately, this can now be done without the need for hospital admission using devices such as the Gynoscann.[11]

Nausea When nausea occurs with an oral oestrogen medication, a change to another method of administration such as a patch or an implant may help. If this occurs during the period in which a progestogen is being taken, a different preparation should be tried.

Breast tenderness Tenderness of the breasts sometimes occurs at the start of therapy. A temporary reduction in oestrogen dose may help, but if the problem continues, the addition of a progestogen may help to reduce the breast discomfort. There is no convincing evidence that HRT increases significantly the risk of breast cancer. There is some suggestion that women with a strong family history of breast cancer or a past history of benign breast disease may be at slightly increased risk.

I am still menstruating but I have started to develop flushes and fluctuating moods. Should I take HRT? HRT may be used for relief of flushes and psychological symptoms, and is based on women's natural cycle (day 1 is the first day of menses). For this purpose a progestogen, e.g. 10 mg Provera, is added from day 14 to day 25. There is then a tablet-free interval for about one week before the anticipated period. If you are offered this treatment you will need to understand that this therapy is not contraceptive and that conception is an unlikely but possible outcome. Pyridoxine or vitamin B$_6$, 50 mg a day, may be helpful for some women in the treatment of flushes and breast tenderness.

My periods have stopped and I have an intact uterus—what HRT should I take? If the menstrual cycle has stopped you may be offered continuous daily oestrogen, e.g. 2 mg oestradiol valerate. In addition, a progestogen, e.g. 10 mg Provera, can be taken for twelve days a month. For convenience, the Provera can be started on the first day of every calendar month, and bleeding starts one or two days after the progestogen has finished. You may be told that you can move the progestogen course so that bleeding can occur when it suits you. Commonly the progestogen will be given on a monthly basis, though there is no evidence that progestogens given every two or even three months would not be effective.

An alternative method of HRT in this group of women involves taking continuous combined oestrogen and progestogen if the woman does not want withdrawal bleeds and is prepared to put up with spotting for the first three months.

I have had a hysterectomy. What HRT should I take? F o r those of you who have had a hysterectomy and wish to take HRT it is common to be offered continuous daily oestrogen on its own. If there is a personal or family history of breast cancer, a low dose of progestogen, such as Provera, may be added. However, the evidence of the benefit of this combination in such patients is still unclear.

Where oestrogens cannot be used in a woman who has had a hysterectomy, progestogens, such as Provera 10–20 mg/day, will relieve hot flushes, but will not help to increase the libido or urogenital symptoms such as frequency or incontinence.

Jenny's story

Jenny is a 50-year-old professional working in an administrative role. She is fair-skinned, has fair hair, and has a strong family history of osteoporosis. She has had chronic arthritis for over 25 years and for the past eight years has taken prednisolone to control joint destruction and pain. Prednisolone is one of the steroid group of drugs and thus is an additional risk factor for Jenny's potential development of osteoporosis.

Jenny had a hysterectomy three years ago. This followed several years of severe menstrual pain which was crippling at times. Before the surgery she had experienced several years of extreme irregularity and the development of flushing and breast tenderness.

The hysterectomy was carried out only after several failed attempts were made to control her unpleasant symptoms with drugs. Bone density scanning carried out at the time of the hysterectomy showed her bone density to be at the low end of the normal range when compared with standard groups of women of her age and a standard group of young women.

Although the hysterectomy immediately stopped her period pain and flooding she continued to complain of breast engorgement and flushing. It had been hoped that leaving her ovaries intact might provide sufficient oestrogen to assist her with these symptoms.

After long and detailed discussions with her specialist it was decided that, since she had no uterus, unopposed oestrogen should be tried, and she was given Premarin 0.625 mg tablets to be taken daily. Unfortunately the flushes and breast tenderness were only marginally improved and Jenny developed troublesome constipation alternating with diarrhoea.

Next she was given Estraderm patches in varying doses. No gastrointestinal problems this time, but she did not get complete control of breast tenderness or flushes which she still found very distressing, particularly when she was at work. The patches were increased in strength from 25 mg to 50 mg and she developed severe skin reactions—blistering and severe itching.

Jenny was determined not to give up on the HRT, and her most recent prescription has been for Trisequens Forte. This preparation consists of varying doses of natural oestrogen—oestradiol—and also has a combination of oestrogen and progestogen mid-cycle. At last she is able to have HRT, which is vital to counteract the bone-robbing effects of the prednisolone.

She still experiences flushing and some breast tenderness, particularly with the lower doses of oestrogen in the last week or so of her cycle of medication, but she is more comfortable on this medication than on all previous HRT preparations.

Her most recent DEXA bone scan has shown little or no further deterioration in her bone density, despite her continued use of steroids.

Some non-hormonal help for flushing

Drugs such as Catapres or Inderal—both very different medications used in the treatment of blood pressure—have been tried as a remedy for flushing with indifferent results.

Lubricating jellies may facilitate penile entry, but the vaginal skin remains wasted and thinned and inelastic without the use of oestrogens. This may lead to intercourse being painful and further reduction in libido.

Other therapy

As we have discussed, all women should be advised to have a minimum 1000 mg of calcium per day. We have seen calcium supplements alone have little effect on bone loss after the menopause. Weight-bearing exercise such as walking for half an hour three times a week is advisable, and women should be advised to stop smoking and reduce fat and alcohol intake.

Unless depression is clinically severe, women should have an adequate trial of hormone therapy before antidepressant or tranquillising drugs are given for the psychological symptoms associated with the menopause. This will require a detailed psychological history to be taken by your medical adviser. It is necessary to know your coping style and history before a diagnosis of depression is considered.

However, if the following are present, medication for depression may be unavoidable:

- Severe sleep disturbance, particularly difficulty in getting off to sleep, waking through the middle of the night, or early in the morning and being unable to get back to sleep.
- Appetite disturbance. Recent changes in appetite with rapid weight loss or weight gain.
- Loss of interest in children, family, employment and hobbies.
- Loss of interest in sex.
- Chronic lowered mood.
- Increased irritability and tearfulness.
- Feelings of helplessness or hopelessness.
- Feelings of unworthiness or self-guilt.
- Suicidal thoughts or ruminations on the worthlessness of life.

Follow-up care

After starting HRT, you should be reviewed every six to eight weeks until a suitable treatment program has been found. Once this is established, six-monthly reviews to check blood pressure and examine your breasts may be suggested. Once in every twelve months a Pap smear and pelvic examination may be repeated. Mammography is repeated every two years or more frequently if this is indicated. Despite two recent well-publicised cases in which it was claimed that Pap smears failed to diagnose cervical cancer, the Pap smear is currently claimed to have a 90% accuracy rate. New tests are reportedly ready to be used, with the hope that, together with the Pap test, accuracy in predicting and detecting these cancers will be further improved.

How long to continue?

There is evidence that the longer oestrogen therapy is continued the greater its benefit, and the more cost-effective it is. Therefore, it can be suggested that as long as a woman is active and well, she should continue therapy. Many experts advise you to take HRT for at least ten years to prevent osteoporosis and protect your cardiovascular system. Other specialists believe some women will ultimately use HRT for as long as 30 years. With increasing age, the endometrium becomes less responsive to oestrogen stimulation; at age 65, only about 60% of women continue to have withdrawal bleeds on cyclical therapy. This percentage may fall with different methods of progestogen administration.

Are there non-medical alternatives to HRT?

Dr Sandra Cabot, a medical practitioner writing under a nom de plume, has written another excellent book on menopause, writing from her interest in women's health and 'natural' medicine.[12] Dr Cabot introduces her readers to the range of alternative therapies and plants which are claimed to contain natural oestrogens. She maintains that women unable to use HRT for a variety of reasons may yet benefit from these alternatives.

She points out that many alcoholic beverages contain these plant oestrogens. But, she adds, drinking these beverages will do little to replace these essential hormones. Plant oestrogens are said to be 200 times weaker than normal human oestrogen. Among the plant foods containing oestrogen and listed by Dr Cabot are linseed, pumpkin, olives, parsley, garlic, clover and red clover.

Among the herbs suggested by Dr Cabot and her naturopath collaborator are sage, licorice, sarsparilla, dandelion, St John's wort, and damiana. Many of these herbs can of course be taken as herbal teas.

Along with these are listed a variety of minerals, vitamins and herbs which have a vitamin C-like action to enhance the circulation.

A final word in support of HRT

A recent newspaper report quoted Professor Norman Beischer, Chairman of the University of Melbourne's Department of Obstetrics and Gynaecology, in support of HRT.[13] Professor Beischer is claimed to have said menopausal women should automatically be placed on HRT and the therapy should be continued for the rest of their lives.

> The consensus on this is that HRT is perfectly safe and does not increase a woman's chances of developing breast cancer. Even women who have had breast cancer are able to undergo HRT.

The quotation continues:

> HRT not only prevents the onset or rate of deterioration of orthopaedic and cardiovascular disease but also improves bladder and sexual function, general appearance and morale, as well as being a cure for hot flushes and sweating attacks.

Summary

Based on what we now know, women at high risk of osteoporosis should consider using HRT at menopause. Obviously this will depend on the presence of factors which should preclude the use of such medication. To protect against excessive bone loss and cardiovascular and cerebrovascular disease, women should begin to take oestrogen within one or two years of starting menopause—at the time of cessation of the menses.

Many women will find short-term relief of hot flushes and vaginal dryness with one or two years of HRT. Should these problems affect quality of life, HRT can be reintroduced for as long as necessary.

Importantly, it is now widely accepted that HRT should be

continued for up to ten years after menopause. There are experts who even believe HRT can be given indefinitely. The risk of breast cancer with HRT has been recognised but is widely believed to be a minor risk compared with the risks of osteoporotic fracture and cardiac disease. Both of these are significant robbers of life and quality of life for innumerable women.

11

Counselling in osteoporosis

When pain or discomfort persists, either intermittently or continuously, effects produced by the autonomic nervous system are less prominent in chronic conditions than in acute circumstances. This is due to fatigue, exhaustion and some adaptation in organ systems within the body.

However, this does not mean that patients with osteoporosis get used to chronic pain or discomfort. In fact, they may suffer more as time goes by, as mental and physical depletion occur. This leaves the individual suffering from chronic pain or discomfort, increasingly less well-equipped to handle the mounting problems associated with coping with constant pain.

To help the chronic sufferer cope with the most negative notable adaptations to their pain, a counsellor's major roles are to assist in correcting the following:

- Incorrect or inefficient motor function, with pain as the major focus for the inability to function.
- Alterations of mood, particularly the presence of depression, but also anxiety, fear, guilt feelings, grief, hurt, anger and helplessness.
- Decreased self-esteem, alienation and hostility towards the sufferer's own body.
- Impaired working capacity and interpersonal relationships, withdrawal and social isolation.
- Sexual dysfunction due to pain or to depression.
- Insomnia.
- Challenges to the patient's own belief and value systems.

With the host of psychological and physical problems the role of the counsellor within an osteoporosis centre or clinic setting or in the wider community is accordingly multifaceted and varied.

In clinics such as those dealing with chronic conditions, for example osteoporosis or pain, counselling and patient education represent some of the most important functions of nursing care. This goes hand in hand with teaching relaxation techniques, support, and the maintenance and reinforcement of strategies learned during treatment provided by other team members.

Frequent formal and informal team meetings should ensure evaluation of progress and consistency in treatment approaches. In the pain clinic this can be reinforced by the patient having a common or shared history file for all team members.

Since many people coming to such a clinic present with frustration and hopelessness, the management is usually initiated with gentle, non-directive counselling with emphasis on promoting the patient's self-esteem and with the aim of giving the patient a sense of value. When rapport is established, a comprehensive assessment of the patient is made following a holistic model.

An integrated approach is needed. This approach integrates levels of discomfort, life stressors, the meaning of the condition or discomfort for the person experiencing it, beliefs about the condition, coping styles (active or passive) and motivation for improvement.

The site of the problems and whether pain is present or not are also important aspects of the assessment, not only due to the specific disabilities of the patient, but also because it is always of importance in the elaboration of the person's behavioural and psychological responses to the condition.

Explanation

Initially, the most important way is to relate to the patient about his or her physical problems, as most patients suffering from pain are usually very sensitive to any implication that there may be no physical basis for their pain. Education about the new concepts of osteoporosis, shaped in accordance with the patient's beliefs and fears about osteoporosis, is often helpful in itself in reducing fear and anxiety. Along with this is the general sharing and explanation of the process of osteoporosis and its sequelae.

After a solid therapeutic relationship is established between counsellor and patient, identified problems can then be clarified, named and then worked on in agreement with the patient. At this time or later in the relationship more complex aspects of the patient's behaviour and beliefs can be related to reported pain levels and other problems if these exist.

If these aspects of counselling are introduced too early in the treatment program, before emotional problems have been voiced, clarified and to some extent worked through, there seems to be less adherence to the implied treatment contract.

It can be an almost super-human challenge to identify and change well-learned behavioural responses to pain or disability. This demands the greatest awareness, support and flexibility from the therapist. Sometimes the treatment approach has to be modified to non-directive counselling only, focusing on support and maintenance of the present condition.

Patient understanding

Treatment models used in pain management use modification or changes in the way the patient thinks to reduce the perception or awareness of pain. When integrated into counselling by the team nurse, the aim is to give the patient a new understanding of his or her pain, introduced with an explanation of the influence of maladaptive thinking patterns and emotions on the experience of pain.

Patients are brought to understand that complaints and behaviours related to pain need not be the central focal points of the patient's life. The importance of decreasing the amount of thinking of the pain as catastrophic, increasing self-control and self-efficacy are also seen as being significant in reducing pain.

Setting realistic goals

Once the problem is identified, the patient's realistic goals are chosen and set and with the help of the nurse counsellor they are then broken down to smaller attainable ones. These can then be accomplished with reasonable effort and within an agreed time limitation.

This is aided by the patient keeping a diary, which is reviewed at regular intervals. Reflecting the patient's problems, diary entries appear most often to focus on reports of pain levels, emotional factors related to the onset of the pain, the level of pain-killers, activities of daily living, exercise and objectives related to interactions with significant others, appearance, diet and sexuality.

With altered levels of function which accompany osteoporosis, re-education or the establishment of meaningful hobbies are essential for improvement.

Appropriate local government agencies are often contacted for provision of support for this purpose.

Improving the patient's ability to cope

The overall aim of the counsellor, as it is with the others in the clinic team, is often an overall improvement in the patient's capacity to cope with the condition and its sequelae rather than an overall reduction in the condition and accompanying discomfort.

However, a treatment approach which aims at healing emotions, promoting self-esteem, maintaining or optimising levels of functioning, will in itself relieve some pain and suffering.

The need to relax

A wide variety of relaxation approaches is available from an equally broad range of therapists. For many of you seeking to add this approach to the management of your osteoporosis there are a confusing number of people offering what they consider to be the answer to helping you cope with stress.

These range from the fairly simple relaxation approaches adopted in the osteoporosis education programs run by the Arthritis Foundation of Victoria to more sophisticated approaches offered by medical hypnotherapists and psychologists.

Relaxation training is also offered by a number of properly trained physiotherapists and occupational therapists.

Techniques taught may vary from the classical Progressive Muscular Relaxation (PMR) techniques of Jacobsen and Schuldt to the more sophisticated Biofeedback approaches which are usually the province of psychologists.

PMR involves teaching you to relax the muscles of your body from the feet up to the top of your head or from the head to the feet if that is more acceptable to the therapist and you. This will be coupled with suggestions of increasing warmth or deepening mental relaxation.

Biofeedback training combines relaxation training with the use of electronic metering devices. These devices feed back information on the function of those parts of the nervous system which are affected by stress. Some of the functions measured in this approach include the electrical conduction of the skin, muscle tension and skin temperature.

Stress or its absence is fed back to you as an audible tone or buzz, a series of light-emitting diodes, or as a display with a needle that swings according to the level of stress.

This form of relaxation training is particularly useful for patients who feel unable to let themselves go sufficiently with PMR or hypnosis.

The only disadvantages to relaxation therapy and biofeedback techniques are the time required to learn the technique and to perform it. As with other meditation-type techniques, a certain degree of discipline is necessary for the patient to become proficient.

Severe depression or other mental illness causing poor concentration or memory would probably make this approach unsuitable.

The major disadvantage of all of these therapies is the cost. As these are usually carried out by a registered clinical psychologist, the medical insurance systems in most western societies—and certainly in Australia—have not to this date reimbursed psychologist's fees.

The fees are appropriate for the time the psychologist spends with the patient. These fees range from about $80 to $100 an hour. Some private health funds rebate these fees at about $15 to $20 per session. When carried out by medical practitioners in Australia these services are likely to be charged at an appropriate consultation fee for the time spent with the doctor. For some doctors using these approaches the fee charged depends on the complexity of the consultation and therefore fees may vary from doctor to doctor and State to State. The major advantage in attending a doctor in Australia for these approaches is the rebate obtained from Medicare—Australia's universal health insurer.

More psychological approaches

These include psychological treatments known as psychotherapy, either individually or in a group. Individual psychotherapy may offer help to change the way the patient feels about his or her pain, or alternatively to employ other supportive measures. It may also seek to find the cause of the problems by using a variety of techniques.

These psychological approaches give both the practitioner and the patient time to explore the patient's personality and behaviour patterns. Also, to determine how the patient's perception of pain affects his or her life. It also helps to define, and measure, the emotional needs of the individual.

Relaxation and osteoporosis

Incorporated in any fitness program should be a program of what might be called 'mental fitness'. In this context mental fitness should incorporate a program of relaxation and positive self-imaging.

What follows is one of many relaxation exercises which could be of value to you in developing your own program of physical and mental fitness. Many of you will benefit from simply making your own cassette using the following script as a model. Others will need to seek out professional help to make use of these types of skills. One of the ways in which you may be able to relax is to follow these suggestions:

1 Find a time and place that will allow you twenty minutes of relatively undisturbed quiet. Padded earphones may be of assistance in tuning out the world. Some people find it helpful to have recorded music of a relaxing nature in the background.

2 Develop a habit of relaxing in the same place at the same time every day. Make it part of your daily schedule. Relaxation is a skill that requires practice.

3 Get as comfortable as you can, preferably sitting in a recliner with your entire body and head supported, or lying down. Wear loose clothing that will assure a sufficient warmth, or cover yourself with a light blanket. Remove your spectacles or contact lenses before beginning to relax.

4 Avoid doing the relaxation exercise immediately after eating a full meal or when you are tired, as you may fall asleep and not benefit from the relaxation practice. However, relaxation itself may be used to substitute for a nap as a source of renewed energy, or it can be used to combat insomnia which is associated with anxiety.

5 After you have relaxed to the recorded script several times, you will find you are able to obtain the same deep state of relaxation without tensing your muscles at all. If you find yourself becoming impatient with the length and sequence of the tape, you might try starting your relaxation sessions midway through the tape, beginning with the deep breaths. It is also recommended

that you occasionally go through the entire relaxation sequence on your own without the tape. Eventually you will be able to achieve the same deep relaxed state merely by imagining your calm scene.

A typical relaxation script

Find yourself a comfortable position lying on the ground or in a recliner chair. If you lie on the floor make sure you have a comfortable pillow or rug beneath you. If you have neck pain or discomfort, use a shaped pillow or triangular pillow to give you neck support.

Spaces indicate where you can pause for periods upwards of five seconds. Timing of the script is best determined by taping it and then relaxing to your own recording.

Make yourself as comfortable as you can. Close your eyes. Now stretch your legs as far as they can go, turn your toes under, tighten the muscles very tight and hold . . . . Now, tighten the muscles in your calves and those in your thighs. Make your entire leg as tight as a drum and hold it . . . . Hold it . . . . And now relax all the muscles in your toes, all the muscles in your calves, all the muscles in your thighs. Let your legs go completely limp. And now let yourself feel that wonderful relaxation coming up from your toes, up your calves, up your thighs. You are feeling wonderfully relaxed, beautifully relaxed, very calm, very relaxed . . . .

Now stretch out your hands and make a fist. Feel the tightness. And now make it tighter, tighter, tighter, and hold it . . . . And now also tighten the muscles in your wrists, in your forearms, in your upper arms . . . . Hold it, hold it . . . . Now let go and get the wonderful feeling of relaxation right through your fingers, your hands and now through your forearms and your upper arms. Let your arms go completely limp, and you are now feeling wonderfully relaxed, beautifully relaxed, very calm, very relaxed and feeling just beautiful . . . .

Now arch your back backwards, raise your chest, tighten your neck and shoulder muscles, and your stomach muscles but keep breathing regularly. Make all those muscles as tight as you can, tighter, tighter, and hold it, hold it . . . .

Now let go, just let go and get that wonderful feeling of relaxation. Just feel the muscles relax from your back, from your shoulders, from your chest, from your stomach: all over your back. And all the muscles are feeling wonderfully relaxed . . . .

Now tighten the muscles in your face. Make a funny face. Tighten the muscles around your mouth, the muscles in your chin, around your eyes and your forehead. Wrinkle your brow. Make them tighter, tighter, tighter, hold it, hold it . . . . All right, now let go, just let go. Let go and get that wonderful feeling of relaxation from all the muscles in your forehead, the muscles around your eyes, the muscles of your cheeks, the muscles of your chin, and the muscles around your mouth.

And you are feeling wonderfully relaxed, beautifully relaxed. Very calm and very relaxed, wonderfully relaxed . . . . Now take a very deep breath and hold it. Hold it, hold it . . . . Now slowly let it out and you are letting out all your tensions, your frustrations, your anxieties and you're feeling wonderfully well . . . . Once again, take a very deep breath and hold it, hold it, hold it . . . . Now slowly, slowly let it out and relax your tensions, your frustrations, your anxieties and you are feeling wonderfully well, wonderfully well . . . .

You will now proceed to relax every part of your body progressively. And while you are doing this, you will hear your voice or your own thoughts clearly and distinctly. You will be aware of your surroundings, although you will care less and less about what goes on around you . . . .

Now, direct your thoughts to the top of your head, your scalp, and think that whatever tension exists there is rapidly vanishing. Your scalp is becoming less and less tight and the top of your head is becoming completely relaxed . . . .

Now think of your forehead and let all the muscles in your forehead relax and become loose and limp . . . . And now your eyes, and all the small muscle groups around your eyes. Just allow them to become loose and limp and relaxed. And just relax more and more and let yourself go completely . . . . Now your facial muscles, the muscles in your cheeks and around your nose and the muscles around your mouth and teeth. Just let them all relax and let them all go very loose and limp . . . . Now relax the muscles in your throat area, your speech mechanism and your swallowing apparatus and all the other muscles in your neck and just allow them all to relax . . . .

Now think of your shoulders, and permit your shoulder muscles to relax . . . . Relax the muscles in your upper arms, your elbows and your forearms and all the muscles up and down your arms. Just let them go loose and limp . . . . Your wrists, your hands, your very fingers; completely relaxed . . . .

And now your chest. Relax all the organs and muscles within your chest . . . . And the muscles in your stomach area, your abdomen and all the muscles and organs within that region. Allow them to become comfortable and relaxed . . . . And the pelvic region fully relaxed . . . .

Now think of your back and all the muscles up and down your back, the long muscles and the small muscles up and down your spine and let all these muscles relax completely . . . .

Now think of your thighs and relax all the muscles there, your knees and the calves of your legs. And just let all those muscles up and down

your legs relax completely . . . . Your ankles, your feet, your toes
. . . .

Relax now and let yourself go completely. Just go limp all over. Permit every organ and every fibre of your body to become completely and profoundly relaxed. It feels so restful, so pleasant to be completely relaxed. You hear your voice or your own thoughts clearly and distinctly. But nothing else seems to matter to you . . . .

Your arms and legs, if you think of them for a moment, feel rather heavy and they are so relaxed and also quite numb and dull, though quite pleasantly so. In fact, your entire body feels heavy in this position. Heavy, so heavy, that it seems it would require a super-human effort to move a muscle . . . .

Now count down from ten to one silently and to yourself and while you are doing so, think of a scene that makes you feel calm, that makes you feel relaxed and that gives you a feeling of wellbeing.

Think of that scene in all its details. Put yourself into it and let yourself relax more and more deeply and profoundly and enjoy the calm and peace of that wonderful scene . . . . Now, with your eyes closed, see that scene in all its details and as you count down from ten to one you are going to find yourself deeper and deeper relaxed and you will have a feeling of wellbeing . . . . Calm and relaxed and wonderfully well. Very relaxed
. . . .

Ten—just let yourself go completely now . . . . Nine—deeper and deeper relaxed . . . . Eight . . . . Seven—very deeply relaxed . . . . Six—deeper and deeper . . . . Five—deeply relaxed . . . . Four—very calm and very relaxed . . . . Three—deeper and deeper . . . . Two—deeper . . . . And—one, very deep and sound relaxation.

Think of nothing now but relaxation. Feeling wonderfully relaxed. Calm, feeling wonderfully well. And now, like a wave, feel that relaxation spreading from your toes, up your calves, up your thighs, and into your stomach and chest muscles. And now it's spreading from your fingers, up your arms, into your shoulders, neck and head region, relaxing every part of your body until you are involved in a wonderful feeling of relaxation . . . .

You are feeling calm, feeling relaxed, feeling like you are floating on a sea of tranquillity; completely calm and at ease. . . . . And now, just enjoy that wonderful feeling of relaxation and wellbeing for a few moments
. . . .

Soon, you will count to five silently and to yourself and you will open your eyes. You will continue feeling as calm and wonderfully in control of your feelings as you feel now. Your mind will be clear and alert and your body will feel very well in every way. You will look forward to your next relaxation session.

One—feeling fine. Two—coming up now, feeling very good. Three—

feeling very relaxed, but alert. Four—and five—open your eyes, feel relaxed, feel calm, feel wonderfully well.

Mirrors of your mind

The foregoing process makes use of a number of well-tried approaches to relaxation. These include the techniques of PMR and self-visualisation. Visualisation and the use of visual imagery were well-covered in an earlier book by your author. The book, *Mirrors of the Mind*, suggested a great number of visualisations and imagery-based techniques to assist in the production of self-hypnosis and deep relaxation.[1]

In that book, I showed how looking into a 'mirror' in your mind could provide you with the means to change behaviour and thoughts, particularly those which might be having a negative effect on your relationships with yourself and others. By changing the self-image as seen in the internal 'mirror', external changes might follow.

A visit with Gandor

One of the approaches which has proved very popular over the years and which was originally described by the American psychologist and author Don Gibbons is the image he called Gandor's Garden.[2] In this visual imagery exercise, instead of being given direct suggestions for change you are allowed to get in touch with your internal resources in the following manner. I have adapted this exercise over the past decade since publication of Gibbons's book.

After you have placed yourself in a relaxed state, you are asked to:

Imagine yourself paying a visit to the elf—Gandor—in his underground garden.

After looking at your surroundings you discover a tiny reflecting pool. As you gaze into the pool you see an image of yourself, not as you have been but as you would like to be. As you continue to concentrate on this image it starts to speak to you, telling you something about yourself you have not previously realised. This will be something you need to help you change towards the person you wish to become. [Give yourself 20–30 seconds and then move on.]

After a while you continue to walk along the path through the magic garden. You come upon a small child skipping a rope. Perhaps you recognise yourself as a small child, brimming with health and energy. As you come close enough, you hear the child telling you something from your own past, your own childhood, which you need to remember now so you can live more fully in the present. Perhaps it is to recall the boundless energy and vitality you experienced as a young child. Perhaps it's to recall how you felt as a child, without care, without too many concerns for the world around you. [Give yourself 20–30 seconds and then move on.]

Next, as you continue along the pathway through the garden, you come across three birds hovering over a clearing. They appear to be humming a tune to accompany their flight and as you approach you imagine you can make out the words to the tune they hum. It's a song about happiness and about the true secret of being happy. [Give yourself 20–30 seconds and then move on.]

You leave the clearing and continue your journey along the garden path. You still have one secret in store, for there, sitting beside the path, is a figure whose face you cannot see clearly. It is either an old man or an old woman sitting by the path with eyes closed, as if meditating. As you approach, the face breaks out in a smile, as if you have been expected. Then this old, perhaps familiar, figure begins to speak, giving you special advice about something specific which has been of particular concern to you.

You will then continue to the end of the path where you will find Gandor waiting for you. He issues you with an invitation to return as often as you wish. You are told that you will return to the normal outside world and will remember with a special fondness everything which has occurred in the garden. You will always find new insights and new skills waiting for you when you revisit this special garden.

This image recalls the idea of developing an 'inner guide', with the old figure in Gandor's garden providing an example of this guide. The inner guide represents your own inner wisdom which can provide you with access to all of the resources which have been present but perhaps unused over your life. This process is used extensively in the management of cancer with hypnosis and imagery and is described in detail in *Mirrors of the Mind*.

These techniques can be utilised with or without the use of hypnosis or auto-hypnosis. Hypnosis is basically an altered state of awareness, different to sleep, produced either spontaneously or as a result of repeated suggestions. In hypnosis many people will experience deep relaxation, a special peace of mind and an increased ability to respond to their own suggestions or to those of the therapist teaching them to use this natural talent.

Hypnosis is not something which is done to you; it is something you can learn from early childhood until advanced age. It can be used by up to 80% of the population to enhance relaxation, control anxiety and pain, along with reduction in unwanted habits.

Hypnosis itself does have some application in the overall management of osteoporosis, although it probably is not one of the major approaches. Producing an altered state of awareness, in which you can concentrate more and more on less and less, can be particularly effective in the application of suggestions of change leading to self-improvement, self-confidence and self-esteem. These in turn may be of assistance in assisting you to cope with pain or stress.

As long as hypnosis is used to assist in the overall management of pain and discomfort and not simply to mask pain it should not create problems. If pain is acute, removing it or masking it may lead to a worsening of the condition causing the pain. On the other hand, in chronic pain and when used in conjunction with other treatments, hypnosis may be invaluable in assisting you to cope with pain and discomfort.

Visualise bone strength

Many other exercises have been developed by experts in the field of relaxation and imagery-based approaches to stress and personal development. Many of these do not require any form of deep relaxation and can be used simply by recording them on a cassette and playing them back through headphones on a personal walkman-type cassette player.

Try this exercise, based on one originally described by Dr Beata Jencks for imagining or visualising your bone strength.[3] Place yourself in a comfortable position, sitting or lying, and play to yourself a tape recording you can base on the following:

Think about your bones and how superbly their construction serves their purpose. They are the supporting elements of your body and must be rigid, but not too rigid, since they must yield to a certain extent under stress and not break.

Imagine carrying two heavy suitcases and feel the bones of the arms stretch and draw apart at the joints due to the weight. Imagine this as you breathe out. As you breathe in, draw in the strength necessary for carrying the heavy load.

Now imagine as you breathe in, running down a flight of stairs, two steps at a time. Allow yourself to feel the bounce of the compression of your bones and their elasticity. Try the same with your out breath and feel the difference. Now allow yourself the relaxed bounce with each outward breath.

Your bones must be strong. Imagine they are made of steel or stone, and feel the weight of your body. Imagine them being made of wood, having suffered permanent compression and wear after a lifetime of walking, running, jumping and moving.

Now think of their porous structure with a total weight of only 9–10 kilograms—20 pounds. Feel the lightness and let yourself appreciate the relatively weightless strength of your superbly sturdy, supporting structure.

Think of the way which your joints join together, one bone after the other, and allow yourself to feel the looseness, flow and mobility.

Finally, remember that your bones are alive and that they are constantly active, producing new blood cells, building up new bone and breaking down old bone every minute of the day. Think of the blood flowing to your bones, bringing oxygen and nourishment to aid in the maintenance and growth of your bones.

Allow yourself to feel the elasticity, the very life in your bones as you focus and meditate on your bone structure.

Reduce pain

Another exercise, based on Gibbons's work and used by your author over many years, can be used to reduce pain, stress or discomfort. Adapting this imagery exercise to many other purposes is simple and very effective for many patients.

When used by a therapist it goes like this:

Visualise yourself seated before a control panel which has one large dial. Continue to hold the image in your mind as I describe it, and soon you will be able to experience the scene just as if you were really there. The dial can be turned to any setting from zero to ten, representing all the various levels of tension and relaxation, discomfort or comfort which your body is able to experience, with the number zero standing for all the relaxation or comfort it is possible for you to feel and the number ten representing as much tension or discomfort as your body is able to experience at one time.

Now you can begin to look closely at this dial which monitors and controls the level of tension in your body. See what the dial reading is now on the scale from zero to ten, and see yourself reaching over to turn it down. See yourself turning the dial down ever so slowly, down and down, just a millimetre at a time, and let yourself feel your body relaxing more and more as you do.

Feel the tension or discomfort in your body lessening more and more as you turn the dial as far down to zero as possible at this time. Turning the dial as far down to zero as possible, as all the tension or discomfort in your body ebbs away. Soon the dial will be turned as far down to zero as possible, and your entire body will be just as relaxed as it can possibly be. And all your previous tension and discomfort will be replaced by peaceful feelings of total relaxation, tranquillity, and calm.

Now the dial is as far down to zero as possible. Your entire body is *completely relaxed and free of tension. It's as if all the tension and all the worry and all the care that you have felt previously have been driven out by soothing currents of peace and tranquillity and relaxation. And you can allow yourself to feel these currents gently coursing through every muscle and every nerve and every fibre of your being.*

From now on, you will be able to relax just like this whenever you wish, merely by sitting or lying down and closing your eyes for a few moments while you visualise yourself turning down the dial on your control panel, just as you have been doing.

And as a result of your new ability to relax whenever you wish, you will be able to rest better at night and to sleep more soundly, awakening each morning completely refreshed and ready for each new day. You will be able to work more efficiently, without being bothered by people or situations which might otherwise tend to upset or annoy you. And you will be able to derive a great deal more enjoyment out of your leisure time activities, because you will be so much more able to relax and just let go.

Rest, work, and leisure, every aspect of your life will be considerably improved and enriched by your new ability to relax whenever you wish, and you are going to be absolutely delighted at the results.

And the more you practise your new ability, the more deeply and the more easily you will be able to relax, and the longer these feelings of relaxation will remain with you.

Therapy in groups

Formal group therapy is a treatment approach which encourages the patient to interact with others also experiencing difficulties in their personal or group interactions. This formal therapy is unlikely to be of any benefit for the patient with osteoporosis.

The sharing of experiences and feelings, resulting from such group therapy, helps patients to readjust their thinking and to develop new ways of coping.

A far more practical approach is that offered by the Arthritis Foundation of Victoria which has been adopted by other Australian States. This program incorporates the approaches of goal setting, relaxation training, and the passage of information vital for osteoporosis prevention and for the management of established osteoporosis. A full reference to the course manual and the location of your local Arthritis Foundation is to be found in the resources section of this book.

The osteoporosis course is now widely in use throughout Australia and interest in the program has spread overseas as well. The title of the manual is *Osteoporosis: Prevention and Self-Management*

Course. It is based on a program which has been in use in the United States of America for more than a decade. More than 100 000 had participated in the program before its introduction in Victoria in 1991.

The program is carried out in Australia under the auspices of the Arthritis Foundation and its state branches. Small groups of people gather together for four sessions of 2–2½ hours over four weeks. Specific goals are set for these sessions. The aim is to provide information to both those at risk of and those with osteoporosis. Participants are given a handbook containing a wealth of information about osteoporosis and its prevention, recognition and management. A leader's manual is available for those leading the program.

12

Optimum fitness and osteoporosis

The effect of gravity on bone and the tension of contracting muscles help to maintain a positive balance between bone formation and resorption. Physical inactivity causes an increase in bone resorption and reduces bone formation.

In the osteoporosis caused by immobilisation, therapeutic exercise and physical activity tend to slow the loss of bone mass. At the time of remobilisation, exercise aids in the reversal of the process, even though a complete restoration of bone mass does not seem to occur.

The mechanism by which gravity and muscle contractions affect bone formation is not clear. There is some evidence that the pull of contracting muscle causes minute electrical currents in your bone. Bone formation occurs as a response to these currents.

The osteoporotic syndrome of postmenopausal women has multiple causes: hormonal, metabolic, and nutritional. A reduction in physical activity may be a significant contributory factor. Sedentary occupations and avocational pursuits decrease the level of physical activity. The widespread use of cars for transportation diminishes the time spent walking. Our modern lifestyle and the use of mechanised aids has reduced the need for physical exertion in our daily lives.

The loss of physical fitness including bone health is the price we pay for relying increasingly on modern conveniences. It follows that a carefully planned exercise program will be an important aid in the prevention of excessive bone loss in postmenopausal women.

Several studies have shown that exercise programs, usually extending over several months, increase bone mineral density in postmenopausal women compared with non-exercising controls. These women were at a phase of their lives when bone mass loss over time is considerable.

Exercise appears to stop the rapid decline of bone mass. It is effective as a preventive program; there is no evidence, however, that bone once lost is restored by physical exercise. The beneficial effect of exercise on bone is regional within the body. Strengthening of the back muscles will benefit the vertebras but not the bones of the forearm. However, the mineral density of the radius just above the wrist will be enhanced by exercising upper extremity muscles.

In the postmenopausal osteoporosis syndrome the vertebral bodies, the neck of the femur, and the radius of the forearm are particularly susceptible to fractures. Vertebral bodies consist of trabecular bone encased in a thin shell of compact cortical bone.

The stresses on the vertebral bodies are high. In a standing position the upper lumbar vertebras and lower thoracic vertebras support approximately 60% of the body weight. If the stress of contracting back muscles is added, the load is almost equal to body weight. Vertebras that have become osteoporotic over time may not be able to tolerate this load.

With sudden increases of stress, such as by lifting or movements that may cause torsion, fractures may ensue, either microfractures of trabeculae or a collapse with anterior wedging. At this point in time osteoporosis becomes symptomatic and disabling. In an advanced stage many of the upper thoracic vertebras may have become wedged anteriorly. The result is the marked forward bending deformity of the upper and middle thoracic spine or 'dowager's hump' (kyphosis).

At this stage of osteoporosis, the posture of the body is badly distorted, height is lost, and eventually the rib cage may sit on the pelvic brim, a condition that causes considerable discomfort. The marked kyphosis and distortion of the rib cage may cause severe breathing problems, simply because the chest is no longer capable of expanding or contracting.

The neck of the femur is another area of the body where a small volume of bone carries a large amount of weight. As it becomes osteoporotic, it may fracture with minimal trauma. The neck of the femur is particularly vulnerable because it is at an angle with the vertical line of gravity of the trunk. If this angle is increased (coxa vara), the bending and shear stresses on the femoral neck become greater, thus causing the bone to be more susceptible to fracture.

Since the women at most risk are middle-aged and of unknown cardiovascular fitness, an evaluation of effort tolerance needs to precede the inception of the exercise program. Your medical adviser should obtain a medical history inquiring about cardiovascular or pulmonary disease by name and symptoms. This is followed by a physical examination of your heart and lungs, a blood pressure determination and an electrocardiogram.

Any consideration of a proper exercise program involves its contributions to your overall health. Your program will involve a set of planned physical activities which together exercise all the systems of your body. This type of program will assist in the functioning of your heart and lungs, and in strengthening your muscles and bones. You will also benefit from the stretching of your joints, tendons and ligaments, which will help improve your overall level of flexibility. In the process you will be improving your levels of balance and coordination and you will be able to enjoy the results of your own efforts. A complete fitness program involves a combination of weight-bearing, flexibility and strengthening exercises.

As you have seen, weight-bearing exercises are carried out standing so the full force of gravity acts through the skeleton. We have already seen weight-bearing exercise is a major factor in increasing bone strength. Examples of this type of exercise include walking, jogging, and climbing up and down stairs. It also includes sports such as tennis, basketball, golf, bowls, and athletics.

Non- or partial weight-bearing activities are not as effective in increasing or maintaining bone strength, but, if done regularly, may contribute something to bone health. They include swimming, aquaerobics or cycling, where some or all of the body's weight is supported by the water or the bicycle.

Exercises which involve working specific muscles against resistance use the pull of muscle where it attaches to bone to create some stress on the skeleton. This contributes to bone strength.

Next come those exercises which aim to increase your flexibility. These exercises involve moving joints to the extreme limits of their range so joints with their ligaments, muscles and tendons are mobilised and stretched. They contribute to a greater ease and efficiency of movement. A number of the exercises described in this chapter make an important contribution to maintaining or improving the flexibility of your muscles and joints.

In addition to these exercises you should include in your exercise program aerobic exercise. Aerobic exercise stimulates the heart and lungs by using large muscle groups continuously for at least 20–30 minutes at moderate intensity. This type of exercise results in an increase in the pulse rate and rate of respiration indicated;

you are also exercising the vital muscles of your heart and arteries. When this is carried out three to four times per week, aerobic exercise helps improve your overall physical and mental wellbeing.

Aerobic exercise will contribute to good circulation and blood pressure, will assist you to control your weight, and protect you against heart disease. Examples include walking, jogging, swimming, dancing and cycling.

All of these factors can be combined in many of the day-to-day things you do without conciously realising you are exercising. These include walking, jogging and stair-climbing, which are both aerobic and weight-bearing exercises.

Swimming is an aerobic activity which also improves your shoulder flexibility and table tennis is a weight-bearing and aerobic activity which develops balance and coordination. Weight-training for those who are capable of this activity is good for your bone and muscle strength, and dancing is a weight-bearing activity which also develops aerobic fitness, balance and coordination.

Normal daily physical activities

The many physical activities you may do as part of your daily routine such as shopping, housework or gardening make an important contribution to your overall fitness and bone health. However, nowadays, they are generally not sufficient by themselves to provide complete fitness. There are many ways you can improve this contribution by including more general physical activity in your daily life. You might consider walking rather than using the car for short journeys, using the stairs rather than lifts, or walking more briskly when you can.

You will obviously take into consideration other factors such as other chronic illness which may impair your breathing or strength such as chronic shortness of breath or arthritis.

General exercises

The following exercise program is recommended:

Walking

Walking is an excellent exercise. It combines the stimuli of mechanical impact on spine and lower extremity bones with intermittent contractions of back muscles. The rate of walking should be somewhat above what is a comfortable walking speed for you. You should maintain an even stride length and arm swing. If feasible, you should walk daily for 30–40 minutes.

As in many exercise programs, compliance may become a problem. Walking is boring, especially if the same territory is covered each time. Wearing a small radio or portable cassette player with earphones on your daily walks can help to reduce boredom. Try to walk with a group of friends.

You should be able to talk as you walk. Aerobic exercise, or any exercise for that matter, should be done in such a manner as to enable you to talk with others or to yourself while you exercise. Shortness of breath sufficient to prevent you from talking or even singing to yourself is an indication you may be pushing yourself too hard.

Slow down if this happens and allow yourself to catch your breath without ceasing the exercise if possible. This 'aerobic exercise' ensures you give your heart muscle and respiratory system a good working out. Your pulse rate should be rapid enough to allow the heart to be working hard.

Try and keep your breathing rhythm as regular and even as possible as you exercise. Try not to hold your breath during more complicated or difficult activities.

Swimming

Swimming exercises the back muscles as well as the lower and upper extremities. The stroke employed is not important, and the choice can be left to the individual. It helps if you are a moderately good swimmer. A beginner, unless properly instructed, may expend more energy than is necessary or good for him or her.

Apprehension will compound the problem and make swimming an unpleasant rather than an enjoyable experience.

An acceptable alternative is to join a hydrotherapy or aquadynamics class. These exercise many parts of your body and the resistance of the water and its cradling effect enable you to increase stamina and flexibility at the same time. Importantly, a properly run hydrotherapy class should be more than physically beneficial—it can be a great opportunity for you to socialise and it is usually good fun.

Cycling

Most women will prefer an exercise bike for use at home. Initial instructions by a physical therapist are essential. The instructions should deal with the proper cycling posture, the height of the seat, the resistance and the speed of cycling. You should also be taught to count your pulse so that excessive stresses will be noted and avoided.

Pain in exercise—a warning and a benefit

Pain or severe discomfort should warn you of impending problems. Consult with your doctor or physiotherapist if pain persists. This is particularly important if joints or tissues become swollen or hot, as this may indicate inflammation in joint or soft tissues such as tendons, ligaments or muscles. However, some discomfort and stiffness is normal after unaccustomed exercise. Cut down a bit next time. But remember 'no pain—no gain' in the early part of your exercise program.

Good posture can be assisted by 'thinking tall' during all activities including standing, sitting and arising from a seated position. Try and be aware of the various elements of your body as a harmonious whole during these activities.

Treat injury promptly

Should they occur, sudden injuries such as sprains and strains require immediate attention. You should immediately stop your activity and apply Rest, Ice, Compression, Elevation and Diagnosis or RICED. The affected area should be immediately rested. Ice should be applied to prevent bleeding into the tissues or bruising occurring. This may be a commercially available icepack, which can be kept in the freezer at home, or a towel full of ice cubes. A pack of frozen peas or beans makes an emergency icepack if necessary.

A firm compression bandage should be applied to the affected area, which should be placed in an elevated position. For a wrist or arm this will usually mean a sling and for the leg or ankle a support to keep the leg from hanging down. As soon as possible, medical attention should be sought to make a diagnosis of the damage.

It is important to treat injuries promptly. Most injuries are preventable by following the guidelines set out in this section: starting at a comfortable level, building up gradually, exercising regularly, warming up and cooling down, wearing good footwear.

Injuries which occur as a result of exercise fall into two categories. The first of these are the acute strains and sprains which have already been mentioned. The second group are those injuries which occur as a result of unaccustomed and repetitive exercise. These are often known as overuse injuries and they develop over time. They often start with a niggling pain which gradually becomes more constant and severe. Such injuries are commonly seen in the upper limbs and in the shoulder girdles—the area at the top of the shoulders, around the shoulder blades and the shoulder joints. The most common of these are pain located at the outside of the elbow, commonly known as 'tennis elbow', and the painful condition of the shoulder joint known as 'frozen shoulder'.

If you develop persisting pain in any area associated with repetitive exercise you may need to slow down, vary your activities or check your technique. If pain persists consult your doctor.

If you become aware of swelling or increased heat in an area you should stop exercise of that area at least on a temporary basis until you obtain medical advice.

Once swelling and pain start to subside as a result of medical or physical treatment (about 24–48 hours) start exercising gently. Increase activity gradually, using pain as your guide. Seek professional advice for the best way of returning to full function.

Exercise for people who have osteoporosis

It is important for you to take care when exercising if you have osteoporosis. You will have to avoid activities that involve bending, twisting, lifting or jolting. You should be aware of the possibility of falling and avoid situations that involve slippery or uneven ground or put you at risk in other ways.

As already emphasised, gentle exercise in a heated pool may be the safest way to start exercising. This will be particularly important if you are recovering from a fracture, although it will not provide the weight-bearing exercise necessary to prevent bone loss.

You will need to include exercises that work and stretch your trunk and back muscles. Extension of your spine or bending backward will help to keep your back straight and back muscles strong. This will help counteract the forward slumping associated with osteoporosis of the spine.

If in any doubt, you should consult your doctor or physiotherapist regarding suitable physical activities.

It may help to keep a log or diary of your excursions, recording time and distance covered. As training progresses, you may find greater distances will be covered in the same period of time. In inclement weather, the length of an indoor shopping mall may provide an excellent alternative to walking outdoors. The risks here are not of the canine variety but of a more monetary type!

Warming up and cooling down

One essential component of exercise occurs at the very beginning and the other at the end of your specific exercise program. These are known as the 'warming up' and 'cooling down' phases of exercise. To 'warm up' means you start the session at an easy pace and gradually build up in intensity. This does not imply an increase in temperature.

In this phase, flexibility and strengthening exercises can be done or you can carry out an aerobic activity at an easy pace for the first five minutes. 'Warming up' helps prevent injury and gets muscles and joints working more effectively.

When you 'cool down' you slow down gradually from the peak of your exercise activity. You shouldn't just stop suddenly after vigorous exercise. The 'cooling down' process helps relax your body and prevents stiff and sore muscles. Warm up and cool down activities are discussed in more detail later in this section.

It is important you work at your own level and also listen to what your body is telling you and don't push yourself too hard. You need to rest or slow down whenever this need becomes apparent.

The benefits of individual exercises include:

- 'warming up' your muscles and joints—reducing wear on the muscles;
- 'cooling down' following exercise—prevents development of muscle cramp;
- creating beneficial stress on bones and joints—to stimulate bone growth;
- nourishing and lubricating joints—keeps you mobile;
- improving your balance and coordination—reduces chances of falling;
- enhancing your muscle strength;
- stretching tight muscles, tendons and ligaments;
- relieving strain on your back and your other joints; and
- improving your posture.

Specific exercises

Exercises for the back are intended to strengthen the extensor muscles of the spine. These muscles attach directly at the vertebras and their contractions stimulate bone formation and reduce bone loss. For the best effect, the exercises should be dynamic and repetitive. Some of the exercises described below have isometric components.

Isometric contractions tend to raise heart rate and blood pressure to a greater extent than dynamic (isotonic) exercises. They may be hazardous to patients with heart disease. However, if the intensity of contraction is moderate and if the duration is brief, the risks are minimal.

Exercises for individuals who are middle-aged or older should be designed with care, taking into consideration the purpose of exercising and an individual's structural and functional impairments. Exercises demonstrated on television or performed in health clubs may not be suitable and may even be harmful.

For osteoporotic women, vigorous dance exercises or aerobics may be contraindicated, especially if they include forceful jumping and twisting. The movements may damage weakened bones.

Flexion exercises of the back are contraindicated in women who are known or suspected of having osteoporosis. Osteoporotic vertebras will not tolerate exercises which lead to forward flexing and may fracture.

I have outlined below a suggested exercise program.

Exercise 1 Spine extension

Purpose: Counteracts kyphotic posture in which there may be excessive forward distortion of the spine. This exercise strengthens the muscles which extend the upper spine.
Position: Sitting on a firm chair but without leaning against the back of the chair. Elbows at side of chest, forearms horizontal, hands pointing forward.
Movement: Pull your shoulder blades backward, hold to the count of five.
Repeat ten times.

Exercise 2 Strengthen upper back

Purpose: Strengthens your back extensors, encourages deep breathing, stretches the pectoral muscles at the front and top of your chest.

Position: As in exercise 1 except that your hands are behind the back of your head.
Movement: Push elbows backward while your hands remain in position at the back of your head. Breath in deeply while performing this motion. Breath out with relaxation.
Repeat ten times.

Exercise 3 Increasing upper back strength

Purpose: Strengthen back extensors.
Position: Lying on your stomach with a firm pillow under your chest and abdomen. Arms extended behind your back, legs extended with toes touching floor.
Movement: Raise head and upper part of trunk while the chest remains on the pillow. Hold to the count of five.
Repeat ten times.

Exercise 4 Hip extension

Purpose: Strengthen lumbar back extensors and hip extensors.
Position: Kneel on floor. Support your trunk on extended arms.
Movement: Lift one leg off the floor with hip extended and knee slightly flexed. Hold to the count of five. Do five repetitions, then do the same exercise five times with the other leg.

Exercise 5 Abdominal muscle strength

Purpose: Strengthen abdominal muscles by isometric exercise.
Position: Lie on your back on a hard surface. Heels touch the surface, arms across the abdomen.
Movement: Raise both your legs with knees straight 10–12 inches. Hold to count of five. Repeat ten times.

Exercise 6 Spinal extension and lower limb movement

Purpose: Strengthen back extensors. Improve range of motion of hips and knees.
Position: Lie on your back on a hard surface.
Movement: Pull your knees up and bring them as close to your chest as possible. Hold to the count of five.
Repeat ten times.

Exercise 7 *Increase back and abdominal strength*

Purpose: Strengthen back extensors and abdominal muscles. Stretch back into full extension.
Position: Lie flat on your back on a hard surface, arms extended overhead.
Movement: Stretch your arms upward and toes downward, pressing your abdomen inward. Hold to count of five.
Repeat ten times.

Exercise 8 *Increase back and abdominal strength*

Purpose: Strengthen back extensors and abdominal muscles.
Position: Lying on your back on a hard surface. Knees flexed to 90°, upper arms away from your body, elbows flexed to 90° supported on surface, forearms pointing upward.
Movement: Press elbows downward. Hold to count of five.
Repeat ten times.

Exercise 9 *Strengthen hip muscles*

Purpose: Strengthen hip abductors. The main abductor muscles of the hip, the gluteus medius and minimus, insert at the greater trochanter of the femur. The distance from the trochanter to the femoral neck is short and the contraction of these powerful muscles can be expected to stimulate bone formation and reduce bone resorption. The abductor muscles of the hip are those which enable you to separate your thighs.
Position: Lying on your side on a hard surface, both hips and knees are held straight. Rest your head on your arm.
Movement: Raise the uppermost leg through full range of motion, keeping hips and knees extended. Hold to the count of five, then lower the leg slowly. Repeat ten times, then turn over and do the same exercise with the other leg. When the muscles have become stronger you may be able to do the exercises with a cuff weight above the ankle. The maximum weight should be about two kilograms.

Exercise 10 *Doing the twist*

Note: This exercise is definitely not suitable for people with severe spinal osteoporosis.
Purpose: Improves the flexibility of your spine.

Position: Lie on your back with your knees bent, your arms outstretched. Keep your shoulders on the floor.
Movement: Roll your knees from side to side.
Do this five to ten times with five repetitions.

Exercise 11 Pelvic tilting

Purpose: Improves the strength of your back and thus your posture.
Position: Lie on your back with your knees bent and feet apart.
Movement: Tighten your buttocks and your stomach muscles and try to press your bellybutton to the floor (you are trying to press your back into the floor in this exercise). Then release and gently arch, pushing your bellybutton towards the ceiling.
Do this five to ten times with five repetitions.

Exercise 12 Holding on—pelvic floor exercise

Purpose: Will assist you to strengthen your bladder control.
Position: Lie on your back with your knees bent.
Movement: Squeeze your upper thighs together. Try and feel as if you are pulling some object up inside you. Hold for three counts and relax.
Do this five to ten times with five repetitions.

Less formal exercise

What are the alternatives to a formal exercise program? Many people enjoy alternative forms of exercise. For those who have retained their fitness, veteran athletics competitions in athletics, golf, and cycling offer a means of continuing stimulus to the skeleton. For others, dancing, bushwalking, regular tennis or low-impact aerobics or stretch classes may be appropriate.

Appropriate clothing

As part of the development of your own particular program of exercise you should plan to wear appropriate clothing and footwear. This should suit the planned exercise activity and the weather conditions. Your footwear should give you firm support and absorb shock from contact with the ground.

Fortunately, we live in an era where the science of footwear has developed to the point where a wide variety of footwear specifically designed for light exercise and even aerobics is available. Coupled with a wide variety of inner-soles and support material such as sorbothane you will readily be able to find appropriate protection and support for your feet. If you wish to walk or bushwalk as part of your exercise program, walking shoes now have tractor-like treads on the soles, comfortable inner-soles and ankle support if you require this.

If you have foot problems or notice that you wear down the soles of shoes unevenly, seek advice from a well-trained podiatrist. Pain in the feet, shins, knees or even hips and back may be due to inappropriate footwear. Most problems can be easily corrected, avoiding greater problems later on.

A recommended nutrition guide

One of the unfortunate facets of a weight-conscious society is the proliferation of fad diets. The irony of the situation is that in an effort to achieve a healthier weight, most fad diets put an individual's health at risk.

Diets such as the Israeli Army Diet, the Beverly Hills Diet, the Grapefruit Diet, the Atkins Diet, the Drinking Man's Diet or others that promise rapid results all threaten your overall nutritional status. They should be avoided just as you would avoid a 'get rich quick scheme'. There is a better way. And it's a lot more interesting and, believe it or not, simple.

One of the most appealing things about good nutrition is that it offers so much variety, and it's something in which the whole family can share. It is based on what nutritionists call the five food groups. Each group has a specific role in our health—eating too much of one or not enough of another isn't good for us. The basis of a healthy diet for people of all ages is simply balance, moderation and variety.

The five food groups

Group 1: Bread and cereals

They provide fibre, starch for energy, protein, vitamins (especially B), thiamine and minerals.

Group 2: Fruit and vegetables

They provide fibre, vitamins (particularly C and A), minerals, and some starch and sugar for energy.

Group 3: Meat and meat alternatives

This group, which includes poultry and fish, provides body-building protein, fat for energy, vitamins (particularly niacin (B_3) and B_{12}), and minerals (especially iron and zinc). Eggs, dried peas or beans and nuts are also included in this group.

Group 4: Milk and dairy foods

These foods give you protein, energy, vitamins and minerals. They are our most important source of calcium for strengthening teeth and bones, and riboflavin (vitamin B_2).

Group 5: Butter and table margarine

This group provides fat for energy, essential fatty acids, and vitamins (particularly A and D).

Each day you should choose a variety of foods selecting from each of the five food groups.

The Commonwealth Department of Health thinks good eating is so important they have drawn up a set of guidelines for healthier Australians. They are based on the three principles of good nutrition—balance, moderation and variety.

These guidelines are:

- Choose a nutritious diet from a variety of foods.
- Control your weight.
- Avoid eating too much fat.
- Avoid eating too much sugar.
- Eat more breads and cereals (preferably wholegrain) and vegetables and fruit.
- Limit your alcohol consumption.
- Use less salt.
- Encourage breastfeeding.

One of the first hints for healthier eating is to balance intake of food to match your level of physical activity and metabolic needs. Or, if you are relatively inactive, increase your energy output to match your kilojoule input. But there are other traps to watch out for if you want to maintain a healthy body. Try to avoid:

- skipping meals;
- irregular meals;
- eating high fat, high sugar snacks on the run;

190

- eating too much over breakfast or lunchtime meetings;
- drinking too much alcohol; and
- drinking too much coffee.

If you can, try having a nutritious lunch. For example, a sandwich, a piece of fruit and a carton of milk or yoghurt can draw on each of the five food groups. Or if you prefer, a salad lunch with a piece of chicken, cheese or tuna, is a well-balanced meal which packs a crunch. It will also contain some of the necessary calcium you require.

If you eat out at a restaurant, fast food outlet or cafeteria, try to choose foods that aren't deep-fried or too sweet or salty. There are usually salads to choose from too. If your menu is limited, try approaching the management to improve the choice of foods offered.

If you're running around, meeting deadlines or working long hours, you're going to need plenty of energy. But apart from the physical component of energy expenditure, energy is needed to fuel normal bodily functions.

We obtain most of our energy from starches and sugars, which are carbohydrates. Starches are found in bread, flour, cereals and vegetables, while most of the sugar in our diet comes from table sugar and foods prepared with it.

Fruit and milk also contain sugars, but in addition they provide other nutrients such as vitamins and minerals. Ideally, your diet will draw on a combination of starches and sugars to ensure an adequate intake of energy as well as essential nutrients.

Fats are also energy-giving foods. Some, such as butter, margarine and vegetable and marine oils, contain essential fatty acids in addition to fat-soluble vitamins such as A, D, E and K. But, because they are concentrated energy sources, you must pay attention to how much you eat. And remember that one of the dietary guidelines is to avoid too much fat.

Here are some hints on how to cut down on your fat intake:

- Trim visible fat from meat.
- Cook meat on a rack.
- Cook homemade soups, stews or casseroles and skim the fat from the surface.
- Steam vegetables.
- Make gravy from meat juices only—removing fat first.
- Avoid fried foods and snacks such as potato chips.
- Substitute non-fat yoghurt for cream in cooking.

- Restrict butter and margarine to one tablespoon daily.
- Limit the oil in salad dressings if you make your own or buy no-oil products.

A good supply of protein is needed to maintain muscle strength and repair damaged body tissues. It also contributes to your energy intake. Foods differ in the quantity and types of proteins they provide, so it is important to choose a variety of protein-rich foods. The best sources of protein are meat and meat alternatives, milk and other dairy foods such as cheese or yoghurt. Breads and cereals are important too.

If you follow the guidelines in this section, you'll get the right combination of proteins.

The importance of vitamins and minerals

Stress, smoking, alcohol, skipping meals and other habits which tend to accompany executive life place extra demands on vitamin and mineral supplies. Here are the ones to watch.

The vitamin B group has many functions, the main ones being:

- to help release energy from carbohydrates, proteins and fats;
- to ensure normal functions of the nervous system; and
- to assist in the formation of red blood cells.

The best sources of B-group vitamins are leafy vegetables, wholegrain cereals, meat, fish, dairy products and eggs. Vitamin B_{12} is found in adequate amounts only in animal foods such as liver, kidney, red meat, eggs, seafood, milk and cheese. So, if you're a vegan and do not eat animal products, it would be wise to ask your doctor about a supplement.

Vitamin C is necessary for maintaining the structure of the body including bones, teeth, ligaments, tendons and blood vessels. It also increases the absorption of iron from the digestive tract, protects vitamins A and D from being degraded, helps the body make essential hormones and builds the body's resistance to infection. A deficiency usually occurs in people who don't eat enough fruit or vegetables—so make sure you eat plenty of both.

If you're working night and day and missing out on fresh air and sunshine, vitamin D deficiency may occur. Indoor types should look to tuna, salmon, sardines, eggs, whole milk, butter and table margarine instead. Select a wide variety of foods from the five food groups and you can forget the vitamin and mineral supplements. But do try to get out into the fresh air as often as possible.

Vitamins can, however, be lost in storing, preparing or cooking food. Try and store food appropriately—dry food in a dry place, fresh foods in a cool place, and buy smaller quantities of fresh foods more regularly, rather than storing. When you are preparing food, avoid peeling, cutting or soaking prior to cooking. And last but not least, don't overcook food. Use the minimum of water and cook for the shortest possible time.

Irregular working hours often prohibit regular shopping. So it's wise to have 'emergency' food supplies on hand. For example, powdered, canned or long-life milk, or canned or frozen fruits, vegetables and meats.

The minerals to watch are calcium and iron.

As we have seen, calcium is extremely important. It is needed to maintain bone and teeth strength, nerve impulses, muscle activity and healthy blood. However, the iron in green vegetables and cereals tends to be in a form that is not as easily absorbed by your body as that in meat and some other protein-rich foods

Dairy products are your best source of calcium. One cup (250 ml) of milk a day, plus a 200 g tub of yogurt will provide enough to meet around three-quarters of your daily calcium needs. Or, if you prefer, you can eat cheese and yogurt. And don't forget there is a large variety of low-fat dairy products available for those who need to keep their fat intake down.

Iron deficiency can lead to anaemia and the associated symptoms of appetite loss, tiredness and heart palpitations. It has an essential role in carrying oxygen around the body.

You have 'iron stores' in your body which should always be maintained because disease can severely deplete them, leading to further problems later on. Meat is the most important source of iron, although iron is also found in legumes, green vegetables and bread and cereals.

Fibre for 'internal' fitness

Numerous studies have shown that an increased consumption of fibre may lead to a decreased incidence of disease, such as constipation and diverticular disease. Dietary fibre may not sound all that appetising, but when it comes in the shape of delicious juicy fruits, vegetables and wholegrain breads and cereals, it sounds a lot more tempting, doesn't it? And that's exactly where you'll find plenty of fibre.

Water

Water is very important to good health. It helps get rid of waste products from digestion and prevents constipation. Try and drink 1.5 L (eight glasses) a day, either as plain water, weak tea or coffee, fruit juices or mineral water.

Summary

An optimum fitness program aimed at preventing or treating osteoporosis must comprise an appropriate exercise routine together with a balanced diet. Exercise must include activities which use gravity to stress your skeleton and those which assist general fitness. Diet should comprise food from the five food groups together with a proper balance of vitamins and minerals.

13

Osteoporosis and pain

Pain is often a late feature in people suffering from osteoporosis. Yet what has been described as 'the paradox of pain' is prominent in osteoporosis. Pain is at the one time a warning of impending or real damage, and yet it may come too late to protect the sufferer. Certainly, the first warning of osteoporosis is the pain associated with fractures of the spine and the limbs.

The most common pain symptoms associated with osteoporosis may be the pain felt in the spine associated with bone fracture or damage. When the degeneration or fracture of the spinal vertebras causes pressure on the contents of the central spinal canal, this may cause a variety of pain complaints. The spinal canal runs behind the body or main part of the flexible spinal architecture. Its contents, the spinal cord and the nerve roots, are sheathed in several layers of membranous tissues that contain the spinal fluid.

Pressure on the spinal contents or the nerve roots will often cause back pain. The same pressure may be responsible for pain experienced at a distance from the problem area—so-called referred pain. Thus, in the lumbar or lowest part of the spine such pressure will often cause sciatica or pain running along the surfaces or interior of the legs. In the cervical spine or neck vertebral pressure will cause pain to be felt in the arms and hands, or even in the area of the upper chest or shoulders.

In the thoracic area or chest pressure on the spinal contents or nerve roots will often cause pain to be felt in a spreading fashion around the chest just like a girdle of pain. These painful symptoms may be accompanied by other abnormal sensations including pins and needles (paraesthesiae), electrical shock type feelings, areas of numbness or increased sensitivity to light touch.

This chapter will describe the range of individual treatments, their advantages, disadvantages and factors which would prevent their use as well as their approximate costs and where these treatments can be obtained.

The advent of acupuncture

Some 5000 years ago the ancient Chinese discovered that fine objects used to penetrate the skin could bring about a return to normal function or health in their subjects. The first recorded writings about acupuncture were published in the five centuries before the Christian era began its influence in the West.

Ancient acupuncture texts and charts were inscribed on stone—even the ancient city walls of Beijing—and can be seen in the museums of Beijing today. Over the millennia an elaborate philosophy developed to explain why illness occurred and how it could be regulated or controlled by altering the flow of vital energy—Qi or Chi—through the meridians or channels which flowed in imaginary lines over the surface and internal organs of the body.

Acupuncture was brought back to the West by Portuguese and Dutch missionaries impressed by the results of this treatment method in China and Japan. Some of the first European medical texts to mention acupuncture as a treatment for arthritis were published in the seventeenth century. The Dutch author Willem Ten Rijne is credited with being the first westerner to write enthusiastically about acupuncture.

The great American surgeon and medical educationalist William Osler wrote about acupuncture's role in the treatment of backache in the late nineteenth and early twentieth centuries. Acupuncture was practised on the Australian goldfields a hundred years ago. It was rediscovered by the western world in the early 1970s. The Australian Medical Acupuncture Society (AMAS) was founded in 1973 by the handful of Australian doctors who had started to use acupuncture in their medical practices.

The initial instruments used by the Chinese were probably bone or stone shaped into needles. In the past 2000 years needles of bronze, gold and copper were used, until in more recent times it became possible to manufacture stainless steel needles.

These fine needles, which are only millimetres thick in the shaft and quite flexible, are easily passed through the skin into the fatty

196

tissues beneath the skin and into the muscles. They are fine and have specially designed tips, so they push through the body tissues rather than tearing or cutting as do the much thicker hypodermic needles used to give injections.

Over the past 20 years or so acupuncture has become more readily accepted in Australia and other Western countries. In Australia, acupuncture training has been carried out for more than twenty years by the AMAS.

Over 2000 Australian medical practitioners are said to have lodged claims to Australia's Health Insurance Commission for acupuncture-related medical services. There are approximately 1000 members of the AMAS spread throughout Australia and New Zealand. To become a Fellow of the AMAS a doctor has to attend 200 hours of supervised training then pass a two-part written examination and a searching oral examination.

In addition, there are many 'lay' or non-medical practitioners of acupuncture with varying degrees of training and competence. Unfortunately, there are few laws to protect the public against untrained operators.

Fortunately for the public, however, two university-based courses in Medical Acupuncture are about to commence in Melbourne, Victoria, with others in the planning stage at other centres.

In this era of acquired immune deficiency syndrome (AIDS) and the human immunodeficiency virus (HIV) and the various forms of hepatitis it is both opportune and necessary that the old reusable needles have been replaced by pre-packaged and sterile needles.

The medical acupuncturist will assess you by taking a full medical history, reviewing all previous investigations and performing a complete physical examination. He or she will then determine whether or not acupuncture is an appropriate form of therapy for your individual needs.

The average number of treatments necessary to assess the potential benefits of acupuncture for an individual patient will depend on the condition being treated and the individual response to the treatment. Our experience is that within five to ten treatments with acupuncture you should be able to see a response. This is likely to take the form of a decrease in pain or an improvement of function in the affected area of the body or limbs.

If no positive response occurs after the initial assessment course the treatment will be stopped, and if the response is positive treatment may be continued until response ceases or an alternative therapy is found.

You should not be overly surprised when the acupuncturist places some or all of the needles at a distance from the site of your pain or stiffness. You may even have small needles placed in your ears or in your scalp. The therapist will probably make use of some of the thousands of years of experience of the ancients and will also make use of their specialised anatomical and physiological knowledge.

Laser—the healing light

One development which has eased the anxiety of potential acupuncture patients has been the introduction of laser acupuncture. Low level laser acupuncture therapy (LLLT) has become commonplace in the surgeries of medical practitioners, physiotherapists and some chiropractors in the past fifteen years.

This form of treatment is harmless to patient and operator alike, owing to the low energy output of the lasers used. There is no sensation from the laser—a very pure light produced by the electrical stimulation of gases, crystals or semiconductor substances.

The laser produces energy in the form of light which is said to interact with the nervous system. The only precaution taken with laser therapy is the wearing of dark glasses to protect against stray beams of laser light entering the eye of therapist and patient alike. This is less important in the more commonly used low level lasers than in the modern lasers of over 10 mW output.

The laser light, produced by these machines, is used in a number of ways. The practitioner may use the traditional principles of acupuncture or use a variety of techniques which include stroking the laser pen along the affected nerves or tissues. There is no heat or damage generated by this treatment and most patients feel no sensation.

The major use for acupuncture in the treatment of osteoporosis would be the treatment of pain associated with crush fractures in the spine and the consequent nerve root pressure or spinal canal narrowing which may follow.

The cost of acupuncture varies— from approximately $20 to $45 according to the practitioner. There is currently a token Medicare rebate of $18. Some Australian private health funds reimburse the cost of this treatment by lay therapists and physiotherapists.

Electrical stimulation of the skin

Transcutaneous electrical nerve stimulation (TENS) developed from the observation that electrical stimulation of acupuncture needles appeared to have increased benefits in the treatment of disease. It was also found that direct stimulation of the skin could have beneficial effects in controlling pain and some disease states.

With the development of microelectronics in the past two decades, smaller and smaller TENS units have been developed, making them more convenient to carry and to use. TENS units are typically small, portable, sophisticated electronic devices which deliver a low-energy electrical pulse to the surface of the skin via electrodes. These electrodes may be reusable with attached gums capable of being used many times. The electrodes are placed over localised areas of pain or at distant areas which often correspond to acupuncture points.

The treatment is particularly useful in those conditions affecting the musculoskeletal system. TENS is likely to be used in those patients with osteoporosis with pain resulting from fractures, or associated with nerve pressure or damage when the vertebras collapse.

Patients with established osteoporosis may have a variety of reasons for using TENS as a means of controlling pain, stiffness and disability. Even if there is no specific indication for the treatment of the osteoporosis itself, TENS may be helpful in treating the osteoarthritis or pain resulting from shingles in the individual with osteoporosis.

Patients with osteoporosis are unlikely to be pregnant or to be suffering from undiagnosed malignancies, but such patients should avoid TENS. In addition, TENS should always be used cautiously over the front of the chest, and in the area over the front of the neck.

Most TENS units are small enough to wear on a belt clip or in a pocket. They can be used with the newer self-adhesive electrodes which reduce the need for messy gels and skin tape. The two or four electrodes per unit transmit the electrical current, produced by a nine-volt battery, through the skin to the underlying nerves, muscles and tissues.

You will experience a tingling sensation with most machines. In some cases the stimulation can be strong enough to cause rhythmic muscular contractions. This enhances blood flow and carries increased blood to the area to aid in healing. The treatment has been shown to stimulate the production of natural pain-killers (endorphins).

A very small number of patients claim that they are unable to tolerate the sensation produced by the TENS unit. TENS has very few unpleasant or unwanted side effects but one is the occasional development of sensitivity to the gel of the electrodes. People with a history of allergy to surgical adhesive tapes would do well to rent a TENS unit or try it in the clinical setting before purchase. A potentially difficult problem could be the development of allergic blisters on sensitive or aging skin.

One possible disadvantage for elderly sufferers of pain is the small size of some of the controls on many of the units available. Other patients may not have the flexibility necessary to reach the electrode sites—particularly if these are on the back and not the limbs.

TENS therapy's great attraction, apart from convenience and effectiveness, is that it can make you independent of medical or paramedical supervision. A trial of TENS therapy is available from pain clinics, some GPs and through physiotherapists. In many countries TENS is available only through a doctor's prescription. In Australia no such restrictions exist and many chemists sell TENS units, although some of these are of questionable benefit.

TENS units range in price from about $150 to $500 each. Caution should be taken in buying cheap and regretting it later. The best units presently available in Australia include the Spectrum II at $220, the Dynex IV at $355, Israeli-made Agar 10K at about $395, and Spectrum Plus at $350. The IMPI Eclipse+ is the most fully featured small TENS unit in Australia at present and costs $485. TENS units can usually be rented for $40 to $60 per month on a trial basis.

In addition to the smaller type of TENS units, our experience with the Likon has shown it to be effective in controlling pain in many patients with whom more conventional TENS was ineffective. The Likon is a briefcase-sized battery-powered machine, originating in Singapore and designed in China, which produces very complex yet very effective electrical pulses. Many patients using the Likon feel its stimulations are deeper than conventional TENS stimulation.

The sensation produced by the Likon varies from a tingling or throbbing similar to that found with the smaller TENS units to a deeper massage-like sensation which most patients feel is very pleasant.

What is gained by increased pain relief may be lost, to some extent, by the decreased convenience of the larger unit which cannot be worn by the patient or carried in the average pocket or handbag.

The Likon costs approximately $800 and can also be rented on a trial basis for about $100 per month from some suppliers.

The Quartzo—piezo electric current

At the time of writing this book your author discovered a French invention—the Quartzo—which is yet another way of delivering electrical current to the body with the intention of reducing pain. This device produces intense but very short bursts of electric stimulation which have the effect of reducing pain and muscle spasm. The good news is that most patients are said to achieve pain relief from two minutes of stimulation to the painful areas twice a day.

There are two main versions of this device—a hand-held portable unit suitable for carrying in a handbag, and an electronic version which needs to be plugged into a power socket. They both produce the electric current by the process of squeezing two quartz crystals together. This process is similar to that used by the gas lighters that many people have in their kitchens. Normally, the spark produced in the air is what ignites the gas burner. In the Quartzo, the device is applied to the skin and the electric current is felt as a series of sharp stinging sensations.

If the Quartzo is marketed in Australia it is expected to be priced at $170 for the manual version and $450 for the more sophisticated electronic unit.

Magnetic-field therapy

Humanity has known of the beneficial powers of magnets over the ages. The ancient Chinese believed that magnets had therapeutic powers as well as discovering the use of magnets in the world's first compasses.

Over the past twenty or thirty years machines producing therapeutic magnetic energy fields have been developed, initially in the Eastern European states and then in the western world. Studies in the United States of America by Bassett and others have discovered that applying these magnetic fields to living organisms may assist in the healing of fractures and many acute injuries.

The magnetic fields generated by these machines have been shown to increase the flow of blood through tissues and to increase the amount of oxygen available to the tissues. Scientific studies have also shown the ability of pulsating magnetic fields to produce flows of calcium and phosphorus ions across bone fracture sites, encouraging the healing process.

We have used this treatment for over ten years in patients with spinal pain secondary to osteoporosis, with reduction or cessation of pain in some patients in whom other therapies had been unhelpful.

There are a number of locally made magnetic field therapy (MFT) units, and units are also made in Italy and Germany. The most common type of MFT device consists of a cylindrical magnetic coil which sits over the affected area. Most commonly you will be sitting on a chair with the coil positioned around you. You will not have to remove your clothing, although it will be wise to remove your watch because of the powerful magnetic energy used in the treatment.

A console or keyboard allows the operator to alter the frequency of the pulses of the magnetic energy, its intensity and the treatment time.

MFT is used extensively in Europe to treat sports injuries and in the rehabilitation of patients suffering from many painful medical conditions including osteoporosis, migraine and varicose ulcers. It has been extremely successful in the treatment of injuries to racehorses in Australia, and received much publicity in racing circles in the early 1980s.

MFT has few contraindications. Patients with unstable diabetes or undiagnosed bleeding from the bowel should avoid it. The presence of tumours or cancer should also reduce its use.

The only major disadvantage is the time it takes for MFT to show any positive effect. You may have to return for treatment either on a twice-weekly or daily basis for a minimum of ten to fifteen treatments before any results are obtained.

MFT is currently available from a few medical practitioners in most Australian States and from some physiotherapists. It is usually classified as a 'physical treatment', which may attract no Medicare rebate if the doctor does not carry out the treatment. It can legitimately be billed as a 'consultation', providing the doctor spends some time with the patient during each treatment.

In these circumstances, the treatment cost ranges from approximately $10 to $15 for each session with a medical rebate of approximately $10–15 for each treatment.

Although the wearing of magnets in various bandages, jewellery and gadgets has received widespread publicity in Australia, there is little or no clinical evidence that these are anything other than an expensive placebo. The only so-called static magnets found to have any therapeutic effect are the layered magnetic foils which come from Europe.

These are generally supplied by sports medicine clinics and, although they may be more expensive, scientific papers on their use in painful conditions have been presented to meetings of medical scientists and have therefore been available to their scrutiny. They are usually supplied as oblong or rectangular plates with a shiny surface facing the outside world and a sticky self-adhesive surface to attach them to the skin. They cause an increase in the local blood flow immediately below the surface of the area being treated, allowing the body to mobilise its natural healing and pain-killing abilities to be brought to the injured site.

Medication used in the treatment of pain

Before any discussion of the medications used in pain or stress relief associated with osteoporosis is carried out, the risk of falls should be re-emphasised. All medications prescribed in the elderly group most likely to be affected by osteoporosis carry with them the risk of producing problems with concentration or balance. This may occur with individual medications but may be increased with the multiple medications likely to be prescribed.

There are several classifications of pain-killers available, ranging from the most simple over-the-counter medications to those belonging to the most powerful narcotic groups. Since pain is one of the more common late complaints of patients with osteoporosis, a proper discussion of this class of drugs is important information for those readers who experience pain and wonder 'What more can be done?'

Simple analgesics

Among the most commonly used and, for that matter, abused drugs purchased over-the-counter are the various preparations of aspirin and paracetamol. Preparations such as Aspro, Disprin, Panadol, Dymadon and others are household names in Australia and other countries.

The proper use of these drugs should always be the first step in a three-stage ladder of pain relief. Aspirin and paracetamol are both relatively safe medications when taken in proper quantities, and for the right reason. Aspirin is slightly more potent as a pain-killer than paracetamol but is also likely to produce unwanted and unpleasant side-effects.

These include stomach upsets involving the production of acute damage to the stomach or gastric lining—known as acute gastritis. If the aspirin intake is continued in the presence of severe heartburn, or in the presence of reflux of the acid contents of the stomach up the gullet, ulcers may result. It is not uncommon for microscopic amounts of blood to be shed regularly after aspirin is taken, and more severe bleeding or haemorrhage may occur if the medication is continued.

One method of preventing this problem and at the same time ensuring that the benefits of aspirin are obtained is to enclose the aspirin in a special coating. This is called an enteric coating and does not dissolve until the medication has passed through the acid contents of the stomach and into the first part of the small intestine, where it can be attacked by the enzymes produced by the pancreas gland—the sweetbread.

The other major problem caused by taking an excessive amount of aspirin is the development of noises in the ears—known as tinnitus. This is usually a sign that the aspirin levels in the bloodstream have reached dangerous or toxic levels. In most cases, this is reversible upon stopping the medication for two or more days and then restarting at a lower level.

Paracetamol may be 'gentler to the stomach' than aspirin but is also less potent and not without problems for the person who abuses it. The most worrying unwanted effect for patients taking in excess of six 500 mg paracetamol tablets a day is the potential for liver and kidney damage. This may in fact be severe enough to require kidney transplantation.

Provided that these simple pain-killers are taken with proper medical supervision they are a safe way of providing increased mobility and pain relief for many sufferers.

Compound or mixed pain-killers

The next common group of over-the-counter medication is the mixed or compound analgesic. This group is represented by the popular Codis, Veganin, Panadeine, Dymadon Co, and other variants consisting of mixtures of aspirin and codeine in small amounts, or of paracetamol and codeine. The same precautions apply to this group of drugs as to the simple pain-killers, with the addition of potential problems associated with codeine, which is a synthetic narcotic or morphine-like pain-killer.

Codeine adds the unpleasant effects of constipation and drug dependence or its potential to those of the aspirin and paracetamol. Although these medicines produce more pain reduction they come with extra risks.

Mersyndol is another compound pain-killer which is available over-the-counter but it adds a muscle relaxant to the paracetamol and codeine. It is commonly recommended for severe headache but may be useful for pain associated with muscle spasm. It must not be taken with alcohol as it produces drowsiness even on its own. The drowsiness caused by this relatively mild pain-killer could be enough to increase the risks of unsteadiness or of falls in the elderly.

The next group of pain-killers are available only on doctor's prescription. These either increase the amount of codeine or add a similar preparation—propoxyphene—to the aspirin or paracetamol. The most common forms of these are Digesic, Capadex, and Doloxene. Those containing codeine in higher quantities include Panadeine Forte and Codral Forte. Propoxyphene is available on its own in the form of Doloxene capsules.

The more potent Mersyndol Forte joins Panadeine Forte and Codral Forte in increasing the risks of dependence and even addiction. All are potentially addictive if taken in excessive amounts or for prolonged periods of time.

Some pain-relieving medicines in this stronger class may even contribute to the chronic pain experienced by making the patient seek bed more and more. This increases immobility, which may lead to further weakening of the bone due to calcium loss and thus greater osteoporosis.

The narcotics

These potent and potentially addictive drugs are unlikely to be prescribed for patients with pain associated with osteoporosis. They would probably be used only in patients whose pain is caused by pressure or damage to the nervous system caused by fractures in the spine or by associated degenerative arthritis in the spine—osteoarthritis or spondylosis.

The most common narcotics used in Australia are pethidine or morphine—available as injections or tablets. Morphine is also available in syrup form and is sometimes used in a combination with aspirin. Recently a longer-lasting form of morphine tablet—MS Contin—with a twelve-hour effect has been introduced in Australia.

At the time of writing this book a twelve-hour duration of action morphine developed by an Australian company is reportedly due for release. This medication—to be known as Kapanol—will enable those experiencing the intractable pain of cancer and other terminal illnesses to have proper day-long pain relief.

Another narcotic drug, oxycodone, is available as Endone tablets, Proladone rectal suppositories, and in combination with aspirin as Percodan.

Their addictive potential means these drugs require the treating physician to obtain a permit to prescribe them on an ongoing basis. This recognises the role the medical practitioner must have in protecting the patient from harm while prescribing the most appropriate form of treatment.

Non-steroidal anti-inflammatory drugs

Another exciting development in the treatment of severe pain has been the introduction of the potent pain-killing non-steroidal anti-inflammatory drug (NSAID) Toradol—ketorolac. This is available as an injection into the muscles or as a tablet.

Like all anti-inflammatory drugs, Toradol can cause severe stomach-lining ulceration and it is more likely to cause this in the age group likely to be having pain from osteoporosis. It is also reported to have caused damage to the liver and kidneys in some elderly patients. Recently, Australian doctors have been advised to be extremely cautious in prescribing Toradol in the elderly or in those with poor liver or kidney function following a number of deaths in susceptible patients in the United States of America.

Toradol is not addictive, as it is not a narcotic, and is therefore not subject to the restrictions necessary for narcotics. As yet, Toradol has not been released as a subsidised pharmaceutical benefit and is quite expensive.

NSAIDs are important and effective medications prescribed for pain and for the treatment of inflammatory conditions such as forms of arthritis.

The most commonly prescribed NSAIDs in Australia include Feldene, Tilcotil, Orudis SR, Voltaren, Clinoril, Brufen, Naprosyn, Indocid and Surgam. Recent trends have seen the use of these drugs made more convenient by the development of potent single dosage per day drugs such as Feldene and Orudis.

A topical gel of the medication used in Feldene capsules which can be rubbed into painful areas of the body is available in Europe and New Zealand. There are also rectal suppository forms of the two most commonly used anti-inflammatory drugs, Naprosyn and Indocid. The suppositories may assist in reducing the problem many patients have when using oral forms of these medications—unpleasant side effects of gastric irritation or gastric ulceration.

The suppository, formulation of the anti-inflammatory medications bypasses the delicate stomach lining, so they can be extremely useful with patients who cannot tolerate oral medication. However, it is recognised that no matter how the NSAIDs are absorbed into the bloodstream some patients will develop the stomach ulceration and bleeding seen with the oral forms of the drugs.

The anti-inflammatory drugs have been shown to have a pain-relieving effect which is equal to, or sometimes greater than that of the simple analgesics mentioned above.

In Australia, the only NSAID medications which appear to be free of gastrointestinal problems are Difflam gel and cream and Indocid Spray. The latter is available only on a doctor's prescription, but Difflam is available in both over-the-counter and prescription strengths.

The dangers of liver and kidney damage together with the gastrointestinal problems mentioned earlier have led the prescription of these drugs on the Pharmaceutical Benefits Schedule (PBS) or subsidised benefits scheme to be severely and some would say unnecessarily restricted in Australia. They may now be prescribed only for long-term usage in patients with proven inflammation—such as in those with rheumatoid arthritis.

A recent addition to these preparations in Australia is the topical NSAID Voltaren Emulgel. This is applied to the skin and is claimed to produce pain relief and reduction of inflammation without the side-effects produced by oral preparations. Your author has recently trialled another topical preparation with promising effects on pain and apparently few side-effects on the stomach and other organs. The preparation, to be manufactured by a new Australian company, Hyal Pharmaceuticals Australia Limited, appears to reduce pain in osteoarthritis when rubbed into the skin. Years of clinical trials will probably be needed before this is released to the public.

Tricyclic antidepressants

The antidepressant drugs are typical of what are known as adjuvant pain drugs. Over the years, older drugs such as Tryptanol, Tofranil and Sinequan were found useful in the treatment of chronic pain. They not only treat the depression commonly associated with any lasting pain, they also treat the pain by influencing the chemical messengers which produce or modify pain experience.

They therefore act as a non-addictive pain-killer by improving the patient's pain tolerance. They show none of the associated unwanted effects of the commonly used pain-killers. In part they are believed to help reduce pain by stimulating the brain's natural pain-killers (the endorphins). They also affect the balance of other brain and nervous system chemical messengers such as noradrenaline and serotonin.

The commonly used antidepressants have long-term safety records and are among the most widely used drugs in medicine. They do not have any addictive potential and do not affect other approaches to pain reduction such as TENS or other physiotherapy approaches.

Antidepressants can be highly effective in relatively small doses of between 50 mg and 100 mg at night, though dosages of up to 200 mg a night (eight tablets) may be necessary before control of pain and depression is reached.

More recent antidepressants include Anafranil, Prothiaden and Pertofran. Tolvon is another older drug having similar effects but fewer gastric and cardiovascular side effects than the other antidepressants. Tolvon is considered safer in the elderly because it causes less sedation, constipation and dryness of the mouth than the other drugs mentioned above.

Other more recent drugs introduced in Australia for the treatment of depression are Prozac, Aropax, Zoloft, and Aurorix (moclobemide). These new antidepressants have differing but very specific effects on the brain levels of serotonin—a chemical messenger which has important roles in the experience of depression and of pain. They act only on this chemical, so they are what are known as 'clean drugs'—they have very few side effects.

Prozac is now the most widely prescribed antidepressant drug in the world. At the time of writing this book, more than five million Americans and ten million other people around the world are said to be taking this drug for the treatment of depression. In the elderly depressed, Prozac appears to cause far less sedation and confusion than other drugs used in the treatment of depression.

Despite continuous attacks on Prozac by certain media spokespersons, Prozac has stood up to the most intense scrutiny of any newly introduced medication over the past few decades.

Tricyclic antidepressants available in Australia are listed below with their dosages and generic names.

Brand name	Generic name	Average daily dose for pain (with evening meal)
Allegron	Nortryptiline	25–150 mg
Anafranil	Clomipramine	25–150 mg
Deptran	Doxepin	25–150 mg
Endep	Amitryptiline	25–150 mg
Nortab	Nortryptiline	25–150 mg
Pertofran	Desipramine	25–150 mg
Prothiaden	Dothiepin	25–150 mg
Sinequan	Doxepin	25–150 mg
Surmontil	Trimipramine	25–150 mg
Tofranil	Imipramine	25–150 mg
Tryptanol	Amitryptiline	25–100 mg

The doses of the other antidepressants are:

Brand name	Generic name	Dosage
Prozac 20	Fluoxitene	20–60 mg
Aropax 20	Paroxitene	20–40 mg
Zoloft	Sertraline	50–100 mg
Aurorix	Moclobemide	150–600 mg

Tranquillisers

There are two major groups of tranquillisers used in treating chronic pain. The first group is the so-called 'minor tranquillisers', of which Valium and Serepax are the most well-known. Despite their adverse publicity these drugs have a limited yet real role in the treatment of pain and its sequelae. In most cases these drugs are useful and relatively safe when used according to the instructions of the doctor and the manufacturer.

Recognition of their extensively reported side effects and potential withdrawal problems is now widespread. Despite the fact that dependency problems occur in a small but definite group of people taking the medication for more than a short period, it is common for many elderly patients to have taken their small regular dose of Serepax for many years. Some of these people have adapted to their minor tranquillisers so that more damage may be caused by attempts to cease that dose of what for them is an innocuous sedative than to continue them.

Such agents are useful to reduce anxiety in patients, particularly those with acute pain. They can also be of value in reducing muscle spasms in chronic pain patients. One drug in this group—Rivotril or clonazepam—has been used extensively in the treatment of pain caused by damage to the nervous system, such as occurs in the painful state following an episode of shingles.

When used in chronic pain cases they may uncover what is known as a 'masked depression' leading to apparent depression which is not caused by the medication but was already present in a hidden form. Members of this group of drugs include Valium, Ducene, Serepax, Rohypnol, Mogadon, Euhypnos, Normison, Dalmane and Halcion.

Major tranquillisers—possible major side effects

The 'major tranquillisers' are more commonly used in the treatment of severe mental illness. The best known are Largactil, Melleril and Stelazine. The major tranquillisers have little or no role in the treatment of the age group most likely to be suffering from pain associated with osteoporosis. They produce excessive sedation in the elderly and therefore increase the risk of falls with the consequent risk of increased fractures and other injury. Their only potential application is in the elderly person with associated severe mental illness or great confusion.

They may also cause uncontrollable muscular twitching—a condition known as tardive dyskinesia—in a significant number of patients. This condition can be extremely troublesome and can prove very difficult to control. It sometimes develops after relatively short courses of the medication and in relatively small doses.

This, therefore, limits the use of such medications in the treatment of all but the severest forms of chronic pain.

Anti-epileptic medications

Anti-epileptic drugs have recently played an important role in the treatment of pain caused by disease or injury to the nervous system. Drugs such as Tegretol, Rivotril and Epilim all share this role, although they have a variety of effects which may limit their use in the treatment of pain caused by osteoporosis.

As most of these drugs may cause confusion or drowsiness in the elderly, their use should always proceed with caution on the part of the prescribing physician as well as the patient.

Steroids

Cortisone-like drugs, which are often injected into joints or into inflamed areas, have limited or no role in the management of pain associated with osteoporosis.

Since one of the major side effects of such drugs is the development of osteoporosis there would be no reason to use these drugs in this condition. Steroids may need to be used in the treatment of other conditions, which may be present at the same time as the osteoporosis in the same patient. Drugs such as calcitriol or Didrocal may be required to prevent the further loss of bone caused by treatment with steroids.

Anaesthetic approaches

The anaesthetist plays an integral role in many of the pain-relieving techniques used in pain clinics. In particular, the anaesthetist will be involved in giving patients with chronic pain a variety of nerve blocks. These usually consist of the anaesthetist injecting pain-relieving local anaesthetic or other drugs into the nerves thought to be transmitting pain messages to and from the nervous system.

These range from the intravenous blocks used in the treatment of RSD to special spinal blocks where local anaesthetic and steroids are placed over the spinal cord or over the emerging nerve roots. In the treatment of cancer pain and other terminal pain conditions the anaesthetist may be involved in positioning special devices into the spine which allow the continuous injection of morphine into the spinal space.

Neurosurgery

Neurosurgery has a limited place in the treatment of non-malignant pain. In treating patients with uncontrolled pain the neurosurgeon will at times be involved in the cutting of specific nerve pathways. They may also be rarely involved in the insertion of sophisticated and extremely expensive spinal cord stimulators. These are electronic devices inserted into the space around the spinal cord and its associated nerve roots in a painful surgical procedure. The current cost of the operation and the associated electronic hardware is over $30 000.

The most likely area of involvement of the neurosurgeon in pain caused by osteoporosis is likely to be that of corrective spinal surgery—to remove bone causing pressure on the nervous system or to stabilise the spine by fusing or joining vertebras together. The neurosurgeon and the orthopaedic surgeon share an involvement in the surgical correction of spinal disorders.

211

14

Help is at hand

The information published below was accurate at the time of going to press. Personnel may have since changed at some centres. Medicare rebates for bone density scanning may be available if government criteria are met.

Support from the arthritis foundation

The Arthritis Foundation of Australia (AFA) can offer assistance to you in your activities to prevent or minimise osteoporosis and with concerns you have about other musculoskeletal conditions. such as arthritis and back problems.

The AFA can help with advice and counselling from trained staff; printed and audiovisual information including brochures, booklets, books and audio and video cassettes; educational and exercise programs including water and land exercise classes and arthritis self-management courses; regular arthritis support group meetings.

Such help can be invaluable in assisting you to take up and maintain the daily activities which will contribute to your health and wellbeing.

The AFA also works to support people through its funding of research into treatment and management of musculoskeletal conditions and lobbying of governments to provide appropriate funding and services for people with musculoskeletal problems.

Arthritis Foundation of the Australian Capital Territory
PO Box 1642
Canberra City ACT 2601
Tel: (062) 57 4842

Arthritis Foundation of New South Wales
PO Box 370
Darlinghurst NSW 2010
Tel: (02) 281 1611

Arthritis Foundation of the Northern Territory
PO Box 37582
Winnellie NT 0831
Tel: (089) 83 2071

Arthritis Foundation of Queensland
PO Box 901
Toowong Qld 4066
Tel: (07) 371 9755

Arthritis Foundation of South Australia
99 Anzac Highway
Ashford SA 5035
Tel: (08) 297 2488

Arthritis Foundation of Tasmania
88 Hampden Road
Battery Point, Hobart 7000
Tel: (002) 34 6489

Arthritis Foundation of Victoria
PO Box 195
Kew Victoria 3101
Tel: (03) 853 2555

Arthritis Foundation of Western Australia
PO Box 34
Wembley WA 6014
Tel: (09) 387 7066

Arthritis Foundation of Australia
National Office
PO Box 21
Sydney NSW 2001
Tel: (02) 221 2456

Support from other agencies

Apart from the AFA there are a range of agencies or services that can help with advice and information regarding osteoporosis. These include:

- hospitals;
- menopause clinics at public hospitals;
- community health centres (where available);
- women's health centres (where available).

NEW SOUTH WALES

Hospitals
St Vincent's Private Hospital
438 Victoria Street
Darlinghurst 2010
Tel: (02) 332 6565
The Osteoporosis Clinic is run on Monday and Thursday mornings. The first visit involves a hormonal profile, biochemical profile, X-rays and bone density scan. Operates a DEXA scanning unit.

St George Hospital
Nuclear Medicine Department
Belgrave Street
Kogarah 2217
Tel: (02) 350 3112
Operates a DEXA scanning unit. A referral from your GP is required.

Royal Prince Alfred Hospital
Missenden Road
Camperdown 2050
Tel: (02) 516 6111
The Menopause Clinic is run every second Friday morning. Patients may be self-referred. There is also a private bone density scanning clinic at Prince Alfred Medical Centre. There is a reduced charge for pensioners.

Prince of Wales Hospital
High Street
Randwick 2031
Tel: (02) 399 0111
Osteoporosis Clinic operates a DEXA scanning unit.

Osteoporosis Prevention Program
Tel: (02) 399 4954
The Osteoporosis Prevention Program is organised by the Health Promotion and Multicultural Health Unit, Eastern Sydney Area Health Service, in conjunction with general practitioners. For further information, contact the Health Promotion Coordinator, Maureen

Strudwick, on (02) 697 8132 or the Bone Densitometry Technician, Ekaterina Zivanovic, on (02) 399 4954.

Maureen Strudwick is also involved in a 'Fitness for Seniors' program which covers diet and exercise and includes a bone density scan.

Royal Hospital for Women
188 Oxford Street
Paddington 2021
Tel: (02) 339 4111
Runs a Menopause Clinic.

NORTHERN TERRITORY

Northern Territory Family Planning Association
Shop 11
Rapid Creek 0810
Tel: (089) 48 0144
Provides counselling for menopause. Has a resources centre of pamphlets, books and videos.

QUEENSLAND

Hospitals
Mater Misericordiae Hospital
Ward Street
Rockhampton 4700
Tel: (079) 273 700
Operates a DEXA scanning unit. Patients need a Doctor's Request Form.

Royal Brisbane Hospital
Herston Road
Herston 4006
Tel: (07) 253 8111
The Menopause Clinic runs on Tuesday afternoons.

Princess Alexandra Hospital
Ipswich Road
Woolloongabba 4102
Tel: (07) 240 2111
The Menopause and Osteoporosis Clinic runs Monday to Friday. The clinic carries out bone density scans, mammograms and hormone replacement therapy (pellets and implants). Operates a DEXA

scanning unit. A referral is required. There is a waiting list of approximately two months.

The Wesley Hospital
Nuclear Medicine Department
451 Coronation Drive
Auchenflower 4066
Tel: (07) 371 5133
Southern X-Ray Clinics Company operates a DEXA scanning unit. They have four appointments per day, Monday to Friday. There is a reduced charge for Healthcare card-holders. Referral required.

St Andrew's War Memorial Hospital
Nuclear Medicine Department
Corner of Wickham Terrace and North Street
Spring Hill 4000
Tel: (07) 839 0822
Has a DEXA scanning unit. There is a reduced charge for pensioners. A referral is required.

Private clinics
Central Queensland Imaging
PO Box 337
Bundaberg 4670
Tel: (071) 524 088
Operates a DEXA scanning unit. A Doctor's Request Form is required.

Queensland Medical Imaging
Morris Towers
149 Wickham Terrace
Brisbane 4000
Tel: (07) 831 4527
Does DEXA scanning for endocrinologists. The management prefers a referral letter detailing patient history and doctor's requirements. There is a reduced charge for pensioners.

Toowoomba Radiology Clinic
125 Russell Street
Toowoomba 4350
Tel: (076) 32 9322
Operates a DEXA scanning unit. A referral is preferred.

Clarke and Robertson Medical Practice
Antenor House
16 South Street
Ipswich 4305
Tel: (07) 812 1688
Has a DEXA scanning unit. A referral is required.

Community and women's health centres
Centacare
79 Woongarra Street
Bundaberg 4670
Tel: (071) 532 532
Centacare is a family and welfare agency run by the Catholic Church. Robin Hunter coordinates a Menopause Support Group that meets monthly at Centacare. The support group invites guest speakers and discusses issues such as diet, osteoporosis, physical management and stress. They also hold two general education evenings a year. Partners and daughters are encouraged to attend. A GP is available to answer questions and videos on the topic are shown. Videos and books are available for loan from the library. The monthly and general meetings are promoted on radio and in newspapers, or contact Robin at Centacare.

Women's Health Centre
165 Gregory Terrace
Spring Hill 4000
Ph: (07) 839 9988
Acts as a resource centre for books, pamphlets and articles on women's health issues. The centre is open 9:00—5:00 Mondays, Tuesdays, Thursdays and Fridays. The centre is open 12:30—7:00 Wednesdays.

For information, call (008) 01 7676 between 10:00 and 4:00 on Mondays, Tuesdays, Thursdays and Fridays. Call between 12:30 and 4:00 on Wednesdays.

SOUTH AUSTRALIA

Hospitals
Royal Adelaide Hospital
North Terrace
Adelaide 5000
Tel: (08) 223 0230

Operates a DEXA scanning unit. A referral is required. Pensioners, Health Card holders, out-patients are not charged.

Queen Elizabeth Hospital
Woodville Road
Woodville 5011
Tel: (08) 345 0222
Operates an SPA scanning unit. A referral is required. There is no charge.

Flinders Medical Centre
Flinders Drive
Bedford Park 5042
Tel: (08) 204 5511
Operates an SPA scanning unit. May refer patients on for DEXA scanning. There is no charge.

Women's and Children's Hospital
(incorporating the Queen Victoria Hospital)
160 Fullarton Road
Rose Park 5067
Tel: (08) 332 4888
The Menopause Clinic runs on Thursday mornings. A referral is required.

Private clinics
Osteoscan
57–59 Anzac Highway
Ashford 5035
Tel: (08) 297 0277
Operates a DEXA scanning unit.

North Adelaide Centre
183 Tynte Street
North Adelaide 5006
Tel: (08) 291 0010
Operates a DEXA scanning unit. A referral is required. There is a reduced charge for pensioners.

Endocrine, Bone and Menopause Centre
130 Sydenham Road
Norwood 5067
Tel: (08) 364 3274
Operates an SPA scanning unit. A referral is required. There is a reduced charge for pensioners and Health Card holders.

Community and women's health centres
Adelaide Women's Community Health Centre
64 Pennington Terrace
North Adelaide 5006
Tel: (08) 267 5366
Runs information sessions on menopause. One-to-one counselling from medical practitioners and nurses is available. Brochures are available on osteoporosis and menopause.

TASMANIA

Hospitals
Royal Hobart Hospital
Medical Imaging Unit
Liverpool Street
Hobart 7000
Tel: (002) 388 237
Operates a DEXA scanning unit. A referral is required.

Private clinics
Hobart Medical Imaging Group
176 Macquarie Street
Hobart 7000
Tel: (002) 21 1311
Operates a DEXA scanning unit. A referral is preferred. There is a reduced charge for pensioners and Health Card holders.

Community and women's health centres
Menopause Service
Queen Victoria Hospital
7 High Street
Launceston 7250
Tel: (003) 37 2833
Contact: Desma Wieringa, coordinator
Provides a resources centre of books, pamphlets and videos. Workshops of eight weeks duration are run three to four times per year as required. The workshops cover menopause and hormone replacement therapy, breast self-examination, nutrition, pelvic floor exercises, osteoporosis and heart disease, alternatives to hormone replacement therapy, self-esteem, relaxation and pain management, and an information session for partners. Sessions can be run throughout the (003) area.

Women's Midlife Health Advisory Service

GPO Box 1102
Hobart 7000
Tel: (002) 33 3508

Provides information and support on topics such as menopause, sexuality, breast self-examination, Pap smear tests, osteoporosis, nutrition and weight management, exercise, stress management, self-esteem and confidence building, and hysterectomy awareness.

Women's Health Centre

326 Elizabeth Street
North Hobart 7000
Tel: (002) 31 3212

Service is available between 9:00 a.m. and 4:00 p.m. Monday to Friday. A library is provided. A counsellor is available to discuss issues such as osteoporosis and menopause. Consultations with the two women doctors are bulk-billed.

The Women's Health Centre runs menopause workshops approximately three times a year. The sessions are two hours a week, for six weeks. The workshops are advertised in the local papers and on the local radio stations.

VICTORIA

Hospitals

Austin Hospital

Bone and Mineral Research Unit
Studley Road
Heidelberg 3084
Tel: (03) 496 3157

Operates two DEXA scanning units. Volunteers—blood and urine samples are required. The patient will receive a letter explaining the results. There is no charge and the results are used for research. Referred patients—there is a nominal charge.

Essendon and District Memorial Hospital

Essendon Osteoporosis Centre
Chester Street
Moonee Ponds
Tel: (03) 342 4000

Operates a DEXA scanning unit. Runs a weekly osteoporosis clinic which provides assessment, clinical evaluation and management.

Royal Melbourne Hospital
Bone Densitometry Unit
Grattan Street
Parkville 3052
Tel: (03) 342 7027

Operates a Logic DEXA scanning unit. A referral is required. There is a reduced charge for pensioners.

The Bone and Mineral Clinic runs a special bone clinic on the first Wednesday of each month.

Royal Women's Hospital
132 Grattan Street
Carlton 3053
Tel: (03) 344 2274

The Menopause Service is open on Thursdays from 1:30 p.m. Patients may be self-referred. The service assists those suffering physical and/or psychological problems attributed to menopause.

St George's Hospital
283 Cotham Road
Kew 3101
Tel: (03) 817 2464

The Women's Health Clinic requires a referral. A DEXA scanning unit is operated at the X-ray Department. There is a reduced charge for pensioners.

Vaucluse Hospital
X-ray Department
82 Moreland Road
Coburg 3058
Tel: (03) 383 6266

This private hospital operates a DEXA scanning unit. A referral is required. There is a reduced charge for pensioners.

Private clinics

Airlie Women's Centre
1 Airlie Avenue
East Prahran 3181
Tel: (03) 525 1941

This private clinic provides bone density scanning.

Baker Institute Menopause Clinic
Baker Lane
Prahran 3181
Tel: (03) 522 4301

Has a resource centre—pamphlets, videos, nursing staff to answer questions. Doctors are available for consultation. The clinic will refer on patients who require mammograms or bone density scans. A referral is required.

Como Diagnostic Clinic
Level 3, 627 Chapel Street
Como Centre
South Yarra 3141
Tel: (03) 826 4300

Operates a DEXA scanning unit. A referral is required. There is a reduced charge for pensioners.

Monash Department of Medicine
Monash University
Body Composition Laboratory
Monash Medical Centre
246 Clayton Road
Clayton 3168
Tel: (03) 550 1390

Operates a DEXA scanning unit. A referral is required. There is a reduced charge for pensioners.

SPA scans are done by the Prince Henry's Institute of Medical Research, at the Monash Medical Centre. Patients do not need a referral. There is a reduced charge for pensioners.

Victoria Parade Radiology
Freemason's Day Procedure Centre
320 Victoria Parade
East Melbourne 3002
Tel: (03) 417 2499

Operates a DEXA scanning unit. A referral is required. There is a reduced charge for pensioners.

Wainer Clinic for Women
366 Church Street
Richmond 3121
Tel: (03) 427 0399

Provides counselling and multidisciplinary treatment for menopause. The medical staff, psychotherapist, physiotherapist, psychologist and naturopath have expertise in the management of menopause. The clinic runs evening menopause and healing groups.

Support groups

Healthsharing Women
Fifth Floor, Victorian Information Centre
318 Little Bourke Street
Melbourne 3000
Tel: (03) 663 3544
Acts as a resource centre for books, pamphlets and articles on women's health issues.

The Victorian Centre for Women's Health
Level 3
627 Chapel Street
South Yarra 3141
Tel: (03) 826 9799
Private centre. Publishes newsletters, provides free lectures.

WESTERN AUSTRALIA

Hospitals
Sir Charles Gairdner Hospital
Department of Endocrinology and Diabetes
2nd Floor, G Block
Verdun Street
Nedlands 6009
Tel: (09) 346 3891
Operates three DEXA and one SPA unit. Referral is required. Apointments are available on Mondays, Tuesdays and Thursdays between 8:30 a.m. and 4:00 p.m. Appointments are available on Wednesdays and Fridays between 1:00 and 4:00 p.m.

Royal Perth Rehabilitation Hospital
Selby Street
Shenton Park 6008
Tel: (09) 382 7142
The Outpatient Department runs an osteoporosis clinic on a Tuesday afternoon, once a month. A referral is required. No charge.

Private clinics
Perth Imaging
8 Colin Street
West Perth 6005
Tel: (09) 321 9666
This private clinic operates a DEXA scanning unit. There is a reduced charge for HBF members.

Perth Thermography and Perth Bone Densitometry
Suite 27, 443 Albany Highway
Victoria Park 6100
Tel: (09) 472 1588
This private clinic operates a Lunar DEXA. A referral is required.

Community and women's health centres
Women's Health Care House
100 Aberdeen St
Northbridge 6003
Tel: (09) 227 8122
Female doctors can assess patients and refer them for tests.

Mid-life and Menopause Support Group
Agnes Walsh House
Bagot Road
Subiaco 6008
Tel: (09) 340 1535
Open on Wednesdays and Fridays, between 10:00 a.m. and 4:30 p.m. Can provide pamphlets and videos for viewing, books and videos for purchase. Holds evening meetings on mid-life topics.

ASSOCIATIONS
Australian Menopause Society
Royal Hospital for Women
188 Oxford Street
Paddington 2021
Tel: (02) 339 4246 or (08) 33 9134
Publishes a quarterly newsletter. Membership is open to doctors, nurses, paramedical and community workers.

Endocrine Society of Australia
Sir Charles Gairdner Hospital
Nedlands WA 6009
Tel: (09) 346 3822
Fax: (03) 389 2816

Australian and New Zealand Bone and Mineral Association/Society
145 Macquarie Street
Sydney NSW 2000
Tel: (02) 256 5462
Fax: (02) 241 4083

15

Taking the fight to osteoporosis

Despite the gaps which still exist in our understanding of how and why osteoporosis occurs, we have seen the development of some broad guidelines to reduce the profound impact this condition has on individuals and on the cost of healthcare to the community.

Prevention of osteoporosis is known to be preferable to treating the established condition. We have no proven therapy that will re-establish bone mass once it has been lost. Prevention should start early in life. During childhood and adolescence the emphasis should be on an adequate dietary calcium intake (800 to 1000 mg/day elemental calcium). This additional calcium should ideally be provided by adequate dairy foods or soft-boned fish. The addition of calcium supplementation should not be necessary, but many proprietary foods now have additional calcium as part of their processing and manufacture. Appropriately structured physical exercise should also be part of this program. However, young women involved with excessive physical training may develop amenorrhoea and hasten development of osteoporosis.

We now recognise that oestrogens in the early postmenopausal period will undoubtedly halt progression towards osteoporosis. In women with an intact uterus they should be given cyclically with a progestogen, which will minimise or abolish the potential risk of the development of uterine cancer. There should also be an adequate calcium intake throughout the menopausal and postmenopausal period.

HRT should preferably be instituted within three years of menopause and may need to be continued for perhaps ten years. In older women and in those in whom oestrogen is contraindicated, the use of certain progestogens in a continuous manner is recommended.

The universal use of hormones is not recommended. Rather, hormone therapy should be directed at high-risk subjects, those with low bone density or with risk factors that accelerate bone loss.

For the treatment of osteoporosis to be ideal we require identification of women at high risk for osteoporosis. This needs to be done at or about the time of menopause. Bone densitometry with the new DEXA technology, with its low radiation and convenience, is the ideal approach to this end. This technique is becoming increasingly available in Australia but is not yet subject to rebate for screening, diagnosis or therapeutic management.

At the time of writing this book the Australian Government has announced the introduction of a bone density scanning rebate. Certain circumstances have to apply before the cost of any individual test may be claimed back from the Government's universal health scheme—Medicare. The rebate of $75 per test will not be available for tests carried out to screen women for the possibility of osteoporosis. It will be available only if the method is used to confirm the diagnosis of osteoporosis after other investigations have raised the possibility of the disease being present. The other indication will be the monitoring of treatment in patients with established osteoporosis.

An exciting development, recently announced in Australia, is the discovery of the gene which determines the genetic risk for osteoporosis. In the future it may be possible to identify those at risk with a simple blood test. We should then be able to target those at risk more precisely.

We now have access to a number of non-hormonal bone-preserving agents, including calcitriol and the bisphosphonates for those in whom HRT is inappropriate or who do not tolerate HRT. Although it is too early to assess the full impact of these drugs, a number of trials have indicated their potential value. The calcitonins may also have a greater role in the future, particularly if the new intranasal forms prove effective in patients with osteoporosis.

The maintenance of an adequate level of regular physical activity, weight-bearing, fitness and mobility, should be part of any preventive program. Other lifestyle measures which should assist in preventing or delaying the development of osteoporosis are: avoidance of smoking, a reduction in alcohol intake, and a reduction in excessive caffeine, protein and salt intake.

It is suggested that the investigation and initial management of established osteoporosis should remain the province of experts or well-informed general practitioners. However, the precise indications for the available therapies are not established, and objective evidence of efficacy of the various treatment regimens needs to be obtained in a rigorous way.

Associate Professor Deborah Saltman, writing in *General Practitioner*, January 1994, finishes her article in this way:

> It is clear that the health of women during the transition from reproductive to reproductive-free state involves more than the management of an 'illness'. Empowering women with health knowledge and the means to effect health changes will help them achieve greater control of their own health issues.

Menopause should be viewed simply as a transition period for women. **Menopause is not a disease**. It can therefore be argued that menopause should not be treated in all women. However, those women requesting HRT or choosing to use it in an informed manner to protect their bone and cardiovascular fitness should be allowed to do so without being made to feel guilty.

Osteoporosis, in contrast, is both an unnecessary disease for most women and a major health issue which will continue to add to the economic and health burden for this community into the 21st century. Osteoporosis is a health issue which will become increasingly more important with the aging of the population.

Present knowledge about osteoporosis suggests further research should be directed at increasing our understanding of the biology of bone formation and destruction, at identifying those at greatest risk for development of osteoporosis, and at developing the means of assessing a variety of effective strategies for prevention and treatment of this largely preventable silent epidemic.

Notes

Chapter 1 Introduction to osteoporosis—the silent thief

1 Dr Philip Sambrook, *Modern Medicine of Australia*, vol. 34, no. 8, August 1991, pp. 21–32.
2 'Osteoporosis: its causes, prevention, and treatment', *Modern Medicine of Australia*, vol. 34, no. 8, August 1991, pp. 37–46.
3 Patricia Coney, *The Menopause Industry*, Spinifex Books, Melbourne, 1993.

Chapter 3 More problems with bone

1 C.D. Forbes, and W.F. Jackson, *A Colour Atlas of Clinical Medicine*, Wolfe Publishing, London, 1993, pp. 154–5.

Chapter 4 Osteoporosis: what are the features and risks?

1 N.A. Pocock, et al, 'Genetic determinants of bone mass in adults: a twin study', *Journal of Clinical Investigation*, vol. 80, no. 3, 1987, p. 706; Mundy Gregory, 'Boning up on genes', *Nature*, vol. 367, 20 January 1994; N.A. Morrison, et al, 'Prediction of bone density from Vitamin D receptor alleles', *Nature*, vol. 367, 20 January 1994, pp. 284–7.
2 A.F. Stewart, et al, 'Calcium homeostasis in immobilisation: an example of resorptive hypercalciuria', *New England Journal of Medicine*, vol. 306, 1982, p. 1136.
3 P.B. Mack, et al, 'Bone demineralisation of foot and hand of Gemini–

Titan' IV, V and Vll astronauts during orbital flight', *American Journal of Roentgenology*, vol. 100, 1967, p. 503.
4 'Calcium and exercise: how much do bones need?', *Medical Observer*, 4 February 1994, p. 14.
5 Susan Vale, 'Smoking linked to fractures', *Australian Doctor Weekly*, 4 March 1994, p. 14.
6 Ann Klibanski, 'Male hypogonadism and osteopoenia—Diagnosis and response to therapy', unpublished lecture notes.
7 E.S. Orwoll, et al, 'The Rate of Bone Mineral Loss in Normal Men and the Effects of Calcium and Cholecalciferol Supplementation', *Annals of Internal Medicine*, vol. 112, no. 1, 1 January 1990, pp. 29–34.

Chapter 5 How is osteoporosis diagnosed?

1 Dr Richard Prince, 'How Should Osteoporosis be Diagnosed?', *Patient Management*, vol. 17, no. 1, Jan/Feb 1993, pp. 10–11.
2 L.J. Melton, et al, 'Epidemiology of vertebral fractures in women', *American Journal of Epidemiology,* vol. 129, 1989, pp. 1000–11.
3 Philip Sambrook, 'Bone Densitometry', *General Practitioner*, April 1993, p. 16.
4 Sandra Coney, *The menopause industry*, Spinifex Press, Melbourne, 1993, p. 126.
5 Sambrook, op cit.
6 R.L. Prince and S.R. Langton, 'Clinical validation of dialysable calcium in relation to other methods of serum calcium measurement', *British Medical Journal*, vol. 290, 1985, p. 735.

Chapter 6 Preventing osteoporosis

1 N. Dalen and K.E. Olsson, 'Bone mineral density and exercise', *Acta Orthopaedia Scandinavia* vol. 45, 1974, pp. 170–4; R. Chow, et al, 'Effects of two randomised exercise programmes on bone mass of healthy postmenopausal women', *British Medical Journal*, vol. 295, 1987, pp. 1441–4; B. Krolner, et al, 'Physical exercise as prophylaxis against involutional bone loss: a controlled trial', *Clinical Science*, vol. 64, 1983, pp. 541–6.
2 Professor Lance Twomey, 'Physical activity and aging bones', *Current Therapeutics*, January/February 1993, pp. 31–4.

Chapter 8 Treating osteoporosis

1 Dr E. Farrell, and Ann Westmore, *The HRT Handbook*, Ann O'Donovan Publishing, Melbourne, 1993; Dr Sandra Cabot, *Menopause—Hormone*

Replacement Therapy and Its Natural Alternatives, Women's Health Advisory Service, NSW, 1991.

2 Sandra Coney, *The Menopause Industry*, Spinifex Press, Melbourne, 1993.

3 Marie Chapuy et al., 'Vitamin D$_3$ and Calcium to prevent hip fractures in elderly women', *New England Journal of Medicine*, vol. 327, no. 23, pp. 1637–42.

4 Professor Philip Sambrook, 'Calcitriol and postmenopausal osteoporosis', *Medical Journal of Australia*, vol. 157, 21 September 1992, pp. 364–6.

5 Murray W. Tilyard, George F.S. Spears, Janet Thompson and Susan Dovey, 'Treatment of Postmenopausal Osteoporosis with Calcitriol or Calcium', *New England Journal of Medicine*, vol. 326, no. 6, 6 February 1992, pp. 357–62.

6 A. Caniggia, et al, *Metabolism Clinical and Experimental*, vol. 39, no. 4, Supplement 1, 1990, pp. 43–9; J.C. Gallagher and D. Goldgar, *Annals of Internal Medicine*, vol. 113, no. 9, November 1990, pp. 649–55.

7 P. Sambrook, et al, 'Prevention of corticosteroid osteoporosis', *New England Journal of Medicine*, vol. 328, pp. 1747–52.

8 Carlo Gennari and Louis Avioli, 'Calcitonin therapy in Osteoporosis', *The Osteoporosis Syndrome*, Grune and Stratton Inc., 1987, pp. 127–42.

9 J.Y. Reginster, et al, '1-year controlled randomised trial of prevention of early postmenopausal bone loss by intranasal calcitonin', *Lancet*, vol. ii, 1987, pp. 1481–83.

10 Nelson B. Watts, et al, 'Intermittent cyclical etidronate treatment of postmenopausal osteoporosis', *New England Journal of Medicine*, vol. 323, 12 July 1990, pp. 73–9.

11 Dr Tommy Storm, et al, 'Effect of Cyclical Etidronate Therapy on Bone Mass and Fracture Rate in Women with Postmenopausal Osteoporosis', *New England Journal of Medicine*, vol. 322, 3 May 1990, pp. 1265–71.

12 Stephen T. Harris, et al, 'Four Year Study of Intermittent Cyclic Etidronate Treatment of Postmenopausal Osteoporosis: Three Years of Blinded Therapy Followed by One Year of Open Therapy', *American Journal of Medicine*, vol. 95, December 1993, pp. 557–67.

13 B.L. Riggs, 'A new option for treating osteoporosis', *New England Journal of Medicine*, vol. 323, 1990, p. 124.

Chapter 10 The HRT controversy

1 Jo Chandler, interview with Dr Elizabeth Farrell, *The Age*, 1994.

2 T.L. Bush, et al, 'Cardiovascular mortality and noncontraceptive use of oestrogen in women. Results from the Lipid Research Clinics Program Follow-up Study', *Circulation*, vol. 75, 1987, pp. 1102–09.

3 Sandra Coney, 'The Exploitation of a Fear—The selling of HRT', Healthsharing Women, Papers and Proceedings, 1992, pp. 4–11.

4 ibid.

5 Dr Suzanne Silberberg, 'Clinical and Research Issues of Hormone Replacement Therapy', Healthsharing Women, Papers and Proceedings, 1992, pp. 12–14.

6 Dr Susan Davis, Letter to the Editor, *Sunday Herald-Sun*, 28 November 1993, p. 34.

7 A.H. McLennan, et al, 'The prevalence of oestrogen replacement therapy in South Australia', *Maturitas*, vol. 16, 1993, pp. 175–83.

8 A.H. MacLennan, 'Hormone replacement therapy and the menopause. A consensus statement of the Australian Menopause Society', *Medical Journal of Australia*, vol. 155, 1991, pp. 43–4.

9 Dr Elizabeth Farrell and Ann Westmore, *The HRT Handbook*, Anne O'Donovan Publishers, Melbourne, 1993.

10 National Osteoporosis Society, *Menopause and Osteoporosis Therapy —GP Manual*, Bath, UK, 1993.

11 G.T. Kovacs, et al, 'A new method of endometrial cytological sampling—Gynoscann—a comparison with Vabra curettage', *Medical Journal of Australia*, vol. 148, 1988, pp. 498–503.

12 Dr Sandra Cabot, *Menopause—Hormone Replacement Therapy and its Natural Alternatives*, Women's Health Advisory Service, Sydney, 1991.

13 Julie-Anne Davies, 'Push for hormone therapy', *The Age*, 6 March 1994, p. 6.

Chapter 11 Counselling in osteoporosis

1 Dr Leonard Rose and Peter Fitzgerald, *Mirrors of the Mind*, McCulloch Positive Health Guides, McCulloch Publishers, Melbourne, 1989.

2 Don E. Gibbons, *Applied Hypnosis and Hyperempiria*, Plenum Press, New York, 1979.

3 Beata Jencks, *Your Body-Biofeedback at its Best*, Nelson Hall Paperbacks, Chicago, 1979.

Recommended reading

A critical look at Hormone Replacement Therapy: Research Forum Series 2, Health Sharing Women Papers and Proceedings, Victoria, 1992

Avoiding Osteoporosis, Dr Allan Dixon and Dr Andrew Woolf, Optima Positive Health Guide, London, 1989

Manage Your Pain, Dr Leonard Rose with Peter Fitzgerald, Angus & Robertson, Sydney, 1987

Menopause—Hormone Replacement Therapy and its Natural Alternatives, Dr Sandra Cabot, Women's Health Advisory Service, Sydney, 1991

Mirrors of the Mind, Dr Leonard Rose with Peter Fitzgerald, McCulloch Publishing, Melbourne, 1989

Osteoporosis: Prevention and Self Management Course, Leaders' Manual and Participants' Handbook, Ben Witham with Jenny Davidson, Arthritis Foundation of Victoria, Melbourne, 1991

Overcoming Pain, Dr Leonard Rose, McCulloch Publishing, Melbourne, 1990

Stand Tall, Morris Notlevitz, MD, and Marsha Ware, Secker & Warburg, Melbourne, 1982

Staying on your feet: information and suggestions for older people on preventing falls, Falls Prevention Project Team, Central Sydney Health Service, Southwood Press, Sydney, 1992

The HRT Handbook, Dr Elizabeth Farrell and Ann Westmore, Anne O'Donovan, Melbourne, 1993

The Menopause Industry, Sandra Coney, Spinifex Books, Melbourne, 1991

The Osteoporotic syndrome: detection, prevention and treatment, Avioli, L.V. (ed.) 2nd edn, Grune & Stratton, Orlando, Sydney, 1987

Understanding Osteoporosis, Wendy Cooper, Arrow Books, 1990

Index